Yachting in the Arctic Seas, Or, Notes of Five Voyages of Sport and Discovery in the Neighbourhood of Spitzbergen and Novaya Zemlya

James Lamont

YACHTING IN THE ARCTIC SEAS.

28

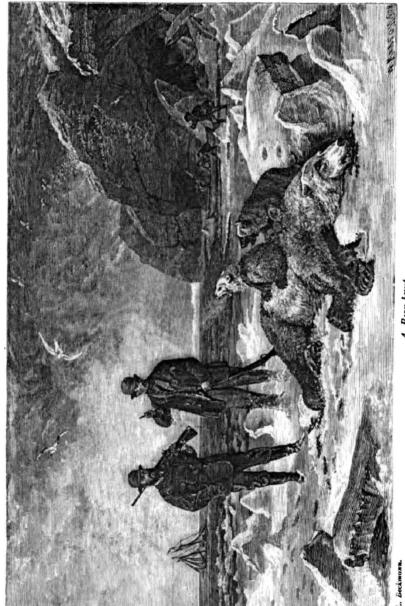

L. Beckmann.

A Bear hunt.

YACHTING IN THE ARCTIC SEAS

OR NOTES OF

FIVE VOYAGES OF SPORT AND DISCOVERY

IN THE NEIGHBOURHOOD OF

SPITZBERGEN AND NOVAYA ZEMLYA.

BY

JAMES LAMONT, F.G.S., F.R.G.S.

AUTHOR OF 'SEASONS WITH THE SEA HORSES.'

EDITED and ILLUSTRATED by W. LIVESAY, M.D.

𝕷onbon:

CHATTO AND WINDUS, PICCADILLY.

1876.

PREFACE.

THE POLAR REGIONS will always be an inexhaustible mine of scientific interest, and it is hoped that the present record of the summer voyages of a sportsman may stimulate many men of leisure and means to continue the exploration of the Arctic Seas.

The scattered meteorological records are selected from a very numerous series made, and may be so far relied on that the instruments were constructed by Messrs. Negretti and Zambra, and were kindly selected and corrected by Mr. Glaisher at a few days' notice.

The illustrations are, with few exceptions, transferred directly from the sketch-book to the engraver's blocks—faithful reproduction of Arctic scenes, rather than pictorial effect, being aimed at. The maps simply illustrate the text, and are not intended as authorities on debateable questions of geography.

W. LAMONT.

December 1875.

CONTENTS.

LIST OF ILLUSTRATIONS.

SECTION I.

NOVAYA ZEMLYA AND THE KARA SEA

'Mountains of ice that stop the imagined way
Beyond Petsora easterly, to the rich
Cathaian coast'

MILTON

B

NOVAYA ZEMLYA AND THE KARA SEA.

IN 1858 and 1859 I made two pleasant and successful yacht voyages to Spitzbergen, and for years afterwards I continued to be haunted by reminiscences of the excellent sport I had enjoyed and of the interesting physical features of the weird and little-known land I had visited.

In the latter year I had succeeded, with a most weak and unsuitable vessel, in penetrating some distance into the enormously-heavy pack-ice which always more or less impinges on the northern and eastern coasts of Spitzbergen; and I began to think that, with a vessel properly equipped and fortified, and with auxiliary steam-power, it might be practicable in a favourable ice season to force my way to a higher northern latitude than had ever been attained, and by so doing, perhaps, help to clear up some of the difficult problems which give romance and interest to the shadowy regions around the North Pole.

I could at least hope to secure a share of the scientific wealth which every country but my own, with the most laudable emulation, was fitting out expeditions to appropriate.

In an unpretending little work, descriptive of my former voyages,[1] I had enunciated most strongly the opinion that it would for ever prove impossible to approach the Pole of the earth in *ships*; but, from reading the accounts of the subsequent voyages of Norwegian walrus-hunters, from an attentive study of the ever-increasing mass of Arctic literature, and from much conversation and correspondence with those learned theorists who, without ever having left their own firesides, stoutly maintain that there is 'no difficulty whatever in sailing to the North Pole,' I was induced to consider whether my own opinion—however practically formed—might not have been too hastily adopted after all.

So completely did these ideas gain possession of me that at the general election of 1868 I abandoned a seat in Parliament, which had cost much money and three arduous contests to attain, and set to work to build a vessel which should embody all Arctic requirements in a moderate compass.

This was no easy matter; for a vessel whose destiny was so unusual exacted a method of build altogether specific and exceptional; and personal supervision of

---

[1] 'Seasons with the Sea-Horses.'   Hurst and Blackett, 1861.

an infinite number of minute matters of detail was essential to future success and safety.

In spite of numerous delays, however, the 'Diana' was launched in the Clyde in March, 1869. She is a three-masted schooner of 251 tons, with compound engines of thirty-horse power; and in her internal arrangements and fittings she is, so to speak, a cross between a yacht and a modern Scotch whaler. I had to restrict the accommodation for myself and companions to the smallest possible compass, so as to allow the largest available space for coals, as well as provisions and other appliances for a possible Arctic winter.

We stowed 130 tons of coal, and, as the 'Diana' steams seven knots an hour with a consumption of $2\frac{1}{4}$ tons or thereabouts per twenty-four hours, we reckoned upon having fuel for nearly 10,000 miles; or considerably more if we were content to steam at half or three-quarter speed.

She has compound or 'high-and-low pressure' engines, which have since become quite common; but they were then newly invented, and, although much more expensive than the old style of engine, they effect a saving of fuel equal to nearly 50 per cent., an enormous consideration in such a voyage as I contemplated.

Our engine gave us a great deal of trouble at first, from the crank of the shaft always stopping *over the centre* whenever we tried to back or stop the engine. This defect, however, has since been remedied; and a more beautiful and perfect little engine I should never wish to go afloat with.

I had the vessel's hold fitted with seventeen iron tanks, like those of a whaler. These were crammed chiefly with coals for the engine, but one or two were filled with water, and one or two with biscuits; and my intention in having them built was that I might stow in them the skins and blubber of any seals or sea-horses we might kill, and so recoup myself for at least a portion of my heavy outlay on the expedition.

My excellent friend, the late Sir Roderick Murchison, then President of the Royal Geographical Society, took great interest in the proceedings, and made successful application on my behalf to the Admiralty to let me have all stores which I wanted from the Government dockyards at the contract prices. I also got the loan of various instruments from the Hydrographical Department.

We had four boats, three of them whale-boats three feet shorter than those used by the Scotch whale-ships, and the other a common dingey.

There was also a complete set of whaling gear, with gun-harpoons, rockets, and all the most modern contrivances for destroying these monsters of the deep. And as my mate and several of the other hands were

men experienced in the whale fishery, and I myself remembered having seen various large whales in the
Spitzbergen sea on my former voyages, I was not without
hope that we might be able to add one or more of them
to the cargo.

I was not aware at the time that these were not
' right' whales, but ' finners,' a species of fish the capture
of which is never attempted by the most experienced
professional whalers.

During the building of the ' Diana ' I paid repeated
visits to Dundee and Peterhead, to obtain information
as to various points to be attended to in her construction
and appliances. I met with the utmost courtesy from
the owners and masters of the whalers, and I found
them always willing to impart to me their valuable
stores of knowledge.

The 'Diana' is built on what is called the composite
principle; that is, her beams and timbers are of T and
angle iron, and wooden planking bolted to them with
$\frac{5}{8}$-inch yellow-metal screw-bolts. She is braced and
fortified inside with numerous beams and angle-irons,
extending in every direction, especially forward. Outside, instead of copper, she is sheathed with a $2\frac{1}{2}$-inch
planking of Australian gum-tree, or, as the ship
builders call it, 'iron bark.' This beautiful wood seems
to have been intended by Nature for the protection of
ice-going vessels, as it is desperately hard and slippery,

and not liable to be split or abraded by the rough contact of the ice. We also had a heavy iron stem-piece bolted and secured to the stem of the vessel, with numerous broad bands of iron.

The propeller was constructed so as to detach and be hoisted on deck when under sail, but I afterwards found that this gave a great deal of trouble, and was of very little advantage. We carried a spare propeller and a spare screw-shaft—not an unnecessary precaution, as I afterwards found.

Altogether, the 'Diana' has been a great success; and six seasons, during which she has undergone all the vicissitudes of Arctic navigation, gales, ice, and even rocks, have left her as stout and staunch as when she was built. No better-adapted vessel for private Arctic navigation ever sailed the frozen seas.

On the evening of April 17 the hills of Cowal faded from our view, as we steamed away down the Firth of Clyde from Toward lighthouse: the snow that remained on the high hills of Loch Striven and the loftier granite tops of Arran suggesting the Arctic scenery we were bound for.

A rapid steam through the Caledonian Canal, and a short delay at Inverness, prevented our being fairly at sea before the 23rd. We left the port at seven A.M. Proceeding under easy sail, after sending the pilot ashore at Cromarty, there was time to look around and see whom the before-mentioned ' we ' consisted of.

We were in all only fifteen souls, as it was my intention to fill up the crew with six Norsemen from Tromsö, who would add to the ordinary duties of working the yacht the special knowledge of walrus-hunting and boat work among ice. I prefer myself always taking the responsibility and authority of master; Karl Iversen, a Norwegian, who had gained experience in the Scotch whaling fleet, acting under me as sailing master. Charles Edward Smith, who had two years previously wintered with a whaling crew in Davis' Straits, accompanied me as surgeon, and William Livesay, an amateur artist, who joined us at the last moment, occupied the fourth place at the cabin mess. Of the crew, the engineer, mate, and fireman were men of great experience in ice, and the boatswain and steward had both sailed with me before in the Mediterranean, the West Indies, and elsewhere.

I am no advocate for loose discipline, nor do I consider that the fact of a voyage being for pleasure or sport warrants an excuse for laxity; still less so on an expedition of this nature, where, with certain perils inseparable from the climate, there is always a chance of wintering among the ice. Yet I cannot admit the accuracy of an assertion often made, that no expedition can be conducted successfully to the

Arctic Regions, save under naval discipline and control; for it happens to be a fact that the highest point north reached by any *ship* was that of the insignificant ' Polaris,' with a crew of thirty-two persons, belonging to six nationalities, and commanded by a civilian. Dissension among the crew was not the bar to further progress north of the explorers of Smith Sound, of Scoresby in 1806, of the Swedish expedition in 1872, or of Leigh Smith in 1873. In every case it was dense polar ice, or other physical conditions; whereas, on the other hand, naval discipline failed to enable the Rosses, Parrys, McClures, Franklins, and all the other able and energetic naval explorers in command of the numerous and well-found Government expeditions from 1818 to 1860, to penetrate further. All the thrilling accounts of wintering within the Arctic Circle have suggested that high personal qualifications, and these alone, have kept crews together, and have served to make discoveries. I thought it, however, no violation of the strictest rules of discipline to place some special inducements before men engaged in so arduous and so exceptional an enterprise, and accordingly took an early opportunity of reading to the crew a sort of proclamation containing a promise of rewards on a graduated scale for discoveries made or latitude attained.[1]

[1] An old Act of Parliament made in 1818, which has never been repealed, offers a reward to any ship sailing to —

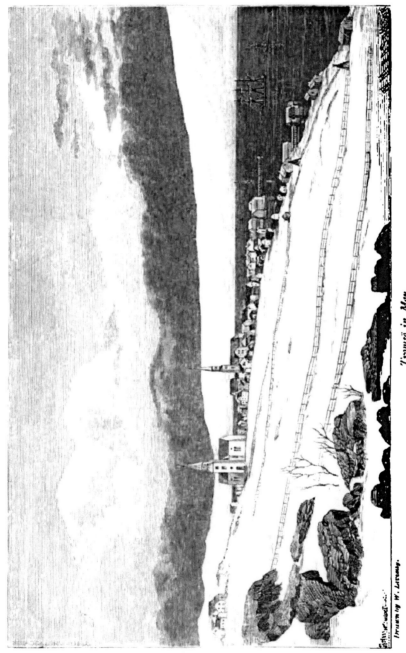

Drawn by W. Leitch.

Tromsö in May.

Two days after losing sight of the Orkneys we sighted the bold cliffs south of Rondö, Norway; and, although I was hoping we might make a quick run to Tromsö by steaming up the quiet water sheltered by the islands of the west coast of Norway, I was not altogether sorry that we had an opportunity of testing the sea-going qualities of the ' Diana ' before we got further north. During a gale of three days, which compelled us to seek more sea-room, we were gratified to find the yacht capable of satisfying every demand which the restless North Atlantic made on her.

After this period of probation we made a call at the rising sea-port of Namsös for a pilot, and steamed up the smooth inland waters to Tromsö, which was reached on May 6. It is for Tromsö that the British tourist leaves his snug villa at Clapham, his peaceful rectory, or his dingy chambers, that he may boast on his return that he has seen the midnight sun; so I may be spared the necessity of describing a place whose only claims to importance, apart from its commercial relations with the cod, the seal, and the walrus, are the fact of its being the seat of a bishopric and the capital of Finmarken.

Nor need I hint to the reader who has visited Nor-

°						£
83 N.	.	.	.	.	.	of 1,000
85 „	.	.	.	.	.	„ 2,000
87 „	.	.	.	.	.	„ 4,000
89 „	.	.	.	.	.	„ 5,000

wegian ports that the day after my arrival was a Saint's day and a general holiday, consequently for me a *dies non*—not a shop open or a person out of church till six P.M. I hardly think I can remember to have arrived at a Norwegian port unless on a Saint's day, or when one was impending.

However, consistently with my experience in every port where I have hoisted the colours of my Yacht Club, I received every attention at the hands of the Consul and chief residents. By their kind assistance, combined with my system of seeing to everything myself, I was able to get our remaining stores on board, to tauten up the standing rigging, to ship my six new hands, and to complete my preparations for sea in two days; and then, bidding farewell to the worthy burghers with whom I had renewed the acquaintance of ten years previous, we weighed anchor at seven P.M. on the 8th.

The Norwegian hands consisted of Helstad, chief harpooner; Hans, harpooner; and four others. These men were all experienced Spitzbergen hands, and had been engaged for me beforehand, at very high wages, by the British Consul. I like the Norwegian seamen very much, and have shipped many of them in my various voyages to the north. I have almost always found them brave, hardy, zealous, industrious, obliging, docile, good-humoured fellows; but I am bound to say, that these six Tromsönians were, in sea-going phrase, the *hardest bargains* I was ever shipmate with, and I verily believe that six lazier, dirtier, sulkier, more mutinous and cowardly rascals never broke a biscuit.

It is very difficult for an amateur voyager to get the best Arctic seamen to accompany him, either from Scotland or Norway, because the best men have generally got some sort of standing engagements with favourite skippers or in favourite ships, and they expect to make more money by the oil and skin allowances or percentage than even extra high wages amount to. I think, upon the whole, the best men, especially for boat work, whom I have had with me have been Shetlanders. The really good men in Northern Norway soon get to be mates and masters of sloops themselves, and rise to become the Tobiesens, the Carlsens, and Johannesens of the walrus fishery.

All the sloops, some twenty-five sail, engaged in walrus-hunting, I found had left Tromsö for Novaya Zemlya. This news induced me to look in at Hammerfest, where I found my old agent Johan Berger more portly and jolly than ever. He seemed rather astonished at being asked for restitution of the boat and walrus-gear I had left in his custody in 1859, and still more so when I produced a list of the articles in his own handwriting! These had long been used up, but he gave me others instead of them.

I learned that the walrus-fishing had so fallen off in Spitzbergen that two vessels having broken new ground near Novaya Zemlya last year, and having returned full in a few weeks, their accounts had induced all the owners to despatch their sloops to the same fishing-ground this year.

As all opinions agreed it would be perfectly impossible to penetrate east of Spitzbergen, in the direction of the shadowy Gillis Land and Wiche's Land (King Karl Land in Peterman's maps), so early in the season, it seemed the more prudent course to explore the seas west of Novaya Zemlya, and that interesting country itself as far north as the ice would permit ; thence to skirt the great ice-pack stretching in a wide sweep from Novaya Zemlya to Spitzbergen ; and, while investigating its character, seize any opportunity which might present itself for penetrating it; allowing me finally, perhaps, to arrive at the east and north-east of Spitzbergen by a route entirely different to that hitherto attempted.

It seemed an excellent programme, even with ominous marks of 'impenetrable pack-ice' on the chart before me in the line of the proposed voyage, and the disappointments and disasters of Barentz, Hudson, Wood, and Lutke fresh on my memory.

The usual course on leaving Hammerfest is to sail north so as to pass outside of the Island of Magerö, whose most northerly point constitutes the North Cape; and here, the inland navigation ceasing, the voyager is fairly on the Arctic Seas, free to sail west to Greenland, east to Novaya Zemlya, or due north to Spitzbergen.

A strong wind prevailing I preferred to steam south of Magerö and reach the open sea by crossing the mouth of the gigantic Porsanger Fiord. On another occasion, when the yacht met a similar north-east gale outside of Nordkyn Point, I found an excellent harbour called Mehaven, twenty miles to the west of the latter Point. I can confidently recommend it as being perfectly land-locked. A vessel may lie quietly at anchor here, unconscious of the fiercest of the north-east gales which sweep this rock-bound coast.

I cannot say as much for Vardö, where, owing to a second gale springing up a few days after leaving Hammerfest, I was compelled to seek such shelter as a harbour fully exposed to the north-westerly swell afforded. No doubt in a northerly gale the east harbour is the more eligible, but few sailors on a strange coast would be prepared to anticipate an island so conveniently shaped like the letter H as to afford an east and west harbour. Such is the form of the island on which Vardö is built. Across the middle of the letter runs the principal street, and so narrow is this bar that the great forty-feet boats, used in the heavy fishing, when drawn up in each harbour, either meet on an anticlinal axis, or thrust their huge prows into the doorways across the street.

A fishing town with more character in it I never saw. Two other streets at right angles to the first, were mere slips of waste ground, with houses so squalid that it might be said of them that they had the misfortune to face each other. Every piece of land not occupied by a hovel or a drawn-up boat was graced with festoons and arbours of drying fish; while the half-frozen sloppy stretches of beach were strewn and blocked with every conceivable kind of fishing-tackle, boats, gear, and personal effects of the ever-changing population of Norwegians, Finns, Laps, Russians, Americans, and English, who stood about and discussed the weather in anxious groups.

The outskirts of the towns were characterised by immense cauldrons, in which codlivers are boiled for the European market, and suggested by their magnitude, on the one hand, the amelioration of insidious disease to thousands, and, on the other, the importance of this branch of industry and the dangers encountered fearlessly in earning a livelihood by the cod-fishers.

Vardö being situated on one side of the Varanger Fiord, of which the other shore is Russian territory, there is a fort in the immediate neighbourhood, with a garrison of thirty-five men under a lieutenant. The object of this armament, we were told, was to stop any sudden attempt at invasion from Russia. Some time ago, when this remote district had less communication with the south of Norway and there was little opportunity of the right hand of the Government knowing what its left hand did, the officer in charge hired out all the men under his command to himself, at a nominal remuneration, and turned their energies, like those of the rest of the inhabitants, to the pursuit of piscatorial gain. He was able for a twelvemonth to reap the profit of this ingenious speculation before it came to the ears of the authorities, when he was compelled to relinquish this appropriate and lucrative way of exercising the garrison.

The fishing industry of which Vardö forms a centre —and which even now had brought some fifty sail of vessels, from a tall barque to the smallest sloop, into its harbour, to fill up—is that known as the heavy or ' lode ' fishing, so called from its depending on shoals of a small sprat-like fish frequenting the shores during the summer months. The cod swim under the lode in such numbers that the fishermen in the boats above have frequently no difficulty in securing two to three boatloads of some 1,800 fish each per day. The reader will not be surprised, then, to hear that we purchased a hundred large cod for a sovereign. Nor do

c

I believe there is any exaggeration in the statement that when feeding on the smaller fry the fish lie
so thick that a stone thrown into the water sinks with
difficulty, only at last slipping from the back of one
fish to another and so gravitating.   The occupation is
not, however, carried on without danger ; as we entered
the harbour a boat capsized in the gale and all five
hands were lost.

Another Saint's day occurred here.   But at last, on
Tuesday, May 18, as the early sun crimsoned the snow
on the hills forming the background to the busy picture
we had watched from the deck for four days, a light
breeze and calmer sea allowed us to leave Vardö.   Three
hundred miles more to the eastward should bring us to
the ice.   And, as far as sport went, we had the comforting reflection that few of the forty walrus-hunting
sloops from Tromsö or Hammerfest had preceded us.

It would cause Mr. Plimsoll's hair to stand on end
even to see these Norwegian walrus-sloops ; often
they are crazy craft, totally unseaworthy, patched up
and heavily insured, and sent over to Spitzbergen to
engage in the most hazardous occupation afloat.   Little
wonder that often nothing further is heard of them, or
that, crushed in the ice, or driven ashore in a gale, the
crew escape with their bare lives to other vessels.   They
are always either sloop or schooner rigged, very broad
in the stern and round in the bilge, slightly doubled as

far as the forerigging with two-inch fir boards, the stem
armed with a strip of iron.   From their shortness and
roundness they are handy to work amidst ice.   As
might be anticipated, they sail better before the wind
than near it.

I hired one of these craft as a tender on my trip to
Spitzbergen in 1859, and for nine or ten weeks existed
with my companion in its cramped and odoriferous
cabin.   The ultimate fate of the ' Anna Louisa,' as the
execrable tub was called, was what I always predicted
—she capsized in a gale—a species of catastrophe unfortunately too common with these wretched vessels.

Advantage had been taken of the comparatively
smooth water of the harbour to set up the crow's-nest,
that *sine quâ non* of every vessel engaged in explorations or sport in Arctic waters.   Its object is to afford a
shelter from the freezing winds to an observer stationed
sufficiently high above the deck to command a wide
sweep of the horizon.   The arrangement is very
essential; in whalers engaged in fishing, or in a vessel
navigating difficult ice, it is often necessary for the
master of the vessel to remain on the look-out for many
hours at a stretch.

In order to realise what the ' crow's-nest ' is, it is
only necessary to imagine an empty cask secured by
proper means to the maintopmast a few feet below the
truck.

Its furniture is sufficiently simple, consisting of a ledge half-way up inside for a seat and a bag and grummet to secure the four-foot telescope when not in use. There is a frame of light ironwork to rest the telescope on, and usually a canvas screen, so mounted as to slide round on the rim of the cask, as a protection against the wind or driving snow.

This ingenious structure is entered by a trap-door or hatch, which, being closed by the occupant, forms the floor: it is approached from the topmast shrouds by a wooden ladder (called by the seamen the 'Jacob's ladder,' from its resemblance to the ladder in the picture of Jacob's dream in old Bibles), the rungs of which are lashed to the main-topmast-back-stays on each side. The sudden termination of the ladder has sometimes in the whaling fleet led to accidents to absent-minded skippers descending precipitately. But its chief objec-tion to a landsman is a see-saw movement given to it by the rolling of the vessel in anything but the smoothest water.

The 'Diana's' crow's-nest was fixed at sixty-four feet from the deck, and as the deck was nearly six feet from the sea level, according to the well-known formula for distance seen from a height,[1] we could see a horizon of about eight miles from this elevation.

---

[1] 'The square root of the height of the eye in feet = the number of nautical miles you have in the radius of your horizon.'

The Crow's Nest.

Hitherto, like Ohthere, the first adventurer who sailed into the Arctic seas, we had had 'upon our steereboord alwayes the desert land, and upon the leereboord the maine ocean.' But now the course of the ships of 890 and of 1869 had to vary, for at noon, crossing the wide entrance of Varanger Fiord, a straight course was shaped for Novaya Zemlya. As the coastline gradually receded from view, its trend suggested more substantially to my mind than a mere perusal of the quaint account of Ohthere's voyage, or even Longfellow's charming little poem [1] had done, the reality of the almost legendary Norwegian. Picture to yourself, as a contrast to the clipper-built 'Diana,' cleaving the crisp Arctic waves under steam and canvas, the mariner of a thousand years ago, without compass or quadrant. each time when a fair breeze had brought him to his most northerly or easterly point compelled to wait till a 'full winde' abaft the beam could enable him to sail along in sight of the veering shore.

I was identifying the deep reach of Varanger Fiord with the coast which, after skirting with a 'westerne winde and somewhat northerly, bowed thence directly towards the south so farre as he could travaile in five dayes,' when my poetical reveries were rudely interrupted by a cry from the masthead, 'A finner in sight, there she spouts!' Though not so acutely interested

---

[1] 'The Discoverer of the North Cape.'

in this huge cetacean as that daring whale-fisher Captain Foin would have been, I turned to the direction indicated quickly enough to see the monster spout, and, after a series of gambols, show his prominent dorsal fin and disappear in the blue depths.

I had not the slightest intention of endeavouring to bag this enormous game, although I was prepared with proper harpoons and lines to make fast to any of his illustrious congeners, the ' right whales ' (Balæna Mysticetus), should they come in our way.

Nor has it been the custom, from the time that the Biscayans in the fifteenth century first hunted the whale on the shores of France and Spain to the great eras of the Spitzbergen and now of the Davis Straits whale fisheries, to look upon these animals as commercially worth the risk of their dangerous pursuit.

Captain Foin, of Vadsö, has lately—all honour to him !—invented a new and exciting sport in the pursuit of the ' rorqual,' as it is sometimes called. His method of attacking the whale is to approach in his small screw-steamer and to fire into the animal a shell harpoon weighing twenty pounds, and containing nearly a pound of powder. If good aim is secured, as will naturally be concluded, the whale is killed outright.

In the year 1868 twenty-four of these mammals were secured by this enterprising cruiser, and with the proceeds, after expenses were paid, and a thousand dollars given to the poor of Vardö, he was able to build another steamer and a tender, and to erect boiling houses for boiling blubber on shore and converting the flesh and bones into manure.

Up to this period it had always been considered that the blubber being much less in quantity and of less value, and the 'bone' far inferior, to that of the right whale, there could be no reasonable hope of remuneration for the destruction of gear lost in hunting an animal about whose amazing strength and power of towing vessels with engines reversed and sails aback such marvellous tales have been told.

Many of these yarns, which are current in Finmarken, I was at first disposed absolutely to scout. I have since, however, had opportunities of convincing myself of the honesty of the narrators, and only withhold from the reader such extraordinary anecdotes lest their seeming extravagance should induce him to doubt the veracity of whatever else I may have to tell him in this volume.

We were bowling away on Captain Foin's favourite fishing-ground, but the fact of a large 'finner' having been secured and towed into a neighbouring harbour a few days previously probably deprived us of the exhilarating entertainment of watching his manipulation of this mighty quarry.

Ever since we had crossed the Arctic circle an exhaustive series of meteorological readings had been taken at regular intervals of four hours day and night.

The sea temperature which, between the North Cape and Vardö (71° 7′ N. 29° 50′ E.), had been 40° Fahr. at a depth of 155 feet and at the surface, now commenced to fall by a beautiful but regular series of gradations till the day before we met the ice, when it stood at 29·5° Fahr.[1]

The fluidity of the sea must not, however, be taken as a criterion of the cold experienced, as I may remind the reader that sea-water freezes at a lower temperature than fresh. Or I may represent this phenomenon graphically by stating I have enjoyed a day's skating in a small inland lake of fresh water in Spitzbergen a cable's length from the shore, while the sea close at hand has been perfectly mobile.

Neither these observations nor the fact of our having to light the stove in the cabin were required to remind us of the walrus-hunting (which usually begins as soon as ice is reached), and of the necessity for making preparations for this exciting sport.

---

[1] There is a discrepancy between observations as to the point at which sea-water freezes. Dr. Walker, in Baffin's Bay, states it to be 28·5°. Dr. Kane, in Smith Sound, gives 29°. I have myself numerous records of a fluent sea in calm weather at 29° and 29·5°, while, on the other hand, when sailing among the Thousand Isles in August, ice was forming in thin flakes in water whose temperature was 31° Fahr. I believe the cause of this seeming anomaly is to be sought in the variation of the saline constituents; though I have not, unfortunately, access to any simul-

All hands were now busy, fitting up, mounting, and painting the walrus-boats, grinding harpoons and lances, paying out line, splicing, serving, and knotting, shaping oars and 'haak-picks,' and I was looking over guns, filling cartridges, and making ready generally by attention to all the hundred and one little matters of insignificant detail which, if now neglected, might later on involve critical consequences.

To describe a well-constructed and well-appointed walrus-boat, as used by the Norwegian fishers and by myself, is to say all that is necessary on the subject of boats and their gear, for, with trifling modifications, a boat of this kind is suitable for the swift pursuit of a bear, for loading up with the jackets of half-a-hundred seals, or a long row of discovery among the icy fiords and islands. A walrus-boat, carrying five hands, then, as she hangs on the davits ready for lowering at a moment's notice in pursuit of game, has the following characteristics :—She is twenty-one feet long by five feet beam, having her main breadth about one third from the bow. She is bow-shaped at both ends, and should be at once strong, light, swift to row, and easily turned on her own centre; this latter quality is attained by having the keel a great deal depressed in the middle. She is always carvel-built, that construc-

taneous observations of specific gravity and temperature which can prove this to demonstration.—ED.

tion of boat being much less liable to damage from the ice and the tusks of the walrus than a clinker-built boat, as well as much easier to repair if actually damaged. These boats have a very thick and strong stem-piece and stern-piece, to resist concussions with the ice.

Each man rows with a pair of oars hung in grummets to stout single-thole pins; the steersman directs the boat by also rowing a pair of oars, but rowing with his face to the bow [1]; and as there are six thwarts, each thirty inches apart, he can, if necessary, sit and row like the others. This mode of steering a boat has great advantages over either a rudder or a single steering oar as used by the whalers, for it not only turns the boat much quicker than either, but it economises the entire strength of a man in propelling the boat. The advantage of each man rowing a pair of oars is that the boat can be turned much quicker, and the oars, being short, are less in the way amongst ice. The harpooner always rows the bow oars, and is, of course, the commander of the boat; he alone uses the weapons and the telescope; the strongest man in the boat usually sits next to the harpooner to hold and haul in the line when a walrus is struck, and it is also his duty to hand the harpoons and lances to the harpooner as required.

There is a deep notch cut in the centre of the stem-

[1] Called 'hammelling' in Norway.

piece, and three others on a piece of hard wood on each side of it ; these are for the lines running through, and great care is requisite to prevent them from slipping further aft on the gunwale than the notches, as, if they do, the boat will probably be upset. Most of the accidents that one hears of occur from this cause.

There is sometimes also a ' bollard,' or little upright post in the bow of the boat for making fast the lines to, but many harpooners prefer to dispense with this, using instead the foremost thwart of the boat.

The boats are invariably painted white outside, in order to make their appearance assimilate as much as possible to that of the ice, and I think it would also be a great advantage to have the crews dressed in caps and jackets of some shiny white material, which would keep its colour in spite of dirt and grease.

Each boat is usually provided with six harpoon-heads, fitting, three on each side, inside of the bow, into little racks covered with a curtain of painted canvas to protect their sharp points and edges from being blunted or accidentally wounding the men. These harpoons are used indifferently for the seal or the walrus, and are, with all their apparent simplicity, the most perfect weapons that can be contrived for the purpose. When the instrument is thrust into the animal and his struggles draw tight the line, the large outer barb takes up, as it were, a loop of his gutta-

percha-like hide, or the tough reticulated fibres containing his blubber, while the small inner barb, like
that of a fish-hook, prevents it from becoming disen-
gaged. The best proof of its excellence is that when
a walrus is once properly harpooned and the line tight
he very rarely escapes. Each of these harpoon-heads
has *grummeted* round its neck one end of a line of
twelve or fifteen fathoms long, each line being neatly
coiled up in a separate flat box under the front thwart,
and the opposite end secured to some strong part of the
boat inside. The lines do not require to be longer,
because the walrus is not generally found in water
more than fifteen fathoms deep; and even if the water
should happen to exceed that depth, he is not able to
drag the boat under, from inability to exert his full
strength when subjected to the pressure of twelve
or fifteen fathoms of water. The lines are made
of two-inch tarred hemp rope, *very soft-laid*, and
should be of the very finest material and best possible
workmanship.

There are generally four shafts for the harpoons,
and it is not customary to keep more than one mounted,
unless when walruses are actually in sight. They are
made of white-pine poles twelve or thirteen feet long,
planed down to about an inch and a half or an inch
and a quarter in thickness, and are tapered to a point
for about four inches at one end, to make them fit into

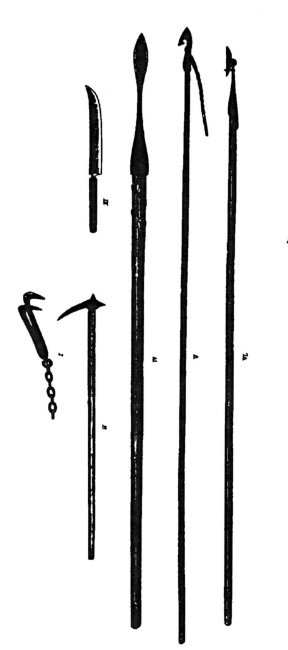

Weapons for the Walrus, &c.

I. Ice Anchor.
II. Haak Pik.
III. Walrus Knife.
IV. Lance.
V. Walrus Harpoon.
VI. White Whale Harpoon.
VII. Harpoon Gun.

the sockets of the heads. After placing a harpoon on a shaft, it is fixed by striking the butt-end of the shaft smartly against a little block of wood which is placed for the purpose between two of the timbers of the boat, about fifteen feet from the bow, and on the starboard side.

The harpoons are used either for thrusting or darting, and a skilful harpooner will throw them with sufficient force to secure a walrus at four or five fathoms distance ; when possible, however, they are always thrust or stabbed into the animal, and in that case it is customary to give the weapon a twist or wrench, both for the purpose of withdrawing the shaft, that it may not be lost or broken, as well as to entangle the barbs more securely in the walrus's skin or blubber. If this precaution be neglected the harpoon may, perhaps, come out by the cut which it made on entering : this is more likely to happen if the intended victim be lying with his skin *slack.*

When there is much likelihood of falling in with white whales (*Beluga* or *Balæna albicans*) it is usual to carry one harpoon of a different construction, and with fifty fathoms of line attached for their especial benefit. The reason for requiring a different harpoon for these cetaceans is that their skin is not, like that of the walrus, the toughest part of their body; but the skin of *Balæna albicans*, on the contrary, is quite tender, gristly, and gelatinous, and the barbed iron, therefore, requires to be driven in until it secures good holding in his flesh beneath the blubber.

Next in the list of the boat's appurtenances come four or five enormous lances with shafts of white pine, nine feet long and one and a half inch thick at the handle, increasing upwards to two and a half inches thick where it goes into the socket of the iron. Formidable as the weapon is, the iron shank is very frequently bent double, or the stout shaft snapped like a twig by the furious struggles of a wounded walrus; so, to prevent the head being lost, it is attached to the shaft by a stout double thong of raw seal-skin, tied round the shank and nailed to the shaft for about three feet up. The reason for having the shaft so disproportionately large is that there may be buoyancy enough to float the heavy iron spear if it should happen to fall into the water, or if a walrus, as often happens, should succeed in wrenching it out of the operator's hands by the violence of his contortions. I have once or twice had a whole boat's complement of lances rendered for the time unserviceable in the despatching of a single walrus. The lances lie on the thwarts, with the blades protected in a box, which is attached to the starboard end of the harpooner's, or foremost one.

The lance is not used for seals, as it is unnecessary and spoils the skins, so that the *coup de grâce* is ad-

ministered to them by the 'haak-pick' being struck
into the brain. Each boat should have five of these
implements, which are also indispensable as boat-hooks,
for pushing and hooking when the ice is too close to
allow of the oars being used.

There are then two axes, one a large one, used for
decapitating the dead walruses ; and the other, a small
handy axe, which always lies close to the harpooner,
is for cutting the line in case anything goes wrong, or
a walrus proves so fierce and mischievous that we
may wish to be quit of him on any terms.

Five or six large sharp knives are for stripping the
skin and blubber off the animals, or 'flensing' them, as
it is called in the fisher's parlance.

An ice-anchor is employed for anchoring the boat
to an iceberg, and also to afford a *fulcrum* by which,
with the help of two double purchase-blocks and twenty-
four fathoms of rope (also forming part of every boat's
appointments), five or even four men can drag the
biggest walrus on to a moderately-flat iceberg for the
purpose of flensing him.

A small compass is indispensable, and ought to be
fixed into a box attached below the seat in front of the
steersman, after the fashion of a billiard-table chalk-
box. So are a telescope, a rifle, and plenty of ammunition, an iron baling-ladle, also answering as a frying-
pan, and a small copper kettle for making coffee.

There is a locker in the fore-peak, and another in the after-peak of the boat,. and in these there ought to be always stowed a hammer, a pair of nail-nippers, a small bag of nails, and a piece of sheet lead for patching the boat if a walrus should put his tusks through her bottom : a bag of cartridges, spare grummets, a box of matches and brimstone, a canister of coffee, and twenty or thirty pounds of rye bread. A mast, yard, and sail are taken if a stay of a few hours from the ship is contemplated; but a boat ought never to leave the ship's side—or even to hang on the davits—without the whole of the other foregoing articles being inside of her; because, if a boat leaves the ship, even if only to kill a seal a quarter of a mile off, you never can be certain that you will ever see the ship again ! You get led on and on insensibly, in the excitement of the chase, from one seal or one troop of walruses to another, and the dense fogs or sudden gales of these regions may come on and prevent your finding your way back.

In addition to all these absolute necessaries we always had one luxury, consisting of a bag of mackintosh cloth lined with fur, and about six feet by three, rolled into a tight bundle and strapped under the after-thwart of each boat. This was to crawl into in case of being long out in severe weather, and although we seldom had occasion to make use of it, still the sense of comfort and security it gave one was very great; because I consider that it made one quite able to defy any cold that might occur in the Arctic regions in summer.

As for provisions, I never felt any uneasiness on that score, as, even if a seal or a walrus could not be immediately obtained, there were always plenty of eider-ducks on the islands and outlying skerries; and the sea everywhere abounded with divers and guille-mots, plenty enough and tame enough to be shot with a rifle. If a stay of many hours from the ship was contemplated I generally took with me a shot-gun and a bag of cartridges for the purpose of killing fowls for food if necessary.

Knowing well from former experience the great difficulty of shooting the walrus—or, at least, of shoot-ing him in such a way as to get possession of him when shot—I had had made by Reilly a double-barrelled C.F. breech-loading rifle of 8 bore, intended chiefly for shell practice. This rifle weighed thirteen and a half pounds, and its proper charge was nine drachms of powder besides three drachms inside of the large conical shell. I found this charge by no means unpleasant to shoot, but its effect was disappointing. My idea in getting this shell-rifle had been that, while the walruses were hurriedly scuttling off the ice and a brain shot at the back of the head not easily attainable, I should be able to lodge an explosive shell in any part of their huge carcases, and that they would thus be disabled and easily harpooned. The result, however, in most instances was, that the walrus was so completely blown up, that he went to the bottom and never reappeared!

Whereas, if I did get a quiet shot at the deadly spot on the back of the head, the terrific blow from the big rifle, either with shot or shell, was no better than that from a smaller and handier weapon. Upon the whole, I came to the conclusion that for all Arctic sport there is no weapon to beat a nine-pound double express of ·450 bore, with solid bullets hardened with tin or antimony for walrus, and soft hollow-fronted bullets filled with wax for deer and seals.

We had not gone through any ceremony in honour of crossing the Arctic Circle—I fancy we were mostly all too old sailors—nor did we now keep any 'fast' or 'feast' of the midnight sun, seen for the first time three quarters of a degree above the horizon on the night of May 18th.

This phenomenon hardly strikes the observer, because, in his voyage north, the twilight has lengthened so gradually that at ten, eleven, and twelve o'clock at night reading on deck has become, without sudden warning, a matter of course. Nor are there any special characteristics to rivet the attention, or distin-

guish a midnight sun from the orb when he approaches
a similar position with regard to the horizon in any
other climate, if the mind be divested of romance or
tricked into oblivion of the solemn hour.

For the next four months no candle or lamp will
be lighted on board; day and night in thick weather
can only be regulated by the chronometer, and although
such a *bouleversement* of the natural course of events is
at first perplexing and finally monotonous, still it is
an arrangement of infinite importance, and without it
Arctic navigation would be utterly impracticable.
During the autumn and winter of 1872, when it was
known that Professor Nordenskiold with his own three
vessels and four Norwegian sloops in addition (the
latter totally unprovided for such an event) were wintering in Spitzbergen, no less than three expeditions,
sent out for their relief, were baffled by the darkness, as
well as by the incessant formation of ice on every part
of the ship, whereby the sails became like boards, and
the running rigging immovably frozen.

To-night we secured the first item of a collection
of birds peculiar to these regions which I was anxious
to obtain; a snowy owl (*Stryx nictea*), pursued and
annoyed by kittiwakes, flew round the ship, and, finally .
alighting on the main truck, was easily shot. Although
by no means a rare bird in Davis' Straits, Spitzbergen,
Novaya Zemlya, and the northern parts of Europe, the

circumstance of this specimen being found so far from land, some 180 miles from the nearest coast—that of Lapland—is worthy of record. The skin being duly preserved, we made the experiment of having the carcase dressed for dinner, and found the cooked flesh by no means unpalatable, the flavour being somewhat between that of roast goose and venison.

Nor were we, although out of sight of land, wanting in the society of other feathered companions; that truly Arctic bird, the 'mollie,' as the whalers term it, also known as the 'mallemucke' and 'Arctic petrel' (*Fulmaris glacialis*), might always be seen flitting like a restless spirit over the waves. The Boatswain gull (*Lestris Richardsonii*) now joined us, and the noisy kittiwakes beguiled the evening hours by their voracious anxiety to swallow the cubes of pork which we cast over the stern with a string attached. In this way we dragged them on board, where they fought and bit like spaniels, till after due examination we set them at liberty again.

The afternoon of May 20 introduced to us another common feature of the Arctic seas. A sunny day had tempted us to remove our mattresses and bedding from the berths, wet from the sweating of new timbers, to dry on deck; suddenly a thick white fog enveloped the whole ship and shut out the welcome sun. These fogs, which from their sudden invasion often place a ship in great peril when near land or in the neighbourhood of icebergs, and endanger the lives of boats' crews which have left their vessels, perhaps, on a bright and un-clouded day, are characterised often by their extremely local character. The explorer enters them as one might venture into the sombre precincts of a dense forest, and after groping about for a short time he emerges from them with just as great surprise to en-counter the same bright weather and clear horizon he has recently left. Occasionally, during the whole time the sun may be discerned dimly through the mist, or he may be shining benignly on the truck and upper rigging. Sometimes moisture is deposited on every-thing, but more often the fog is perfectly dry.[1]

I judged by the fog, by the rapid cooling of the surface sea temperature, by the shallow water (fourteen fathoms) and by our known position—about forty miles north of the island of Kolguev, that we could not be far distant from the ice which last year, we had been told, stretched in an irregular sweep from this island to

---

[1] Local Arctic fogs are doubtless due to the rapid changes in the tem-perature of the air, the results of moving masses of ice. The sun has very considerable power at noon (I have noticed the maximum solar radia-tion in 78° 57′ N. to be as high as 113° Fahr.). This allows the air to take up a vast amount of moisture from the sea by evaporation, and when a large body of ice impelled by a swift current meets this saturated at-mosphere, immediate condensation and fog are the consequences. The condensing agent, ice, being in rapid motion, it is not necessary that the volume of air should move from the locality where it has received its aqueous character.

the south-west coast of Novaya Zemlya. This surmise proved correct. Early next morning a stream of ice was visible from the mast-head, but, a N.E. wind springing up, we were compelled to beat away to the north lest the ice, driven by the gale, should come down in quantity and jam us on the lee coast.

Although we made no further progress during the next few days, merely keeping our own in beating to windward, we soon fairly met the ice which came down with the wind from the N.E.

On the morning of May 22nd we sighted Kolguev; at four o'clock ice was seen from the crow's-nest; half an hour later it could be traced as a broken white line from the deck, and shortly after, in latitude 70° N., longitude 49° 21′ E., we were alongside of a stream of 'brash ice,' composed of small lumps and flat cakes some dozen feet square, covered with snow, and floating in a semi-consolidated mass of half-thawed ice and snow of the consistence of gruel. Between this stream of a mile in width and the denser pack a lane of water intervened, in which, to our disgust, were seen several Norwegian walrus-sloops taking shelter from the gale— this ice, although not known as 'heavy pack,' rendering the sea perfectly smooth to leeward of it, whatever the force of the wind.

Though we were thus anticipated on the fishing-ground, I resolved to turn the circumstance to account by sending a boat away to glean what information they could afford us of the shift of ice and direction of currents in this little-frequented locality. For it must be remembered that in this year, 1869, the Kara Sea, with the ice-drifts round Novaya Zemlya, had not yet become the well-known 'ocean highway' that it has since. Nor had the ships which visited these regions in 1868 and 1869 any but the vaguest sailing directions. There were, it is true, the meagre accounts of the early voyagers of the latter half of the sixteenth century: of Burrough, who discovered the Kara Gates; of Pet, who first sailed through Yugorsky Schar; of Barentz's unfortunate wintering at the north-east of Novaya Zemlya; and of Willoughby, still more disastrously frozen-up 500 miles further south on the coast of Lapland, after he had discovered Goose Land. Admiral Lutke, from 1821 to 1824, was engaged in a survey of Novaya Zemlya, and the Russian Government had mapped all the coast east of the White Sea to Behring's Straits. But while the terrors of ice and dangers of the seas encumbered the accounts of one class of narrators, the more exact information of the shore observers was alike useless for purposes of navigation; and from neither could a useful series of facts concerning weather, currents, anchorages, and the habits of the sea-monsters be culled. Even the Russian traders, who, from very early times, and who still make their way from Arch-

angel to the mouth of the Obi by dragging sledges over
the neck of the Samoyede peninsula, know of nothing
but the narrow lane of land-water which enables
them to pursue their trade before the seas are clear of
ice.[1]

The skipper of one of the sloops informed us these
vessels had been out from Hammerfest three weeks,
but so unfavourable had the weather been that in all
this time the sun had only shown on three days, and
they had fished one day with two reefs in the mainsail.
So thick were the walruses, and so fearless at this
period of the Novaya Zemlya fishing, that, notwithstanding the foul weather he had secured 110 walruses, 32
of which were killed in one day. The other sloops had
each from 40 to 90 walruses on board. Our intelligent informant, who had had thirty years' experience of
the Spitzbergen fishing, considers the walruses smaller
here but fatter. A large bull had a few days ago taken
one of his boats under the ice, the men fortunately
escaping on to the pack. He ascribes the paucity of
walruses in Spitzbergen, where in his early days they

[1] I am aware that between the years 1734 and 1738 the coast between
Archangel and the Yenisei was explored piecemeal by the Russian navy;
but the practical deductions from these expeditions were naturally not in
my possession in 1869, when only chance sent me to Novaya Zemlya, nor
were they known to the Norwegian sloops' skippers. It was not till after
my voyage, when Novaya Zemlya became fashionable, that the information contained in the valuable Russian text, through the enterprise of Dr.
Petermann, became accessible to ordinary readers.

swarmed in thousands, to their having been killed or dispersed to these and other seas. He thinks there is probably plenty of game here yet, but, the ice being partly driven down, the walruses have retreated to the fields of ice which still hang to the coast. Others may have gone into the Kara Sea, which 'he fears to enter, as a current, alleged to run five knots an hour, scours the Kara Straits.' Two sloops, which were observed in the last gale to be drifting down towards Kolguev, are supposed to have been crushed between the ice and the reefs of that inhospitable island, as they have not been heard of since, and no harbours are known in the vicinity.

Of the resources of the land itself he knew nothing, except that the game, including reindeer, was ' strictly preserved, the Russians not allowing any foreigner to shoot within four miles of the coast.' By what system of keepers these desolate preserves were protected he did not pretend to explain. Furthermore 'he believed the Samoyede hunters, who came over from the mainland, were so wild a set of people that it was necessary to shoot some occasionally to keep the rest in order.' I was not alarmed at this account of these poor half-barbarians, whom the skipper honestly believed would kill us to get our clothes; for I had recently heard an authentic account of the wreck of a vessel on the coast of Yelmert Land, whose crew these same Samoyedes entertained, clothed, and finally sledged down to the Petchora. Having offered hospitality, in the shape of brandy, to the worthy skipper (of the beverage, neat, this temperate individual could not be prevailed upon to swallow a drop more than half a bottle), we bade him farewell.

We were destined to sail in company a little longer. The wind now continued to freshen, and, if I describe the circumstances of the next three days, the reader will in future be able to realise the misery of our surroundings whenever the simple announcement of a north-east gale is made.

The summer gales of Novaya Zemlya may be classified as with and without snow. The former are productive of the *most* abject state of despair. Only the crew actually engaged on the deck, and the Norseman who, with his feet in a bag of hay and his beard encrusted with snow, sits like a hoary patriarch at the wheel, need face the snow and sleet which eddy in the wind and are driven into every corner of the ship. With scarcely a rag of canvas set we beat uneasily up and down the edge of the ice; or, apprehensive of the drift by lee-way and unknown currents, slant out through the lugubrious mist to secure an offing. Sometimes the lifting cloud allows us to gaze wearily on the black cliffs, where they run out from the mainland to end in treacherous reefs—on the eternal snows

which cover the dreary uplands and ledges of the cliffs
—or the dark water laden with moving masses of ice,
and on the fog which hardly allows us to steer clear of
them. The damp fog and driving sleet passing over the
deck and rigging freeze and leave a glassy, slippery
covering on every exposed part—sails, ropes, and spars
look as if wrought in glass. Two inches of ice on the
deck in a continuous slide from the cook's galley to the
cabin sometimes reduces the number of courses at
dinner, for the steward is no skilful skater, and the
spilled soup freezes with the rest. We make frequent
tacks to avoid rocks on one side and the grinding stream
of eddying icebergs on the other, and at every tack a
crisp shower of icicles, printed with the pattern of sails
and ropes, clattering to the deck, gives the appearance
of a recently-demolished glass-shop. The noise of the
floating ice crashing against the bows sometimes cul-
minates in a terrific shock, which makes the ship quiver
from stem to stern. The angle at which the ship heels
over to leeward renders ordinary occupations impossible; and, rather than encounter the hazard of
tumbling and rolling against each other in the narrow
cabin, we sit in well-jammed positions, and spend the
time in desultory reading.

These gales, of which I have had several years' experience coinciding with that of other vessels, are most
prevalent early in the season, May and June—com-

mencing at any hour of the twenty-four, they usually last from sixty to eighty hours. The direction of the wind is commonly from some point between E. and N.— I *have* noticed it N.W. when at its height—from the former it veers through N., and finally the gale breaks up with a sou-westerly wind, and cirrus and stratus clouds or actual sunshine. During their continuance the excessive cold and the difficulty of obtaining the ship's position by observation are *the* most serious inconveniences. The cause of these gales is to be sought in the difference in pressure between two large atmospheric districts separated by the mountainous boundary of Novaya Zemlya, nowhere more than sixty miles wide, which difference is modified from time to time by the shifting conditions of ice in the two seas.

Bad ice and the extreme cold prevented our seeing much game till the weather cleared. A few old walruses were observed to wallow about uncomfortably here and there in the half-thawing compound consisting of the wreck of ice-floes. Good walrus-ice is made up of flat cakes, of about double the size of a dining-room, floating sufficiently far apart to admit of easy access by a boat. A hummock here and there is of immense importance to screen an advancing crew. On such masses a single walrus, a family party, or, what sends a thrill to the sportsman's heart, a conclave of several old bulls, will lie and bask in the sun, or display their huge carcases in the limpness of sleep, for many hours together. Where there are more than one, an individual is always told off to act as sentinel while the rest sleep ; and I have seldom if ever caught this sentinel neglecting his duty.

A few snow-gulls (Larus Niveus, Glacialis, Eburneus) and an occasional Burgomaster (Larus Glaucus) alone give life to the ice-edge. Vast crowds of guillemots, puffins, little awks, and other birds frequent the shores of the Northern bays and seas, as their breeding-haunts are seldom found far from the coast.

Seals are always to be seen, and in all weathers troops of the small Jan Mayen seals (Phoca Groenlandica) appeared at the height of the gale raising their human-like faces over the crests of the waves, and a solitary grey seal (Phoca Barbata) was occasionally observed on a cake of ice.

As we neared the sacred Island of Kolguev, with its long line of cliffs, broken here and there by dark narrow ravines so as to give them the appearance of gigantic earth-works pierced by embrasures, flocks of looms, widgeons, pintails, and geese, flying towards the land, indicated the spot as one of the extensive breeding-places of that great army of migratory birds which seeks a milder climate in the colder months of the year.

Kolguev is not permanently inhabited; that is to say, the poverty of vegetation, and its inaccessibility during a great part of the year render it useless for purposes of colonisation; but enterprising Russian traders around the White Sea contrive to obtain a considerable yearly profit from the game which frequent the island. Wandering and houseless Samoyedes are hired and taken here in the spring, provided with every appliance for hunting and existence. Left to themselves they hunt the walrus, seal, bear, and fox, and in summer they rob the nests of the geese and swans for eggs, and those of the eider-duck for both eggs and down. After the breeding-season, before migration south takes place, immense bags of ducks, geese, and swans are made, and the birds are ultimately salted for the Russian markets. From time to time the task-masters visit these self-elected serfs to collect the skins, oil, and other produce; and only then, perhaps twice a year, is there an opportunity of leaving this inhospitable shore.

The only record of any attempt made to colonize Kolguev is that of the year 1767, when a persecuted religious sect took refuge here. Scurvy proved such a scourge that the few survivors were soon glad to leave an asylum where spiritual liberty was only to be purchased at the price of bodily mortification.

A Nor'-east Gale off Kolguev.

Young Walruses Asleep.

At present it was no matter of regret that alternate lanes of water and streams of ice, and finally a belt of fast-ice, prevented all access to this tempting part of the Russian dominions. The shallow water (at one time we observed nine fathoms only) makes its neighbourhood a favourite feeding-ground for walrus, who dive for the mollusca and cancri, on which they feed.

I was gratified on May 27, after steaming nearly all day over this bank among loose ice, to have an opportunity of drawing ' first blood.' The beast killed was a young bull of some two or three years, technically reckoned by Norwegian skippers ' a half-walrus,' but its death was void of any particular interest.

Later in the day a cow and calf afforded some sport, for, after despatching the former, the cub swam round the boat, and was easily captured—a queer little beast not unlike a pig, with the unpicturesque corners of that animal rounded off, and fins substituted for feet. ' Tommy,' as the new arrival was christened by the crew, was slung and hove on board uttering the most discordant cries which ever assailed the ears of man, and never appeared to greater advantage than when he was taken in the arms of old ' Wully,' the mate (not unlike a walrus himself in the Arctic rugosity of his face), and laid gently on deck.

A harsh note—or, more properly speaking, noise, something between a grunt and a bark—henceforth, till we were hardened to the annoyance, broke our slumbers at night and destroyed the peace and quiet of the day. Though particularly anxious to secure and carry home a young specimen of this interesting animal, we soon found that the company of so noisy a shipmate, with the anxiety connected with its weaning, was not an unmixed blessing.

Walrus-skippers are divided in opinion as to the effect of a junger's cries on the older walruses in the neighbourhood. My harpooner on this occasion declared that we should infallibly frighten them all away. On the other hand, many men I have conversed with have averred that there is no more successful trick in the trade than to secure a ' leetle-boy-walrus,' and, by prodding him up with the butt-end of a lance, elicit the plaintive barks which cannot fail to appeal to the clannish instincts of any walrus within hearing. My own experience leads me to subscribe to the latter opinion.

I remember on one occasion, some years ago, falling in with a herd of walruses *in the water*. The mode of attack was to endeavour to harpoon them, by dint of hard rowing after the herd, as they alternately dived and swam on the surface to gain breath. If there are calves in the herd they cannot go much faster than the boat, if so fast; and, the calves having to come up to breathe much more frequently than the old ones, the whole herd generally accommodate their pace to that of the old cows with young ones.

In all my sporting experience I never saw anything to equal the wild excitement of such a hunt. Five pairs of oars pulled with utmost strength make the boat seem to fly through the water, while, perhaps, a hundred walruses, roaring, bellowing, blowing, snorting and splashing, make an acre of the sea all in a foam before and around her. The harpooner stands with one foot on the thwart and the other on the front locker, with the line coiled in his right hand, and the long weapon in both hands ready balanced for a dart, while he shouts to the crew which direction to take (as he, from standing upright in the boat, has a better opportunity of seeing the walruses under water).

The herd generally keep close together, and the way in which they dive and reappear again simultaneously is remarkable; one moment you see a hundred grisly heads and long gleaming white tusks above the waves, they give one spout from their blow-holes, take one breath of fresh air, and the next moment you see a hundred brown hemispherical backs, the next a hundred pair of hind flappers flourishing, and then they are all down.

On, on goes the boat as hard as ever we can pull

E

the oars, up come the sea-horses again, pretty close
this time, and before they can draw breath the boat
rushes into the midst of them; whish! goes the harpoon; birr! goes the line over the gunwale, and a
luckless junger, on whom the harpooner has fixed his
eye, is fast: his bereaved mother, snorting with rage,
charges the boat with flashing eyes, she quickly receives
a harpoon in the back and a bullet in the brain, and
hangs lifeless on the line; now the junger begins
to utter his plaintive grunting bark, and fifty furious
walruses close round the boat in a few seconds, rearing
up breast high in the water, and snorting and blowing
as if they would tear us all to pieces. Two of these
auxiliaries are speedily harpooned in their turn, and
the rest hang back a little, when, as bad luck would
have it, the junger gives up the ghost, owing to the
severity of his harpooning, and the others, no longer
attracted by his cries, retire to a more prudent distance.
But for this untoward and premature decease of the
junger, the men told me we should have had more
walruses on our hands than we could manage. This
curious clannish practice of coming to assist a calf in
distress arises from their being in the habit of combining to resist the attacks of the polar bear, which is
said often to succeed in killing the walrus; if, however,
Bruin, pressed by hunger and a tempting opportunity,
is so ill-advised as to snatch a calf, the whole herd come

upon him, drag him under water, and tear him to pieces with their long sharp tusks.

A hunter told me that he saw an instance of this. The bear was pulled under water, and, as my informant said, 'nothing of him came up again but small scraps of skin with white hair on them.'

I once made the acquaintance of a skipper of a sloop, who had been seized by a bereaved cow-walrus, and by her dragged twice to the bottom of the sea, but without receiving any injury beyond being nearly drowned, and having a deep scar ploughed in each side of his forehead by the tusks of the animal. He thought she did not wish to hurt him, but mistook him for her calf, as he floundered in the water.

No animal displays more strong maternal affection than the walrus. One of my first walrus-hunting experiences, when I was yet under the tutorship of a clever harpooner, one Christian, demonstrated the above fact very forcibly to my mind. We had got fast to a cow-walrus, who was dragging the boat furiously amongst the icebergs, and I was going to shoot her through the head that we might have time to follow the rest of the troop, but Christian called to me not to shoot, as she had a 'junger' with her. Although I did not then understand his object, I reserved my fire, and, upon looking closely at the walrus when she came up to breathe, I then perceived that she held a very young calf under her right flipper, and I saw that he wanted to harpoon it, but, whenever he poised the weapon to throw, the old cow seemed to watch the direction of it, and interposed her own body, and she seemed to receive with pleasure several harpoons which were intended for the young one. At last, when a well-aimed dart struck the calf, and we had dispatched the cow, Christian had time and breath to explain why he was so anxious to secure the calf. Unfortunately, however, we had been so long in getting hold of our poor little decoy-duck, that the others had all gone out of hearing, and they abandoned their young relative to his fate, which quickly overtook him in the shape of a lance-thrust from the remorseless Christian.

Taking into consideration the facility with which a walrus cub may be captured, it seems strange that they are not more often met with in the zoological gardens of Europe. Attempts are made from time to time both by the Norwegian hunters and by the Davis Straits whalers to bring specimens to the European markets, and, indeed, several have arrived alive at the Norwegian ports, and at least three have been safely landed on our own shores; one from Cherie Island, as long as two and a half centuries ago, one in 1853, and a third, brought home in the 'Arctic' whaler, was sold to the authorities of the Zoological Gardens for two hundred guineas. But until some special vessel, with cows on board, or plenty of Swiss preserved milk, visits the walrus haunts and thus solves the difficulty of weaning, it will not be easy to import a young walrus in good condition, and many of the interesting habits and traits of this animal will remain unknown.

Although the calf of the previous season frequently accompanies the dam with her more recent offspring, at that age the ' half-walrus' is too unwieldy a beast to be easily captured alive; if this were practicable, there can be no doubt its nutrition would be a simpler matter.

The walrus is distinctly a carnivorous animal; its natural food consists of the mollusca it obtains about the Arctic coast, either finding them about the rocks exposed by the tide, or more usually diving for them in from ten to twenty-five fathoms of water covering submarine banks. Fish have occasionally been found in the stomachs. An isolated fact of this kind, together with the similarity in form of the walrus and seal, might easily suggest a theory of similarity in seeking food, a theory, however, quickly confuted by a practical study of the comparative clumsiness of the walrus, and a due appreciation of those formidable tusks which are used to plough up the sea-bottom in search of shells.

The form of the long eye-teeth or tusks obeys the law which applies to the modification of the teeth of other animals, viz., that any peculiarity points essentially to the method of feeding, although such peculiarity may subordinately be useful in other ways, notably for protecting the individual, and here for climbing on to the ice-floes from the water.

Walruses use their tusks against one another very much in the manner that game-cocks use their beaks. From the animal's unwieldy appearance and the position of his tusks one is apt to fancy that the latter can only be used in a stroke *downwards*, but, on the contrary, they can turn their necks with great facility and quickness, and can strike either upwards, downwards, or sideways, with equal dexterity. I have frequently observed them fighting with great ferocity on the ice, and the skins of the old bulls, which are light-coloured and nearly devoid of hair, are often covered with scars and wounds received in these encounters. Frequently one or both tusks have been broken in fighting, or in clambering up the ice and rocks, but they soon get worn and sharpened to a point by the sand at the sea-bottom, which they plough up in search of food.

The tusks are very firmly embedded for about six or seven inches of their length in a mass of hard and dense bone, forming the front of the animal's head. This long protuberance is the size of a man's skull, and through it runs the passage by which the animal breathes, the blow-holes lying between the roots of the tusks. That part of the tusk which is embedded in the head is hollow, or rather filled up with a cellular bony structure containing oil; the rest of the tusk is hard and solid throughout.

The calf has no tusk the first year, but the second year, when it has attained to the size of a large seal, it has a pair about as large as the canine teeth of a lion; the third year they are about six inches long. Instances have been known of two tusks growing together in a single socket on one side, while the tusk of the other side has appeared singly as usual.

Tusks vary much in size and shape according to the age and sex of the animal. A *good pair* of bull's tusks may be stated as twenty-four inches long, and four pounds a piece in weight; but I have obtained several pairs above these dimensions, and in particular one pair which measure thirty-one inches in length and weigh eight pounds each. Such a pair of tusks, however, is extremely rare, and I never, to the best of my belief, saw a pair nearly equal to them amongst many thousand walruses, although I always took the utmost pains to secure the best, and invariably inspected the tusks carefully with the glass, before firing a shot or throwing a harpoon.

Cows' tusks will *average* fully as long as bulls', from their being less liable to be broken, but they are seldom more than twenty inches long, and three pounds each in weight; they are generally set much closer together than the bulls' tusks, sometimes overlapping one another at the points, as seen in the stuffed specimen in the British Museum. The tusks of old bulls, on the contrary, generally diverge from one another, being sometimes as much as fifteen inches apart at the points. It is a common belief amongst the hunters that those walruses which have wide-set tusks are the most savage and dangerous, and more particularly if the tusks diverge from one another in *curves*, as is sometimes, though rarely, the case. I can easily conceive that this opinion is well-founded, because it is evident that a walrus with tusks diverging at the points must be much *handier* in the use of them than if they stick straight down, or curve inwards or towards the breast. I remember once going on board a small sloop, and seeing the skull of an old walrus with remarkably wide-set tusks lying on deck. My harpooner remarked to the captain of the sloop: 'That must have been a troublesome customer!' 'I believe you,' said the skipper, 'he put his tusks through the boat and nearly upset us. Look here,' he continued, pointing to the bottom of a boat hanging on the davits, 'and see what the scoundrel did.' A piece had been torn out of one of the planks, and the hole was patched with sheet-lead.

Stor Gamle Oxy Hvalross.

Walrus-tusks are composed of extremely hard, dense, and white ivory. Their small size rendering them inapplicable for many ivory manufactures, they do not command nearly the price of elephant ivory, but they are high in repute for the manufacture of false teeth, and are also made into chessmen, umbrella-handles, whistles, and similar small articles. In the cabin of the 'Diana' during foul weather we found many hours' amusement and occupation in shaping the tusks into very respectable paper-knives with the aid of the carpenter's saw and files.

The upper lip of the walrus is thickly set with strong, horny bristles about six inches long, and as thick as a crow-quill; and this terrific moustache, together with his long white tusks, and fierce-looking blood-shot eyes, gives *Rosmarus trichechus* altogether a most unearthly and demoniacal appearance as he rears his head above the waves. Possibly the old fable of the mermaid may have been originated by their grim resemblance to the head of a human being when in this position.

We were now fairly among the walruses, and I proposed to enjoy a month's sport, while waiting for the genial influences of the sun and Gulf Stream to enable us to cleave a passage through the northern ice.

On the 28th a good many old ones were seen, and I killed three cows, a calf, and a year-old bull. At this time of the year it is quite usual to find the cows with their calves in one part of the seas, while the old bulls are probably still in the recesses of the bays and straits, or even in the Kara Sea.

The walrus is essentially an animal of the coast and shallow water. Little is known of their habits during the winter, but my belief is that they congregate in vast numbers at that season about the S.W. edges of the great ice-packs of Novaya Zemlya and Spitzbergen. A walrus is occasionally found floating on a slab of ice in the open sea, but this is an accidental instance of imprudence on his part, and accounts for the occasional, but rare appearance of a live walrus on the coasts of Norway and even Scotland.[1]

A dead walrus scarcely ever floats until the gases of decomposition have lessened his specific gravity, so that although many which are shot die at the bottom, they are very seldom found floating; the current takes them hundreds of miles away before they are met with. I have only myself found three or four out of many hundreds which I have known to be killed and lost in the water.

[1] Such instances are not by any means so rare on the north coast of Norway. A large bull was killed in Magerö Sound near the North Cape about 1868; but I have not heard of any instance of a walrus being seen on the coast of Scotland since one was killed in the Harris about forty years ago. I made special enquiry about this individual when in the Long Island in the winter of 1860–61, but could not ascertain any further particulars. Although the natives had a distinct tradition of his capture, I could not meet with anyone who had been present on the occasion.

As soon as the ice begins to break up in the spring the walruses move with it. As summer advances and the seas become clear of ice they congregate together in troops, and finally go ashore in some rocky bay, where sometimes they have been found in herds of thousands. Here, towards the end of August, they remain for weeks together in a semi-torpid state, without moving or feeding.

The war of extermination which has been carried on for many years in Spitzbergen and Novaya Zemlya has driven all the Arctic fauna from their old haunts, and, in seeking retreats more inaccessible to man, it is probable that they have had in some degree to alter their habits. For example, up to about twenty years ago it was customary for all walrus-hunters to entertain a reasonable hope that by waiting till late in the season all former ill-luck might be compensated in a few fortunate hours by killing some hundreds on shore ; in fact, favourite haunts were well known to the fishers, and were visited successively before finally leaving the hunting-grounds. Now, although the Arctic Seas are explored by steamers and visited annually by as bold and enterprising hunters as formerly, such a windfall as a herd of walruses ashore is seldom heard of.

Each year better-found vessels and more elaborate weapons are sent out to harry the walrus: as a conse-quence every season there is greater difficulty in obtaining a cargo—for two reasons, those animals which have ventured into what was safe feeding-ground last year meet their enemy, and half are killed, while the other half escaping will be found next year a step farther away. This intelligent retreating of the walrus before a superior enemy will, I believe, preserve the species after its scarcity in accessible waters renders it no longer an object of sport and commerce.

That the walrus, still ranging over the whole of the circumpolar regions and formerly descending as far south as the Arctic Circle, is being driven from every district where the hand of man is felt, is certain. In the ninth century the morse was hunted by Ohthere on the north Scandinavian coast. Up till the end of the fifteenth century it was a regular visitor of our own shores, and it has been assumed from this that the ivory ornaments of the early British horse-trappings and weapons were carved from walrus tusks.

Since the middle of the sixteenth century, when the attempts to find a north-east passage to China led to the exploration of the Arctic Seas and the discovery of Spitzbergen, the walrus has been hunted there by Dutch, English, and Norwegians, and about Novaya Zemlya by the Russians. In the sixteenth and seventeenth centuries they were described as abundant about Bear Island, 'lying like hogges upon heaps.' Captain Thomas Edge, in 1616, killed in East Spitzbergen no less than one thousand. Admiral Lutke, who was engaged in surveying the coast of Novaya Zemlya for the Russian Government in the years 1821–1824, declared that the walruses swarmed in Matoschkin Schar. And in 1834 the mouth of the river Nechwatowa behind Kostin Schar used to be one of the favourite stations from which the Russian hunters made short excursions in their karbassas for slaughter and profit. Von Baer, who visited Novaya Zemlya in 1837, and described its natural history and industries, gave a graphic picture of the hazards and difficulties of the chase by the rough modes of attack known to the Russians, and adds that ' after the walruses have been met with for some weeks on the west side of the south island of Novaya Zemlya, finding it too hot and the ice all melted, they retire in July to the Kara Sea. On the coast of the north island they are to be met with during the whole summer in herds and family parties, but only a few hunters seek them here. On the south island,' he goes on to say, ' herds are seldom met with, only an occasional hermit-like male or female, and, therefore, as the Kara Sea was then seldom penetrated, the next chance for the hunters was to wait at the Kara Gate from the middle of August to intercept the herds which at the approach of autumn return from their basking-grounds in the Kara Sea to the ocean.'

In a voyage to Spitzbergen ten years ago I made a

rough calculation that at that time about a thousand walruses were yearly killed there. It will appear in these pages how the walrus has receded gradually from the seas around Spitzbergen and Novaya Zemlya, where early voyagers found such numbers.

Two days' shooting was succeeded by three days' north-east gale, which condemned us to the cabin, with stove alight and hatches closed. The perusal of Arctic literature and meteorological calculations could only be varied by a visit to the hold or the engine-room.

In the former we found amusement in attempts to wean the walrus-cub, who still proved obstreperous when attempts were made to inject preserved milk into his guzzle by means of a special piece of apparatus borrowed from the doctor's case. In all other respects he comported himself with the 'strange docilite' noted by Master Thomas Welden of the 'God Speed' in 1608. He became a great pet with the men: a dear, loving little creature, combining the affection of a spaniel with the proportions of a prize pig. What struck us in watching its singular dexterity was that there could be any difference of opinion as to the hind-flippers of the walrus being used in conjunction with the forepaws after the ordinary method of quadrupeds for walking on land or ice. 'Tommy' also exhibited a marvellous knack in climbing, or rather wriggling his supple carcase up on to casks and packages in the hold.

During an hour's cessation of the snow we had the harpoon-gun mounted on the rail forward. It consists of a stout barrel fixed to a clumsy stock of teak, with a rough curved handle similar to that of a wheelbarrow. This enables it to be depressed or turned in any direction on the swivel fixed to the gunwale of the boat. They are now in universal use among the Scotch whalers, and it was at the suggestion of my whaling-sailing-master I shipped two of these uncouth fire-arms for a first trial against the walrus. The gun is loaded and wadded in the usual way, and lastly a harpoon, like a pair of tongs with line attached, pushed home. As far as we could ascertain by firing into blank space, it seemed to shoot with tolerable precision and great force, and with so small a charge as one-and-a-half ordinary gun-charges the whole of twenty fathoms of line was taken out.

The last evening of the gale, the wind veering, we were enabled to lay the ship in her right course, N.E. A heavy swell, on which the vessel rose and fell like a cork, rolled us to such an extent that we were in some anxiety lest the boats should break away from the davits: the standing rigging was put to a severe test, and the general churning-up of all the heavy goods and spars in the hold made us glad we had put all delicate instruments in our own berths. So high were the waves that a Lapland sloop sailing in company, when she disappeared in the trough, showed only her truck and some yard of topmast above the intervening wave.

During the following night we passed some streams of the heaviest ice yet seen. Old ice-hands have a curious way of putting the cart before the horse in describing the weight of the ice as causing the swell. Rather does a covering of broken ice further disintegrate on meeting a heavy sea and act like oil on troubled waters, converting a cross sea into a lazy swell. The heavy ice we supposed was part of that being driven out of the Kara Sea through the straits we were fast approaching.

As the gale abated on the morning of June 2 it became clearer, and the south-west land of Novaya Zemlya, with a fringe of fast ice, was sighted from the crow's-nest ten or twelve miles distant. Soon after we saw from the deck a low, dark line of coast, partially lost in the heavy bank of clouds, which the cheery sun was then fast dispersing. The ship was kept on a S.E. course, which was continually changed as we threaded our way among the heavy ice. Standing on and off the land, we saw the islands which lie off the extreme S.W. of Novaya Zemlya, and at one time fancied there was a fair chance of passing through the straits into the Kara Sea; but the absence of any appearances of game induced me to put about for a final scour of the sea about Kolguev before venturing into fresh hunting-grounds.

With some regret we finished the last fresh meat, the remaining morsel of an ox purchased in Inverness six weeks ago. The time meat will keep in these high latitudes is indefinite. The preserving power of the frost is well-known to those who have buried ship-mates on Arctic shores. The following statement, given as narrated in the language of my old mate—one out of many really probable yarns—will illustrate the fact :—'When I was in the old "Advice " I mind going ashore at the Duck Islands with our cooper Geordie Robertson to examine the grave of a man he had known—he had been cooper on board the " Anne " of Leith. We found the coffin, not buried in the ground, but covered with a heap of stones and snow, which we removed. The coffin was blanched; but, upon taking off the lid, the body of the dead cooper was discovered as fresh, to all appearance, as the day he died, though he had been dead no less than twenty-one years : his face was quite fresh; *the hair of his head and beard had grown to a great length!* He had a shirt on, and was happed up in a piece of canvas. Geordie recog-nised his face again directly—his name was cut on the foot-board, but I forget it.'

The 3rd opened light, clear, and pleasant; at five A. M. we commenced ' dodging about' the ice, and soon after breakfast the cheerful announcement of ' walrus' roused the ship to action. Going off I shot a cow with

an explosive bullet in the chest, and gaffed and drew
into the boat alive a second cub by means of a shepherd's-crook-like weapon, which I had myself made and
ground to a point for this purpose so late as the evening
before.

Very little of the actual carnage is seen from the
yacht, and the further she is off the better chance for
the boat stealing up to the game. Often have her tall
masts, or ill-timed blowing-off of steam, warned the
keen senses of the sea-horses that we were in the
neighbourhood.

The usual plan of a walrus-hunt is as follows :—We
are either sailing or steaming among 'likely ice,' with
the captain or harpooner on the look-out in the crow's-
nest. We, reading in the cabin or strolling on deck,
are aroused by a few premonitory words : 'Starboard !'
'Steady !' 'Hard-a-port !' which show the look-out is
using his telescope on some object of doubt, which turns
out to be either 'black ice' or game—if the latter, a
sharp cry of 'Stop her,' and a familiar touch of the bell
to the engine-room when steaming, or an order to
'Back fore-topsail' when sailing, puts all in a bustle.
The men have tumbled over each other into the boat
as it is lowered and pushed off. I am usually so well-
prepared, and everything so ready to hand, that by the
time I have taken a rifle from the stand the boat
is ready to be lowered with all her crew in as I step in

from the rail. My place is in the bows, where I busy myself arranging my weapons or pushing away obstructive ice with a 'haak-pik.' On board they watch us skimming along, as the sturdy Norwegians (fed on fish) or sturdier Britons (fed on beef) bend to their oars—each man rows a short pair, stroke-oar standing or kneeling on the thwart facing the others, and guiding the boat at his own discretion, or by watching the signals I give him by pulling or backing either oar. Away we go, silently but swiftly; a few minutes seem to bridge the distance of two or three miles between the ship and our prey. As the boat nears the beasts, often asleep on the ice, the pulling is more wary. When very near we all make ourselves as small as possible, while the boat-steerer alone, kneeling on the bottom-boards, paddles the boat up to within harpooning distance, *i.e.*, two or three fathoms. Now the harpooner, who has been watching his opportunity, peering over the gunwale, anxiously scans the beast; if still snoring he may be pretty sure of getting fast. Quickly rising, he poises the harpoon, and a rapid thrust from a cool and skilful hand is sufficient to bury the harpoon beneath the tough hide of the walrus. If the harpoon holds well without drawing, the game may be reckoned as bagged.

A single walrus will seldom imperil the crew, but if two old bulls of the bulk and strength of a rhinoceros are towing a boat by the lines, it often becomes a critical question whether one or both must not be cut adrift.

I have described the simplest and easiest way in which a walrus may be killed. More often than not we are greeted by a cunning stare from a beast as wide-awake as we are, and we have had the row for nothing by the walruses plunging into the water before it is possible to get within harpooning-distance or even within rifle-shot.

Often curiosity, or the paralysis and confusion of fear, allow one or more shots to be fired, but the aim is difficult at a moving beast from a moving boat. If the exactly fatal spot in the cranium is reached, which can only be done by apparently firing into the neck when a favourable movement of the beast turns the back or side of his neck towards his assailant, he sinks stone dead on the ice. Then the brain has been penetrated; but, unless this is accomplished, either the animal swims off with his fellows and ultimately dies at the bottom, or in a last convulsive twitch, with the malice peculiar to all beasts sought by man for skin or flesh, throws himself headlong into the water and sinks like lead, disappointing the hunter, without in any way prolonging his own life. The object of the harpooner in cases of this kind is to use the harpoon immediately after the walrus is disabled by the bullet, and, when previously shot in

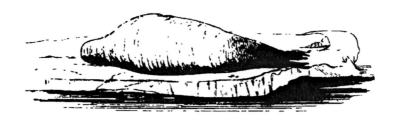

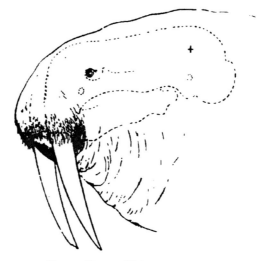

How to Shoot a Walrus.
(The position of the brain is shown by the cross.)

the chest, an opportunity is often afforded by the animal's necessity for coming to the surface to breathe; then the walrus is easily harpooned and secured.

No one who has not tried it will readily believe how extremely difficult it is to shoot an old bull-walrus clean dead. The front or sides of his head may be knocked all to pieces with bullets, and the animal yet have sufficient sense and strength left to enable him to swim and dive out of reach. If he is lying on his side, with his back turned to his assailant (as in the upper figure) it is easy enough, as the brain is then quite exposed, and the crown of the head is easily penetrated ; but one rarely gets the walrus in that position, and when it so happens it is generally better policy to harpoon him without shooting. By firing at an old bull directly facing you it is almost impossible to kill him, but if half-front to you a shot just above the eye may prove fatal. If sideways he can only be killed by aiming about six inches behind the eye, and about one-fourth of the apparent depth of his head from the top; but the eye, of course, cannot be seen unless the animal is very close to you, and the difficulty is enormously increased by the back of the head being so imbedded in fat as to appear as if it were part of the neck. This will be understood by a reference to the plate. If you hit him much below that spot you strike the jaw-joint, which is about the strongest part of the whole cranium. A leaden bullet striking there, or on the front of the head, is flattened like a piece of putty, without doing much injury to the walrus; and even hardened bullets, propelled by six drachms of powder, were sometimes broken into little pieces against the rocky crania of these animals.

When I first began to hunt the walrus long ago in Spitzbergen, many of my failures were attributable to not understanding the anatomy of the animal, and imagining that the brain, instead of being situated as I have described, lay in what appears to a novice to be the head, but which is in reality the massive upper jaw and its connections. At that time—I speak of a period before the introduction of breech-loaders and express-rifles—old Norwegian skippers advised us to refrain from using a gun, as they had a theory it was almost impossible to shoot a walrus dead, and that shooting frightened them and rendered them shy. There is no doubt as to its making them shy, but I soon found out that, when a walrus was shy already, the only chance of bringing him to bag was by firing at his head. At first I failed to do much execution, for the reason given above, and also because, at the advice of the harpooners, I used to refrain from firing until all chance of harpooning the walruses was at an end; and then, when they were all scuffling pell-mell into the water, accurate shooting became next to impossible.

Now that these men can obtain good rifles themselves, our system has been generally adopted. Any successful innovation in sport is always opposed until all can obtain the same advantage.

I proposed to make another innovation, and as this day there were walruses for profit, walruses for pleasure, and walruses for experiments, I took the sailing-master with me on one of my boat-trips to see what we could make of the harpoon-gun. The first trial gave perfect satisfaction. With an ash-shaft about six feet long, fitting the gun and propelled by four drachms of fine powder, a walrus was secured at a distance at which he could not have been got with the hand-harpoon.

Another incident showed the possibility, most unusual, of a dead walrus floating. We had approached pretty nearly to a cow and calf basking in the warm rays of an evening sun: already the mother had looked up at us once or twice, then, lowering her head, sniffed the air, and gave a caressing caution to her cub, and again eyed us apparently without much fear till we got about fifteen yards from her. Now the captain, who stood ready in the bow, fired the harpoon-gun; the harpoon flew over her much too high, a hand-harpoon quickly succeeding also missed, and both animals took to the water. Just as she plunged, however, I gave the cow a shot between wind and water; and the bullet, lodging in her shoulder, compelled her to come quickly to the surface, where I shot her dead before there was time to drive a harpoon. Curiously enough, she floated, and, drifting alongside of the boat, was at last made fast. All the time the young calf was barking round the boat in a most pathetic manner. We had left the gaff behind, and the haak-piks were too short to reach it; so we left it till after the cow had been flensed on a slab of ice, and then had to harpoon and despatch the poor little beast.

After every kill there follows the inevitable process of 'flensing.' The dead beast is towed to the nearest convenient slab of ice, hauled on to this with block and tackle, and divested of its skin and blubber in two halves by deft slashes of large knives in an incredibly short time. The head is struck off to form a trophy, if the tusks are especially good, if not, merely the snout holding the tusks is carried away. The 'krang' or carcase is left on the ice, a feast for bears and the voracious snow-birds and gulls. These latter, by some unknown instinct, have assembled in numbers, and, eddying round in the air overhead, do not wait until we have left the scene of action to commence their feast. So tame are they, that the sailors amuse themselves by knocking them over with the oars.

Thus ended a good day's sport, and I enjoyed a long row back to the yacht with the comfortable reflection that I was six walruses to the good, besides others which had been killed, but, from one accident or another, had been lost.

On the whole, the animals were not so shy as I have seen them, but still were not easy to get, as the ice was unsuitable, and, being in very small pieces, made it almost certain that a walrus when shot would tumble off and sink. Only two *sat* so as to be harpooned without bullets.

While I was away from the ship she nearly ran into two large walruses which were asleep on the ice, and, before the engine could be stopped and a boat lowered, they had scuttled into the water. It was while all on board were intent on the difficulty of pushing through a stream of heavy ice that this over-sight occurred, and, even had the game been seen, no boat could have crept up to them through the dense intervening ice.

Till we had ascertained from experience the good ice-going qualities of the ship it was nervous work ordering a charge through the masses of ice. My sailing-master was not very courageous, and the lion-hearted old mate could not command while we were on board without doing violence to the etiquette of the sea. On myself, therefore, often devolved the respon-sibility of ' taking ' the ice. We often witnessed this exciting piece of navigation from the crow's-nest or mast-head. On went the rakish craft at seven knots

an hour, her bows pointing to the seemingly-impene-
trable barrier, next a dead stop and crash at first
contact with the pack.   The true character of the
obstacle could only be properly estimated by looking
down at it from above, when insignificant cakes of
floating ice were seen to be islands, with treacherous
and sharp-tongued foundations, seven eighths of whose
bulk lay submerged beneath the surface.   After the
first shock the continued force of the screw pushes the
vessel past the first obstacle, and she leaps forward to encounter another, till, hemmed in on all sides, she settles
down to a steady pace, and ultimately ' bores ' through
into more open water.   Among the ice-blocks there is
a great sensation; some of them are made to spin over
each other, while heavier pieces take a downward cant
and are apparently swamped in the black deep.   It is
easy to imagine from this how vessels are often hopelessly
beset.   The ice may prove denser than anticipated, the
ship stops, a few cold nights at the end of the season
freeze all together and the unlucky crew are hopelessly
fixed, fortunate if the pressure which goes on among
the ice, irrespective of season, does not crush their shelter
to pieces before the next summer.

June 5th was the most genial day I have ever
experienced in the Arctic regions.   Light, fleecy clouds
sailed gently across the blue sky, and huge blocks of
ice, gleaming like the purest crystal in the sun, hollowed

out and honeycombed by the water into sapphire and emerald caves, floated gently past us. The absence of wind induced me to get up steam early in the day, in order to make a thorough investigation into the lay of the ice, and as we steamed about all day the throb of the engine alone disturbed the quiet of this agreeable Arctic picture.

On deck, with the steady keel and the agreeable temperature, we passed the morning reading, writing, sketching, and examining anchor-mud under the microscope for diatoms and foraminiferæ.

Our make-believe of a summer's day was but a poor register of the actual temperature, for we found, on consulting the thermometer at noon, that it stood less than half a degree above freezing-point. This discrepancy between appreciated and registered temperature was due to the dryness of the air (as evinced by a comparison of the wet and dry bulb thermometers) and the direction of the little air that stirred, being west, or varying only slightly north or south of it. At noon the solar radiation thermometer stood at 106°. And at four P.M. the ordinary thermometer, hung in the shade, showed a rise of five and a quarter degrees since mid-day. Similar observations of a temperature higher at four P.M. than at noon were recorded on several other occasions. Taken alone, such registers were misleading, for the mean temperatures at these hours during twenty-seven days of May and June, roughly confirmed one of the important conclusions arrived at by a study of Pakhtusof's two-hourly readings, viz., that the mean maximum temperature of Novaya Zemlya from April to October, in common with that of Siberia, Boothia, and other Arctic stations, is greater nearer to midday than to four P.M.—in this differing from the greatest heat of more southern parts of Europe, which is registered about three P.M. Pakhtusof, the Russian explorer, spent the greater part of the years 1832–35 in Novaya Zemlya, and twice wintered on its desolate shores. A long line of Arctic worthies, unknown to ordinary English readers, have immortalized their names in the annals of Novaya Zemlya; and no one has done more for science, and notably for the department of meteorology, than the brave and indefatigable lieutenant sent out by the Archangel merchants.

About noon of this day we passed, what is not altogether a rare spectacle in these seas, a sloop abandoned and beset in the heavy ice. She had probably driven down upon the ice, in the late gales, during a snow-storm, and, not having room to wear, had gone right into the pack and been crushed—a lonely, melancholy object. Her dark hull and shattered mast, standing out sharp against the white background, partly heeling over, water-logged, and fast jammed in the ice, she drifted a helpless wreck.

As we ran along the edge of the pack to gain a nearer view we were convinced the crew had been saved, for the sails had been carefully unbent, and portable property removed. This hope was strengthened by remembering that we had, early in the morning, observed a sloop towing some boats. These, doubtless, belonged to the wreck, and had enabled the crew to put themselves in the way of being picked up. Not being in want of anything we were likely to find on board, we did not care to encounter the labour of getting over the ice to her. Very little of value, I was sure, remained in a vessel deserted by starving Norwegians. The men having evidently escaped, we were indifferent to the fate of the weather-beaten hull.

We had some fine sport with walruses in the course of this day. I got a very large and fat cow (11 ft. 5 in. long), and caught her calf alive. This made the third occupant of the pen we had contrived for the calves in the yacht's bows. In addition I shot dead upon the ice two bulls, one a very large and old animal with fine tusks. One tusk must have been broken long ago, and I unluckily smashed the other with the bullet in trying to shoot between them into his brain, as he lay asleep with his belly towards the boat; my second bullet went through his brain just as he was scrambling to his legs after being awakened by the tremendous concussion of such a blow on the tusk. In the evening I missed another very fine bull—in fact the biggest walrus I had yet seen—and directly afterwards I thought that I had discovered, lying on ice a mile off, a still larger one with superb tusks. We pulled away after him without stopping to use the binocular, and, as we neared him, the bull seemed to grow bigger and bigger, and his tusks to assume enormous proportions. At last keen-eyed Hans (a half-bred Lapp, who was my second harpooner) exclaimed, with a very crest-fallen look, that it was not a walrus at all, but a boat! So it proved to be—a small Samoyede boat turned bottom up on a cake of ice; and what I had fancied to be such a splendid tusk turned out to be a small white oar lying half beneath her.

This was very disappointing, but to make amends we took possession of the coracle, and Hans rowed her back to the ship triumphantly, singing a Lapp song. The boat was of Samoyede make and of the rudest possible construction—she was twelve feet three inches long, and four feet three inches broad, and was built entirely without nails or iron, being literally *sewn together*. Here, whatever the needle may have been, the thread consisted of well-tarred hempen cords running through the timbers and planking.

The karbassas or Siberian coasting-vessels are similarly constructed, the larger, in common with vessels I have seen in Spitzbergen and Vardö, being held together with withies or twigs of twisted birch. Curiously enough the sewing usually outlasts the planking.

In this craft the bottom plank and stern-piece were gouged out of one huge log of pine, the rest of the boat consisting simply of a triangular stern-piece and one board on each side. She was abundantly tarred inside and out. Her gear comprised two small oars, two small iron-pointed boat-hooks, and a greasy seal-skin shoulder-strap attached to her gunwale and evidently intended for the purpose of dragging her over the ice.

We got her on board and had her overhauled and made additionally seaworthy by the carpenter, thinking she would be of service for sketching or solitary shooting excursions in the calm harbours we might anchor in.

While we were out in the boat after walruses, late in the evening, we heard a great many shots some two or three miles away. Looking in the direction of these unaccustomed sounds we perceived the mast of a boat and five or six men standing on the ice firing at something. On approaching we found these to be Samoyedes, with two large boats. and a small one exactly like our prize. They were fast to a fair bull walrus which they killed just as we came up, and were now proceeding to drag it up on the ice, with ice-anchor and block-and-tackle, exactly as a Norwegian crew would do. They evinced no fear of us and jabbered away at a great rate. 'Tabak' was the only word intelligible to our ears, and I signed to them to follow us back to the ship.

As they came alongside and clamoured vociferously for pipes and tobacco we could take more note of their faces. With the exception of a younger one—a fair, chubby, rosy-faced, blue-eyed Russian—they were all dark-skinned, and their physiognomies were decidedly Mongolian, with long dark hair like Eskimos, and with dark, flashing beads of eyes.

Their dress consisted as usual, among these Arctic tribes (Eskimos, Lapps, and Samoyedes), of trousers and long coats of reindeer skin, the latter confined by a girdle round the waist. Underneath they wear an Iceland shirt which seldom or never sees the light or feels the soap.

I could not spare a telescope, which they were very anxious to have, but on seeing a small sheaf of clay pipes and a pound of tobacco, which we handed them, they all raised their hands simultaneously and were so overcome with joy that they pressed upon us every skin and article of value with which the boat was laden. I was loth to take advantage of these poor fellows, but made them happy by accepting a tolerable pair of tusks, as a fair barter for what we had given them.

They did not seem so much impressed as I expected at the sight of the steamer until she blew off steam just over their heads; and at this really startling noise they all seemed to think they were gone men.

We had taken advantage of the sun's welcome appearance in the day to get observations at noon and three P.M. and found ourselves in N. latitude 69° 11′ and E. longitude 53°, Kolguev Island bearing S.W. about fifteen miles distant.

It got gloomy and cold about one A.M. on the 6th, and we banked up the fires and dodged about under sail all night.

At four A.M. I was called up to pursue a small bull, which was killed and brought on board. This beast showed two recent lance wounds and had probably been unsuccessfully attacked by the Samoyedes we had lately seen.

At eight A.M. I was notified from the crow's-nest of a big walrus asleep far off amongst the loose ice. We had a long row up to him, and, as we got nearer, I observed him to be one of the most prodigious bulls I had ever seen.

Helstadt had always been gloomily predicting that the first really big bull we tackled with the Scotch boats would inevitably pull us under water; and I concluded from various significant proceedings on his part that he was very uneasy at the formidable appearance of this beast. He took unusual pains to coil his line, fastened the iron harpoon-head to its handle with great deliberation, gave earnest injunctions to Mathias, the line-holder, and, most significant of all, moved his little axe to a handier place forward, that he might be able to cut the line without delay if necessary. At this last suggestive precaution I remarked to him: 'Meget stour oxy!' ('A very big bull!'), to which he replied that 'it was'—'very'—'and that we must be careful.' His settling of the axe reminded me of old African experiences, where the Kaffirs always give notice of danger by taking off their sandals.

This monster lay asleep with his broad back to us, and I am sure the heart of the boldest man in the boat beat quicker as, cautiously and gently paddling, we stole on him quietly from the leeward. I with my rifle cocked and kneeling in the bow, and Helstadt close to me grasping his harpoon, waited breathlessly, as each moment lessened our distance from the walrus.

All at once, and without any apparent reason—for I don't think he could either have seen, heard, or smelt us—the bull slowly raised his head from the ice, and made a deliberate search all round with eyes, ears, and nose. Certainly the last sniff was not satisfactory, for, although I don't think he saw us yet, he seemed to have a vague suspicion of danger in the air. Possibly, this was the bull I missed yesterday, for he was just about the size, had similar tusks, and was found not far from the same place. He would not lie down again, so we paddled on, and I determined to shoot him if I got a fair chance.

When we were about twenty yards off he showed such a fine side-head shot that I fired, and, the shell crashing into his skull, he instantly fell over on his side and lay kicking and groaning on the ice. 'Hurrah!' 'row iveck!' 'row!' 'row!' shouted everyone; and the three men pulled like mad to reach him, fearing he would tumble over into the water and sink. We reached him in the nick of time, for, just as Helstadt drove his harpoon deep into his side, the bull rolled over into the deep water.

Up to this moment I thought the shell had gone into his brain and that he was dead; but the cold plunge seemed to revive him, for he went off under water with a rush that drew out every fathom of the line and then pulled the boat nearly bows under. I began to think that Helstadt's fears would be realised, and I noticed with some concern that the walrus had towed us into open water. He remained a long time underneath, and when he came up showed so little head, and for so short a time, it was impossible to get a second shot. Again he dived and made a furious rush forward, then back under the boat, the most dangerous thing a walrus can do, for should he see the boat above him he is very like to put his tusks through her, or even try to capsize her.

When he came up again I fired at his head, but the missile only ploughed up his scalp. He was now getting blown, and at his next reappearance I gave him his quietus by a ball through the brain. He was a big beast, and we could estimate his weight by the difficulty we had in getting him on the ice: we five, with two double-purchase blocks and tackle, found ourselves almost baffled, and only succeeded after an hour's arduous labour. We had just finished strip-ping him of his inch-and-a-half hide, his blubber, and his cranium, when the yacht came up and hoisted them directly off the ice without further trouble.

In the afternoon we had some occupation with a fierce old cow, who presumed to attack the boat single-handed and died very game. At the same time I lost another grand bull by his rolling off the edge of the ice and going to the bottom after being shot through the brain. Returning to the yacht we got a ' big seal ' or ' Spitzbergen seal ' (Phoca barbata) which was casually floating by on a cake of ice.

A cold raw fog at night preceded another fine day. Sailing somewhat heedlessly on we found ourselves about eleven A.M. in a cul-de-sac of the ice to the eastward of Kolguev and scarce two miles distant from this island, and during the delay in getting out we amused ourselves as best we could. The doctor was at work dissecting walrus heads and skinning stray birds we had shot; and our three walrus cubs having been posed, some hours were occupied in transferring them to the sketch-book.

I ascended to the crow's-nest, and after the confined horizon from the deck it was quite a new sensation to range over such an extensive panorama of ice, water, and land. From this elevation a seal or sea-horse can be made out at a distance of six or seven miles with the telescope. A large opera-glass, although not nearly so powerful, is far handier to use, owing to the ship's motion, or even the vibration of the screw, making it difficult to hold the heavy four-foot telescope sufficiently steady. Henceforth I passed a good deal of my time in this aërial position, and, besides doing good service as look-out, often watched with keen delight the ease with which the steamer rushed, crashed, banged, smashed, ripped, tore, and bumped through the ice, which would inevitably have knocked my old yacht the ' Ginevra ' into *cocked hats*.

Meanwhile the crew were provided with the greasy amusements of ' making off ' blubber and stowing away skins.

This operation in small vessels is performed on

deck, but as there was ample room in the steamer's hold the men were able to set about their cold and slimy occupation sheltered from the wind. 'Making off' is the process for separating the blubber from the skin, which, as before mentioned, are removed together from the slaughtered beast while warm—that of seals and small walruses in one piece, that of a full-sized walrus in two divisions. A sort of frame or stage about four feet high, its front sloping at an angle of 60°, is set up across the deck; behind it stand two men called 'Specksioneers' (blubber-cutters), clad in oil-skin from top to toe, armed with large knives, sharp as razors and curved along the edge. The skins are hung across the frame blubber side uppermost, like clothes on a line, then the operator slices off the fat, which rolls away from its own weight, like a great white blanket. It is an operation requiring great dexterity to separate the fat from the skin, so as to remove the whole of it and not to cut or shave the skin itself; but, by a sort of mowing motion from left to right of the knife, which is held in both hands, these men do it with great rapidity and neatness. As the blubber is peeled off it is divided into slabs of twenty or thirty pounds' weight each, and thrown down into the hatchway, where two men are ready to receive it and to slip it into the man-holes of the tanks. From its oleaginousness it soon finds its level in the tanks, and when full these are screwed tight up and caulked so as to prevent any noxious effluvium from escaping. The skins denuded of fat are salted to preserve them, and packed away in bales for the market.

Walrus hide is a valuable commodity; it is usually from an inch to an inch-and a-half thick, very pliable in its green state, but slightly spongy, so that I should doubt the quality of the leather made of it. It is principally exported to Sweden and Russia, where it is used to manufacture harness and sole leather; it is also twisted into tiller ropes, and is used for protecting the rigging of ships from chafing. In former times nearly all the rigging of vessels on the north coasts of Norway and Russia used to be composed of walrus-hide. Another more universal and modern use to which it is put, is that of stuffing railway buffers, for which its elasticity admirably fits it. When there is a super-fluity of the article in the market, I believe it is boiled into glue.

When I first hunted in Arctic waters the Hammerfest merchants gave the hunters ten dollars for every walrus, bear, or white fish, five dollars for a big Spitzbergen seal, while a small seal was valued as a quarter. The bargain included skin, fat, tusks—in fact, everything worth carrying away. This was a vague way of transacting business, and the merchants were naturally often taken in. For example, Helstadt, the harpooner, re-

lated, with the pride of a shrewd man of business, that
some years ago he and his shipmates came across and
killed one hundred and twenty large bull walruses among
the Thousand Islands, Spitzbergen. As they were to be
paid ten dollars *per skin*, they merely cut two broad
strips of hide out of each walrus (leaving at least one
third of the hide and blubber upon the carcase) so as
to get as many skins as possible on board (no matter
what size). By this ingenious device they contrived
to accommodate them all, and were of course as well
paid at ten dollars a piece as if they had taken home
the entire skins. After this, two of the merchants
disagreeing, the hides were paid for by weight, and
at this time the market value of them was about two-
pence a pound.

The seal-skins mostly find their way to Scotland,
where, after being split into two or even three pieces
by an ingenious process, about which little is known
out of the trade, I believe they are chiefly used for the
manufacture of patent leather, as well as made into
what the hosiers call 'dog-skin' and 'Dundee kid'
gloves. Their value in Hammerfest is from one to
four dollars a skin, according to size.

The walrus has not nearly so much blubber in proportion to its size as the seal: thus a seal of six or
seven cwt. will carry 200 lbs. of fat; an ordinary
walrus may weigh 3,000 lbs., but his fat will not exceed

that of the seal; a full-sized old bull walrus must weigh at least 5,000 lbs., and such a walrus, if very fat, will produce 650 lbs. of blubber, but seldom more than 500 lbs., which is, I think, the *average* amount yielded by the most obese of our victims. I have heard of examples of heavier beasts. Johan, one of my boat-steerers, asserts that he obtained a walrus in 1868 whose hide, cleared of blubber, weighed no less than four hundred and fifty pounds, and that the whole hide fetched fifty-six dollars, or about twelve pounds English money.

Curiosity led me once to weigh and value the marketable parts of a large bull walrus, and the following results were arrived at :—Weight of walrus blubber = 520 pounds, about one-fifth of a ton, which, at 40*l.* a ton is worth 8*l.*; 300 pounds of skin at 2*d.* a pound = 2*l.* 10*s.*, and 8 pounds of ivory at 5*s.* a pound = 2*l.*, giving a value of 12*l.* 10*s.*

The fat of one of my largest seals weighed 220 pounds, while the seal-skins were never over 60 or 65 pounds while green. The fat of the walrus does not yield so fine an oil as that of the seal, but it is usual to mix them indiscriminately together, and the compound is always exported into Southern Europe under the name of seal oil.

I trust the reader will have patience to wade through this mass of commercial information, because the fact of a vessel like the 'Diana' being able largely to recoup her heavy expenses has an important bearing on Arctic exploration.

As all Arctic navigators and all students of Arctic literature are aware, the chance of making a successful expedition consists in having a well-found and properly equipped vessel in a favourable position when the rare opportunity of an 'open season' occurs. It is well known that in every route towards the Pole hitherto followed there are varying causes which determine an open or a close season, and that such causes act locally, *e.g.* that in Smith's Sound unusual obstacles may present themselves during the same year in which the seas around Spitzbergen may be more free from ice and open to navigation than for many years. Secondly, that we have as yet no data for correctly predicting an open or close season in any one particular route during any particular year or month. What conclusion are we justified in drawing from these premises? I think this, that the only method by which grand success is likely to be achieved is by hammering away at the ice year after year as the walrus-hunters and whalers do, and having, as I have said, the means of making a rapid push forward at the favourable moments, which experience tells us do recur at long intervals.

As this is now an enterprise of prominent in-

terest, it may be asked, who then is likely to penetrate to the North Pole? A Government expedition may happen to hit off an open season, and will
then accomplish a great deal. But any Government
is with difficulty persuaded to increase the estimates for
the mere discovery of valueless regions of sea and land ;
and it is only by the pressure of public opinion, headed
by the Scientific Societies, that they are at last compelled to do something for the honour of the nation.
Finally, after much writing in the newspapers, much
agitation in the scientific world, and much contemptuous
criticism of the opinions of whalers (who alone really
know something about the matter), an Arctic expedition
under Government auspices is resolved on. Double
pay, liberal rations, and the chance of excitement,
attract crowds of volunteers—a Royal personage or
two wave their hands as the ships, gay with flags, weigh
anchor—a great many guns are fired, and the nation for
a year or two forgets all about the Arctic expedition.

Meanwhile the ships, if so far successful, alternately
drag about and winter in ice docks for two or three
seasons, become proficient in amateur theatricals, and
cache out vast masses of provisions, which are unhesi-
tatingly appropriated by the first whaler, who, in the
open season which perhaps immediately follows the return
of the expedition, probably runs over in a few favourable
weeks the ground so laboriously traversed under more

adverse circumstances. The result being limited almost to meteorological readings, geodetic surveys, magnetic observations, and the correction of older charts, no Government who values its popularity will dare to sanction another Arctic expedition for a quarter of a century. The public is impatient at the expense and suspense, and lastly the scientific promoters look blue and turn their attention once more to Central Africa.

Can a private individual, then, hope to succeed in an undertaking where national enterprise is more than likely to meet with failure? Not unless he has means, inclination, and courage to give to this object ten or twelve years of his life, regardless of the perils of wintering in the Arctic seas. Few men who could afford to devote, say, 5,000*l.* a year to such a purpose can be found who would not prefer to spend their time in other and more civilized pursuits.

The foregoing considerations lead me reluctantly to form the opinion that we must not centre our hopes too fondly on the great results to be obtained by the Government Arctic expeditions of any nation, and that consequently we must be content to go on piecing out the mosaic of Arctic knowledge year after year from various sources—often unsystematic and often even unreliable.

Were all walrus-hunters and whalers educated men, like the painstaking and talented Scoresby, or could edu-

cated men be persuaded that hunting, for the sake of
sport (with a prospect of partial re-imbursement), could
be combined with scientific research, and prosecuted
alongside of it, we should have the best possible assurance that the mysteries of the Arctic world would
be gradually unfolded to our view. In the digression
into which I have been betrayed I wish it to be understood that I speak generally only; for no one more
heartily wishes success to the present Polar expedition
than I do myself.

Emerging in the afternoon from the narrow lane
of water we steamed through much favourable ice, and
saw a fair sprinkling of walruses and seals, which
afforded me some excellent sport.

I came to the conclusion this day that the shells
are too soft and pliable to *penetrate* the skulls of the old
walruses. They have not nearly the penetration of a
hardened ball of small size, though, for a body shot,
the effect is terrific. It was found that the three
biggest bulls killed to-day were all merely stunned by
the shells in the head, although all were well-directed
shots. The last one I shot gave an amusing illustration of this. He was a large single bull, and I shot
him through the head, so that he lay on the ice apparently quite dead. Hans struck his harpoon into him,
and I jumped out on the ice to spear him. Jack
Lamont, a stalwart clansman of my own, from Islay,

exclaimed: ' Well, what a splendid shot! If he had been
a fowl he couldn't have been shot deader.' We were
discussing whether it would be better to skin him
where he lay, or to tow him to a more suitable piece
of ice adjacent, when all at once the bull gave a tremendous wallop, and, nearly jumping into the boat,
regained the sea, where he was only despatched after
a fierce fight. This animal was struck in exactly the
same spot as the bigger one whose death has been
previously narrated, viz., on the strong plate of bone
at the side of the head, just below and in front of the
brain, and in both instances the shell had burst in the
flesh, after merely cracking, but not shattering or
penetrating, the skull. They had, in fact, both been
' knocked out of time.'

Acting on the hint suggested by these results, I
had an inspection of all the Britannia-metal utensils on
board, and selected those most easily dispensed with
for melting down. During the evening we turned out
some very good round hardened bullets of No. 12
gauge which promised to smash the skull of the best
bull in the Novaya Zemlya seas.

As we were thus occupied in the cabin the wind
beginning to whistle in the rigging confirmed the
approach of another gale, which had already been
prognosticated by a steadily and rapidly falling barometer. At first we hoped it might be possible to ride

it out in comfort under the lee of the ice ; but, as the wind rose, the heavy ice, issuing from Kara Straits, began to dash with such force against the yacht that it was deemed prudent to get more out to sea.

Heavy rain fell almost incessantly the next day. At noon we made our greatest easting, 58°, in latitude 70°, and we were therefore due south of the S.E. corner of Novaya Zemlya and abreast of Waygat Island. It was too thick to see the land, and we were being blown away from the Straits ; I therefore made up my mind to get out of this horribly stormy Petchora sea forthwith ; and further, being in want of fresh water, a run into some harbour was advisable. Had we been provided with the charts which are now obtainable it would have been possible to have fetched Kamenka Bay, where Pakhtusof wintered in 1832–33.

But, having no knowledge whatever of the coasts and harbours, we shaped a course for Gooseland ; and only learned much later how many good anchorages we must have passed on our way. There were the intricate labyrinths of water about the Reindeer Islands, so ably surveyed by Pakhtusof in 1833 ; Ssachanicha Island, where Lütke's four years of voyages terminated in 1824 with a summer of such unwonted bad luck that, with the exception of the north part of Waygat, the former island was the only part of the Novaya

Zemlya coast not blocked with ice; the convenient anchorage behind an island in Schirotschicha Bay; Meal Cape, so called by Barentz when he landed here in 1594, and found six casks of rye meal which had been hastily buried by Samoyedes, who had fled at his approach.[1]

Black Cape, the last point determined by an exhaustive series of Russian explorations, which, covering at intervals a period of a hundred years, comprised a survey of coast and islands from North Cape, Norway, to Behring's Straits, and which Rogatschew in 1839 left behind him, only to wreck his schooner on the homeward voyage, after fighting the difficulties of two

---

[1] Though Russian hunters, from time to time, pass the winter on the Island of Waygat and even on the larger island, and though scientific expeditions have also remained here during the whole round of the year, it would be incorrect to describe Novaya Zemlya as an inhabited country. Barentz, nearly 300 years ago, found traces of human residence at Suchoi Nos, and at that time the Russian hunters never passed beyond the Orange Islands. Burrough, forty years previous to this, had been told, when at Waygat Island, that the larger island was inhabited by Samoyedes. But the huts and crosses noticed by these explorers, and found by later voyagers far beyond the limits known to them, are no proof of permanent residence. The huts are and were then only erected for temporary use. And a cross is invariably the pious Russian record of deliverance from shipwreck or of an unlooked for slice of good luck in hunting. Of serious but disastrous attempts to colonise Novaya Zemlya, the instances of the Stroganoff family from Novgorod, in the sixteenth century—who left their bones in the bay, which still bears their name—and that of Mawei may be given. The latter, a poor Samoyede, who had lost all his cattle by pestilence, brought his family to Novaya Zemlya, vowing to his gods to winter here. Next season the corpses of the whole family with the exception of Mawei were found, and evidences of their having suffered miserably. No doubt the missing man had ventured out to seek food and perished in a snow-storm.

summers and a winter on the desolate western shores ; Meshduscharrskij, the largest island of the Novaya Zemlya coast, and which, sheltering the warm waters of the ample Kostin Schar, forms a quiet sea, comparable to the Ice Fjord, Spitzbergen, in its early accessibility and prolonged freedom from newly-formed autumn ice ; the prominent gypsum shores of White Island ; South Goose Cape, the southern termination of the long, straight line of coast, where Willoughby first sighted Novaya Zemlya in 1553—all these places of interest are altogether shut out from our sight, or are but dimly discerned occasionally through the driving rain and blinding spray, as the 'Diana' forges her way through the heavy sea. We neared the coast of Gooseland on the 11th, but made very slow progress towards the anchorage at its northern cape. For, although the sea was calmer under the lee of the land, the wind, at times, headed us in such tremendous gusts that the engine could barely force the ship against it.

Nowhere south of the immediate neighbourhood of Matocshkin Schar does the land rise to any great elevation. Gooseland forms the westernmost part of Novaya Zemlya, and is a level plain of about fifty miles by twelve, lying between the mountains and the sea.

Viewed from the crow's-nest it appeared a dreary

expanse of coarse, swampy pasture interspersed with half-frozen lakes and ponds; the latter swarming with geese and swans, and the grassy meadows with reindeer, all enormously magnified by the mirage, and appearing as if close to the shore, whereas miles of impracticable marsh intervened. A long line of low dark hills, now nearly clear of snow, and running north and south, or parallel to the sea, form the background.

Rounding North Goose Cape, we anchored at three A.M. on the 12th within the promontory which constitutes the western boundary of Goose Harbour, this haven itself being one of the subdivisions of Möller Bay. We were in five fathoms of water, but, owing to the force of the N.E. gale, two anchors with sixty fathoms each of chain were necessary to make us secure.

The prospect from our anchorage was by no means a cheerful one. Anything more frightfully gloomy and desolate could not be imagined. Low hills thickly covered with snow, with black earth peeping out here and there, stretched away inland, while the low coast appeared to be ice and blown-over snow in various stages of slipping and breaking away seaward, and revealed only occasional glimpses of black and horrible rocks. Inside of us was a small barren island of slaty rock, almost buried in a covering of snow, and farther up the bay were a few smaller rocky islets.

Drawn by W. Livesay.

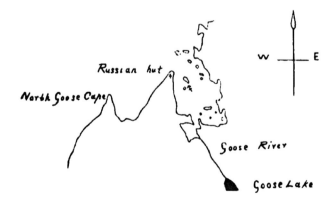

Goose Haven, Novaya Zemlya.

Nearly at the end of the low tongue of land a rude hut, flanked by some tall poles, seemed to indicate this place as one of the resorts of the White Sea hunters, who are attracted to these coasts in summer by the number of ducks and geese, and who dry in the sun a species of salmon (Salmo Alpinus), caught in the neighbouring rivulets and inland lakes. One of the crew, who was ashore here later, found the Russian log-hut to be in ruins, and, strange to say, the apparent drying poles turned out to be the lofty carved crosses peculiar to Russian graves, and here marked the last resting-place of some poor fellows, about whom we could learn no particulars.

While serving out the first allowance of preserved meats on deck, in the afternoon, my attention was called to three dark objects moving about on the snowy shore, about two miles from us, and upon looking through the telescope I had the satisfaction of making them out to be reindeer. A further inspection of the land showed us upwards of a dozen grazing on the black strips of earth, on which background they appeared white; five of them were on an island, quite close to the ship. The supply of fresh meat being at its lowest ebb, the deer were a very welcome and appropriate spectacle, perhaps somewhat tantalising too, as it blew such a hurricane that it would have been madness to have put off a boat for the shore and hope she could fetch the ship again. The crew were so eager to be at the game that I believe if I had called for a crew of volunteers to man a boat, every hand in the ship would have responded, even if it had been to pull through a sea of fire and brimstone. However, I restrained their impatience, knowing the weather must moderate, and that the deer were unlikely to leave the ground.

By four o'clock next morning the wind had dropped to a light breeze, and having steamed up nearer the island, for the convenience of the watering party, Livesay and I, with several of the Norwegian hands, pulled up to the head of the bay, where we landed for a day's exploration. Having hauled the boat a dozen yards or so over the ice, we made her fast by ice-anchors fixed still further in, a very necessary precaution, where the bay ice as here is rapidly breaking off and floating away from the shore.

Three deer had been noticed in a little marsh bare of snow, and by a stealthy crawl I was able to approach about 150 yards. A shot broke the leg of the best, and, signing to the men behind to let loose my pet retriever, we watched him run the wounded animal so far across the frozen plain that the deer became invisible to us, and 'Sailor' appeared like a black dot; but, hearing faint barks in the distance, we followed him up and found him lying beside the deer with its throat cut. The remaining deer made off at a great pace inland. We now divided into two parties and although we must have seen at least thirty deer at a short distance, and many more further inland, scattered like little white dots on the small bits of pasture, which the sun had bared, or moving as specks of shadow over the snow, the day's bag only yielded six head. This contrast to the facility with which they are slaughtered in the Spitzbergen valleys, was due to their wildness, from frequent collision with Russian hunters, and the extreme unsuitability of the ground for stalking. Most of the reindeer haunts I am acquainted with in Spitzbergen are either valleys shut in by rocky mountains or plains at the foot of snowhills. The large streams caused by the immense quantities of rapidly-melting snow scour the low land, and cut the ground in all directions into gullies most convenient for the stalker. By a series of happily-arranged terraces, he can often there work his way up to within easy distance without the slightest difficulty. The abundant herbage so closely occupies the attention of the game, they will browse their way up to the concealed hunter, without once raising their heads. Often, with my finger on the trigger, I have waited till I could hear the *munch-munch* as they tore off the short grass and moss, then, firing, have dropped a couple right and left, and, reloading, have had time to knock over a second, or even a third—double-shot.

Here it was very different, and I could quite understand even a fair rifle-shot having nothing to show for a
long day's hard tramping. Early in the season the
pasture lies in small patches and strips on the tops or
sunny sides of gentle hills; a few minutes suffice the
deer to feed from one end to the other, and while
crossing the snow to the next patch of green, noses in
the air, they cannot fail to detect any object within a
mile of them.

The ground we traversed was everywhere soft and
spongy, except on the more elevated ridges, which
consisted of bare rocks or *débris* of shaly limestone,
veined with bands of slate. The action of the weather
crumbles and converts it into a coarse grit and sand.
No flowers opened their petals so early as this, and
without a very close scrutiny it was difficult to realise
that the withered leaves and sodden seed-capsules,
which adhered to last year's stems, would in a few
weeks be buried in a luxuriant carpet of succulent
grasses and dwarf flowers of every hue. Only forty
botanical specimens were collected, which does not
represent one tenth of the species known, by the re-
searches of Van Baer and others, to represent the flora
of Novaya Zemlya. I need not remind the reader
that there are no trees in these latitudes, the biggest
stem of vegetation, a dwarf species of willow, is not
thicker than a pencil.

In one of the bays a quantity of small drift-wood

was seen, unlike that found on the east coast of Novaya Zemlya and everywhere around Spitzbergen; it consisted of pine *sticks* and birch *branches*, many pieces being marked by some cutting instrument. Scattered amongst these pieces were curious little compact rolls of birch bark.

The lakes and streams were still partially frozen, but could be crossed by wading twelve to eighteen inches deep in slush. A couple of wild swans and a straggling skein of geese were seen apparently waiting at the edge of a lake for the ice to break up. No doubt the season was rather later than usual and had a little interfered with their calculations. The geese return to breed in Novaya Zemlya as early as the beginning of May; for Pakhtusof, wintering on the north shore of the Kara Straits in 1833, saw them as early as May 15, and Moïssejew, in Shallow Bay, on May 24, 1839. The former observer saw the geese and swans coming eastward from Waygat Island in flocks in the middle of May and going into the interior of the island (Novaya Zemlya), where they probably knew of good breeding-places. They left in the middle of October, directing their flight S.S.W., that is, straight towards the Petchora river.[1] Snow buntings were seen in great numbers; in some places they get

---

[1] As many as 15,000 geese have been killed in Russian expeditions to Kolguev.

up at every step and perch on pointed stones a few yards in front; at other times they rise like an English lark, and soaring overhead send down a shower of melody very welcome to a mariner's ears. Snipes flit over the marshy swamps, and on a sunny day the chaste-coloured Arctic terns dart hither and thither and turn excited somersaults in the air, if their nests on the ground are approached. Of ducks we saw three species in the bay as we rowed up—the eider duck (*Anas Mollissima*), the king duck (*Anas Spectabilis*), and the pin-tail.

The puffin, or sea-parrot, and the guillemot are the commonest in the list of migratory birds which breed in Novaya Zemlya—the latter in such numbers as to amount to a full half of the feathered inhabitants. A visit to a 'loomery,' as the whalers call the breeding cliffs of guillemots or looms, is one of the sights of the Arctic regions. These birds sit in countless myriads, tier after tier, on the slight ledges afforded by the horizontal strata of the limestone cliffs. Endless rows of snowy breasts and black heads, with the regularity of soldiers standing on parade, are seen as they sit bolt upright on their single eggs, with their backs against the rocky precipice. Marvellous is the sight when a shot is fired from a boat beneath; then, it is no exaggeration to say, the air is darkened, and as each bird flies out and utters his peculiar cry there is a terrific Babel of sound. In the rush of the guillemots leaving the cliffs numbers of their eggs are dislodged from the narrow ledges and fall crashing to the foot of the precipice, while others are instantly pounced upon by the predatory gulls, which incessantly hover overhead. Most comical is it to observe the male and female guillemot relieving one another in sitting on their solitary egg, one sidles off as the other sidles on, without leaving the egg *for an instant* exposed to the watchful eyes of their enemies above.

We saw a few snowy owls (*Strix Nictea*) still in their winter costume. Those seen by the crew were described in the quaint and exaggerated language of the sea as 'standing three feet high,' and 'having heads as big as the binnacle'! The food of these birds in Novaya Zemlya consists chiefly of the young guillemots and of the lemming, a small animal like a rat, without a tail, and belonging to the order *Rodentia*. It migrates, I believe, in winter.

On my return to the yacht so little 'due diligence' had been exerted in filling the water tanks that I deemed it wise to see what the 'master's eye' would effect the next day, as, the gale having subsided, I was anxious to lose no more time. A watch over the willing but hitherto ill-directed crew produced such happy results that we were full up and steamed out of the haven at 6.30 P.M.

A stroll over the island, when we were drawing water, yielded nothing but a few geological specimens.

A longer excursion was undertaken by Livesay, with two of the Norsemen, after some haunches of venison which, unable to bring down the previous day, he had buried to protect them from the foxes. A wolf was said to have been seen ambling away over a hill, and undoubted tracks of foxes led up to the buried meat. No other facts were added to our knowledge of the Natural History of the district, and a thick fog coming on rendered pursuit of a herd of reindeer which they saw impracticable.

The reindeer shot were in very poor condition, the leanest I ever remember eating. In whatever part of the circumpolar regions they are killed this is always the case early in the summer.

In these desolate regions the early summer brings on a rapid and nourishing vegetation, bright flowers bloom in juxta-position to snow-drifts. Day and night these lean and hungry ruminants browse away on the scanty herbage of scurvy grass, succulent saxifrages, grasses, and carices of the verdant slopes and valleys. From a food point of view the change in the deer during a few weeks is astounding, the rank flesh, devoid of fat, and the loose ill-fitting skin fill out to the proportions of a barrel, with an outside layer of two or three inches of fat. This is a very beneficent provision of nature, for during the long winter the only herbage to be found is a scanty covering of moss and lichen, on such ground as is bared by the wind or so superficially covered with snow as to be reached by digging. The reindeer in reality lives by consuming his own fat laid up the previous summer.

The reindeer of Novaya Zemlya is a much larger beast than that of Spitzbergen, owing probably to the milder climate and more luxuriant vegetation of the former country. I was once consulted by a distinguished naturalist as to the affinities of the reindeer of Novaya Zemlya and Spitzbergen. It is a subject of some difficulty, and I only give my own opinion with considerable hesitation and diffidence.

It seems to me, however, that the reindeer of Spitzbergen is almost identical with the wild and tame deer of Norway and Lapland; whereas the Novaya Zemlya type appears to me more allied to the reindeer of the American continent.

I judge chiefly by the horns, and I must admit that it is extremely difficult to explain how any such affinities as I have indicated can have arisen, because the straits between Novaya Zemlya and the mainland must be always passable to reindeer in the winter, whereas the 480 miles of stormy sea, which never freezes, dividing Spitzbergen from the North Cape, must always form a hopelessly-impassable barrier.

To Liakhov, the Russian trader and explorer, when happening to visit the promontory of Swätoi-Nos. long. 140° E. and lying between the mouths of the great rivers Yana and Indigirka, the sudden appearance of a large herd of reindeer coming over the Frozen Sea from the north gave substance to the shadowy reports of Yakuts as to the existence of more land lying in that direction. With the promptness of a man whose business instincts were aroused he set out with sledges the next month, and, following the deer tracks, discovered the group of islands known as New Siberia, at some fifty miles from the mainland.

This circumstance suggests two points of interest as to the economy of the reindeer, their wandering habits, and their winter quarters. The instincts of this animal, as originally exhibited in both hemispheres, seem to be migratory; in spring vast herds follow up the melting of the snow in their progress northwards for pasture. In the autumn the first fall of snow drives them back to the shelter and herbage of the northern limit of trees. It may, therefore, be assumed that the existence of reindeer in Spitzbergen and Novaya Zemlya, and other isolated lands to be yet discovered, where ordinary yearly migration is difficult or impossible, is an accidental circumstance; in other words, that the reindeer is not indigenous to districts compelling him to the annual five months' starvation, which in a severe season might mean extinction. It may further be taken for granted that the accidental element, whether of deer wandering out of their reckoning on continuous lands or adjacent islands, or of unusual states of ice bridging across areas of part water, part land, may recur yearly or at intervals of years. If this were the case we should expect to meet in Spitzbergen, with, not only the descendants of the first chance inhabitants, but also those brought thither by a recurrence of favourable circumstances.

Again, did we meet with characteristics peculiar to the reindeer of one known district, we might reasonably infer that the deer of Spitzbergen, for example, must have journeyed by a route unknown to us from that district. Now, as I have stated we *do* find in Spitz-'bergen reindeer unlike in horns and general proportion to those of Novaya Zemlya, or the variety hunted by the Eskimos in Greenland and North America, but, on the other hand, approaching very closely in type the tame deer used by the nomad tribes of Northern Europe and Asia.

The inference I draw from this fact, viz. that the reindeer passes over ice and intermediate frozen lands to Spitzbergen, from a point of the continent of Asia almost exactly opposite in a straight line across the Pole, is susceptible of strong confirmation by some remarkable facts, which, as a frequent visitor to Spitzbergen, have come under my notice. More than once in this country I have been struck with the *extreme tameness* of the deer, and in a volume written ten years ago I stated my belief that this was due to their 'never having seen man or anything which could hurt them.' I am now more inclined to think the utter fearlessness of these deer is to be ascribed to *early familiarity with men who have never attempted to shoot or hunt them.* (For the Novaya Zemlya shores—certainly the least accessible parts— are no more harried from the sea-board than the western shores of Spitzbergen, yet in all parts the Novaya Zemlya deer *are excessively wild.*)

Another interesting circumstance in connection with the Spitzbergen deer is the peculiar ear-marks found upon certain of the old stags; these consist of decided 'crops and half-cuts,' similar to those given by a Scotch shepherd to his sheep, and are too distinct to allow a suspicion of their being accidental slits or tears resulting from fighting. Old Spitzbergen skippers have told me that they have killed '*hundreds*' of deer with ear-marks, and they invariably account for this by saying that 'these deer must have come by some unknown connecting islands from Samoyede land.' Several of my own Norwegian crew separately volunteered to inform me of the frequency of these marks being found on deer in

Spitzbergen, and one of them even went so far as to give me a circumstantial account of a deer with letters branded on his side.

I will not vouch for the veracity of this last story, but I was sufficiently interested in the question thus raised to make a particular examination of deer subsequently killed in Spitzbergen, and towards the end of August 1869 I shot in Ginevra Bay two large fat old stags, having each the left ear 'back half cropped.' I showed them to Hans, a half-bred Lapp, accustomed to deal with tame reindeer from his infancy, and he had no doubt whatever of these animals having been marked by the hands of men.

Lastly, we have accounts of large numbers of tame reindeer straying away from Eastern Siberia, which are said to go over the ice, and are never heard of again.[1]

So that there seems to be a strong chain of evidence pointing to the existence of a continent, or tracts of land separated by no great widths of channel, stretching from the neighbourhood of Eastern Siberia[2] across the Pole to Eastern Spitzbergen. Whether Plover Land (north-west of Behring's Straits)—an undefined, unexplored district, about which we cannot yet say

[1] See Baron Wrangell.

[2] The Tunguses and Yakutsks of Eastern Siberia have a firm belief that there lies a country to the north of them which is inhabited by a people like themselves, owning vast herds of reindeer.

that it is or is not inhabited; the newly-discovered Franz Joseph Land, already traced to within eighty nautical miles of Gillis Land; and Gillis Land itself, are parts of this hypothetical continent or archipelago, I will not attempt to prove, although much other evidence might be adduced in favour of such a theory.

The distance a reindeer can travel without food is limited, nor can they probably swim more than a dozen miles. The Samoyedes are in the habit of transporting their tame animals to graze on the Island of Waygat in the spring and taking them back in the autumn in their large flat-bottomed boats, but I have never heard of their being conveyed further north to Novaya Zemlya proper.

The wild deer are compelled, as I have explained, against their natural instinct, to winter in Spitzbergen and Novaya Zemlya, because they can neither travel without food nor swim long distances; and very possibly those passing from Eastern Siberia to Spitzbergen occupy more than one season in performing the journey.

We assume from the miserably-emaciated appearance of the reindeer in June that he has fought a hard battle against hunger where we find him, but we have also the direct testimony of those who have wintered in these regions. A party of Rossmyloff's men, who first visited Novaya Zemlya with the intention of wintering, observed a large herd of deer on the shore of Matoschkin Schar, on the last day of January 1769. Tempted by the welcome prospect of fresh meat the men rushed heedlessly forth in the uncertain twilight 'to shoot as many as the good God meant for them,' and unfortunately losing their way in a snow-storm were buried alive.

We got well clear of the harbour during the night, and were dozing in our berths the next morning at 5.30, when a sharp shock like the bluff blow from a big piece of ice was felt; this was immediately followed by two other shocks, and the familiar grating sound and feel which accompanied them immediately told old sailors what had happened. 'All hands on deck! the ship's aground.' Jumping on deck half-dressed, there was no mistaking our plight. The crew were already busy bringing coals and deck lumber aft, and endeavouring by a process called 'overing' (running in a body from one side of the vessel to the other to make her roll) to ease her off.

The yacht, it appears, was steaming easily in a thick fog when the master felt her gliding over mud, and had just time to get the engine stopped when she struck hard and fast on a rock under her fore-foot. After bundling twenty bags of coal aft, reversing the engine, and spending an hour of great anxiety—not

I

for our lives, but for the safety of the ship and the
summer enterprise—a gentle swell coming to our
assistance lifted the yacht's head off the rock and set
us afloat. Ten minutes' more delay would have
tempted me to heave all the loose coals overboard, to
start the fresh water from the tanks, and to get out a
kedge anchor, which, unless the tide were falling,
would have got her off.

A strong current, unmistakeably observed, driving
us towards the land as we passed Cape Britwin later in
the day, must have had something to do with our
running on the rocks. The course steered should have
taken us farther out to sea. The current, we were
convinced, was one of the two tails into which the
Gulf Stream forks to the north-west of North Cape.[1]

The warm current which laves the western coast of
Spitzbergen has long been known, and its importance
recognised by the early whalers. Here, then, a last
effort of the beneficent ' ocean river,' as Maury has
termed it, was by another arm performing a similar
office in rendering the west coast of Novaya Zemlya
accessible to ships.[2] For the first time since our second

[1] Johannesen as well as Ulve found at Cape Nassau and on Admiralty
Peninsula, glass buoys and pieces of fishing tackle from the Lofoten Isles.
Pods of a West Indian bean were also seen near the Gulf Stream Islands,
a few miles further on the same coast.

[2] The western coast of Novaya Zemlya was unusually free from ice in
1869. It is said to be seldom so before the end of July. Willoughby in
1553 found the coast of Goose Land bristling with ice on July 30th.

day after leaving Vardö, the sea temperature was as high as 34°·5 F. The rise of two degrees was conclusive as to the nature of the current, which was carrying us north at the rate of thirty miles a day.

The fog continuing during the evening, we lay to until morning, when it cleared off and displayed a magnificent panorama of mountain scenery, unlike any we had yet witnessed. The character of these hills was very marked, broken and shafted, rising at places in abrupt cliffs from the sea.

Believing we could identify the higher peaks marked in the chart, we judged the ship's position to be somewhere abreast of Matoschkin Schar and bore up for the land. And now, observing a smart-looking schooner some miles off, we conjectured she might be full of walrus and about to sail for Norway, and, if so, would take letters for us. Upon nearing her, however, and running up our ensign, she showed the Russian flag, and as none of us could speak Russian we were puzzled how we should hold any profitable communication. Seeing our half-bred Lapp, an idea seemed to strike the Russian skipper, who had come off in a boat, for he immediately put back and returned with another

Lutke in 1821 found it impossible to land on the same coast in consequence of the impenetrable wall of ice which girdled the shore with a belt more than six Italian miles wide as late as August. The same voyager three years later was unable to approach any part of the Novaya Zemlya coast to the north of Kostin Schar. It was blocked during the whole summer with masses of ice from twenty to thirty miles in breadth.

Lapp from his own vessel. Conversation was then carried on as follows:—I asked a question of my Norwegian sailing-master, who translated it into his language, which Hans understood; the latter repeated it in his own *patois* to the other Lapp, who rendered it into Russian for his master. Through this laborious medium of conversation, we learned ' they came from Archangel in the White Sea, and had only been at sea a few days; they had coasted a few miles further north, but, getting no walruses, were now bound south for Waygat Island, where last year they killed one hundred and twenty.'

Furthermore, they confirmed my suspicions that we had been carried past the mouth of the Matoschkin Schar during the night by the current. The configuration of the coast about the Straits makes it particularly difficult to hit off the entrance. It should never be attempted save in the clearest weather and with the aid of reliable charts or pilots. Admiral Lutke, we learn, met with the same difficulty on his first voyage to Novaya Zemlya, and for many days groped his way up and down, without being able to detect the inlet. A reference to the lithograph outline will, perhaps, be a useful guide to future voyagers.

Running north to about the latitude of Admiralty Point we encountered dense pack. It was of no use, therefore, attempting to penetrate further in this direc-

tion ; and I knew any attempts to sail into the Kara
Sea through Matoschkin Straits would for the present
be equally fruitless. The only alternatives were, therefore, either to give up Novaya Zemlya for this season,
and endeavour to sail to the east coast of Spitzbergen,
and Gillis Land, or to make a push for the Kara Sea
by way of Kara Straits.

June [1] 17th [2] saw the 'Diana' again in the neighbourhood of Kolguev, and at the edge of loose ice,
marked on the charts as the usual equatorial limit of
drifting ice. Let us, by a brief *résumé* of the position
of ice and the directions of currents observed up to
this time by other explorers, see what hope might be
entertained of reaching the eastern coast of Novaya
Zemlya on the mouths of the great Siberian rivers.

The Kara Sea is a funnel into whose wide mouth
the Polar current sets directly from the great ice-house
of the north. The tendency of this current, like that to
the east of Spitzbergen and to the east of Greenland, is
to pack the ice on its eastern boundary. But, unlike
the seas of those localities, the Kara Sea eastward and
southward is land-locked, and communicates with the
great ocean only by three narrow straits.

---

[1] The reader who wishes to follow the narrative of the 'Diana's' voyage
in 1869 is advised to skip pp. 117–198 and turn to p. 199. On the other
hand the accuracy of observations of changes in ice, &c., due to season, is
insured by the paragraph commencing on June 17th, where the last ended.

[2] 1870.

Great rivers, notably the Obi and the Yenisei, pour more fresh water into this contracted area than drains into the Mediterranean—a volume so great that in the middle of this sea (half-way between Cape Flushing and the mainland) water sweet enough for drinking has been noticed. This river water, several degrees warmer than the Polar current, mingles with it, tending to raise its temperature[1] and to diminish its saltness. Practically the effect of this comparatively warm water is to keep an open 'land-water' all along the Siberian coast, except in winter.

Still the ice-laden current holds its sway : sweeping round the east side of Novaya Zemlya it seeks an outlet through the Kara Gate, and when in spring the local winter's ice around the shores of the Strait breaks up, the heavy masses from the north-east find a passage to the west. At the end of the summer, when the mass of Polar ice may be so far reduced by

[1] In a discussion on a paper of the late Admiral Sherard Osborne's, read before the Royal Geographical Society on April 28th, 1873, a gentleman present was good enough to inform us that 'it was absurd to suppose those river waters could have any influence on thawing the polar ice.' The proof of this statement which he offered the members of the Society was that in an Arctic voyage 'he had attempted to wade through a small stream and found it icy cold.' What degree of Fahrenheit may correspond with a feeling of 'icy cold' I cannot pretend to say, as the feeling would entirely depend on the previous condition of the body. But, if this observer had not noticed for himself, he should have called to mind the experience of others and reflected that fluid river water must be at least three degrees higher (and was probably a great deal more) than the floating ice, and, further, that a difference of three degrees in water, with its immense capacity for heat, means many units of heat as compared with air temperature to act on the ice.

melting as to interrupt the drifting supply to the Kara Sea, the current influence is still felt in keeping the eastern end of the Strait jammed with ice when the whole Kara Sea itself may be clear. A vessel may have a better chance of sailing round the north-east extremity of Novaya Zemlya or through the Matoschkin Schar than through the Kara Straits. The more northern seas may be swept, as observed by Weyprecht, Payer, Tobiesen, and Mack in 1871; but what little ice may happen to enter the Kara Sea must stick to the south-eastern point of Novaya Zemlya and obstruct the navigation eastward of it. Wind alone from the south and west can drive back the dense masses of the early season or break through the feebler barrier in later summer. Ships may creep round the coast of the mainland as the Russian lodgias have done for centuries; as Malygin and Skuratow did in their surveying voyage of 1737, and the Norwegian sloops have done in the last few years; but no prediction can be made of crossing the Kara Sea from the Kara Straits except by favour of the wind.

Few scientific voyagers have entered the Kara Sea, and none have sailed across it to Yelmert Land. The coast eastward of this again (till we meet the track of the vessels which have sailed farthest from Behring's Straits—a stretch of some two thousand miles) we only read of in the records of the Russian surveys made between 1821 and 1843; surveys made partly by land, partly by sledge journeys, and partly by short sea trips from the mouths of the rivers.

Yet the idea of the feasibility of a sea voyage to Behring's Straits, a north-east passage, has been revived by Captain Mack, who established the certainty of a warm current, undoubtedly part of the Gulf Stream, running east round the north-east end of Novaya Zemlya with great velocity. Following up the warm current he reached 81° E., and then saw no traces of ice in any direction. To test the possibility of such a voyage was the first object of the Austrian expedition of 1872. It failed in this, but discovered Franz Joseph land.

One fourth of the east coast of Novaya Zemlya itself has never been explored. The trustworthiness of Gerrit de Veer's account of Barentz's voyage, the first on record round the north-east end of Novaya Zemlya, and his subsequent wintering in Ice Haven, has been established by the Norwegian skipper Carlsen. In 1871 he followed Barentz's track, and landing in Ice Haven found the winter-hut and its contents exactly as it had been left 278 years before. Carlsen, instead of returning, as Barentz was compelled to do, by the route he had come, continued his voyage down the east coast and sailing through the Kara Straits completed the circumnavigation of Novaya Zemlya.

This feat had only once before been equalled, by

the Russian sailor Loschkin. His voyage occupied two winters and three summers, and was accomplished by sailing up the east coast from the south, and finally doubling Cape Desire to the west coast.

William de Vlamingh, in 1760, entered the Kara Sea by the northern entrance and partly sailed across it. Rosmysslow recorded the winter phenomena of the east coast, and of the Kara Sea, at his winter quarters in Matoschkin Schar in 1768–69, and explored as far as his crazy vessel would permit in the following spring.

Pakhtusof stood sentinel a few miles from Rosmysslow's station in the winter of 1834–35, and had previously done similar duty at Kamenka Bay in the winter of 1832–33. During the springs following these winters he and his companions accurately surveyed all that we know of the east coast from Cape Menschikow to Cape Distant.

The latter point has been approached by Captain Johannesen in 1869 and in 1870. In the former year he traversed the whole east coast known to Pakhtusof, the western shore of the Samoyede Peninsula, and sailed across the Kara Sea. In 1870, between August 11th and September 9th, he thrice crossed the Kara Sea, and ultimately reached the west coast in the same manner as Loschkin had done, occupying, however, fewer months than the Russian had taken years for the voyage.

Lastly, Mr. Wiggins, in the 'Diana,' has lately

(1874) reached 85° east longitude in about the latitude of the northernmost point of Novaya Zemlya.

From a study of all these voyages a rough generalisation of the state of the Kara Sea and the climate of the east coast of Novaya Zemlya at each season of the year can be arrived at.

The mean annual temperature of the east coast, which may be taken to represent that of the Kara Sea, is some degrees lower than that of the west coast. It is 14·99° Fahr. being lower than that of West Spitzbergen or the north coast of Labrador.[1] Midwinter occurs about the beginning of February, and midsummer in August.[2] On the one hand, as great cold as 40° Fahr. has been registered; while the medium summer temperature does not equal that of St. Petersburg in October, and is similar to that of Edinburgh in January. Continued frost without a single break lasts from the middle of October to the middle of May; and no month of the year is entirely free from frost. Except during a few weeks of summer, calms invariably mean cold, while wind raises the temperature.

In September only, when the Kara Sea is clear of ice, the east and west coast of Novaya Zemlya assimilate in temperature.

[1] The mean temperature of the year on board the 'Tegethoff,' drifting with the pack between 77° and 80°, was 2·75°.

[2] Even in midsummer snow frequently falls. Seven inches of snow has been noticed in Maschigin Bay on August 2nd (1838).

In October the sun disappears, fresh-water streams
are frozen up, and the Kara Sea is again covered with
ice, while the west coast is comparatively warm.
Winter has come in earnest, and those differences in
atmospheric pressure which manifest themselves in east
winds in the Kara Straits are initiated. As the difference in temperature increases so the wind becomes
more violent. The young ice in the first month of
winter is readily swept away by south and west winds;
and, what is important to note, the whole pack in the
Kara Sea is in motion during the winter. At one time
wind, at another a current, clears lanes of water, and
even occasionally leaves the coast quite free as far as
can be seen in the few daily hours of twilight. ' Water-
holes,' or ' Polynias,' as the Russians term them, are not
peculiar to this sea. Wrangell has observed them at
varying distances up to 170 miles from the coast of
Siberia in the month of March. It may reasonably be
assumed that such spaces of open water occur in all
parts of ice-covered seas. They may certainly be predicted where the air is sensibly moist, and where precipitation in the form of rain or snow is experienced. Those
who have not taken the trouble to investigate the limits
of such areas, or who are acquainted with them only
by report, hastily proclaim a theory of ' open water to
the North Pole'! It is difficult to gauge the motives
of an explorer who, fully convinced of the possibility

of a short sea voyage to the North Pole, deliberately refuses to attempt such an achievement (?).

Constant evaporation goes on from snow and ice, from water-holes, and from rifts in the ice. The air at a low temperature is readily saturated, and, from its small capacity for water, slight changes in the wind produce, according to their extent and the season of the year, deposition in the form of fogs, dense vapour, and falls of rain and snow. Immense quantities of snow[1] during the winter and spring,[2] and more frequent rainfalls than in other Arctic countries, characterise Novaya Zemlya, as a result of the changing, moving mass of ice dammed up in the Kara Sea.

The narrowness of the barrier between the Kara Sea and the Ocean gives rise to other phenomena—gales of wind, which have already been alluded to, and two distinct climates within a few miles of each other.

'On the east coast west winds bring dry weather, and damp only comes with the east wind when the

---

[1] A curious phenomenon is sometimes noticed when the pack splits in the winter, dense vapours arising from the fissure and falling as snow. It is, no doubt, due to air not completely saturated taking up moisture from the water. The process absorbs and renders latent much heat, and this heat suddenly taken from the surrounding air suddenly lowers its temperature and causes precipitation.

[2] In April, Pakhtusof met with so violent a storm of snow his party were unable to keep their feet. They lay down together with their heads to the wind to avoid being buried, and in this position remained three days without food.

Kara Gate is open, and this does not reach the west coast. On the west coast west winds bring damp, and land, i.e. east winds always fair weather.' Proof of this is seen in the journals of Pakhtusof and Ziwolka, who were engaged in surveys on opposite sides of the country at the same time in 1835. 'When one had gloomy weather, the other experienced fair. The very day one could see farthest, the other could make no observations.'

In spring the ice is often swept from the east coast to the horizon, only to close again with a change of wind. In early summer open water is more frequently seen, but the bays are still choked with ice fourteen inches thick, and grounded icebergs encumber the shore. A vessel which has wintered here, may be tantalised by an open sea which cannot be reached; but if clear of her winter harbour *inside the Straits*, may reckon in sailing up the east coast as early as July.

The sun's rays now begin to have power, the snow melts, streams trickle down the mountain sides, inland lakes thaw, and the crash of ice through the Kara Straits commences. Long after the winter ice which has formed about the Straits has broken up and gone westward, fresh supplies block the way and forbid access to the Kara Sea. In some years it has been impossible to sail into this sea. As late as the middle of August, Lutke found the whole coast from Kostin

Schar blocked with masses of ice from twenty to thirty miles in breadth. Violent storms from the west and south partly broke through the ice, and with difficulty he bored through to the north part of Waygat Island. Endeavouring to penetrate further into the Kara Sea he met with a wall of ice, stretching as far as the eye could see from east to west. And after waiting a week he had to turn back. Curiously enough the date, August 13th, is that when Cornelius Bosman was similarly headed off two centuries before.

Admiral Lutke's directions for the exploration of Novaya Zemlya, drawn up some years ago, are worthy of a place here.

'In speaking of the eastern coast of Novaya Zemlya, we must take care to distinguish between the coast of the southern island and the northern island. The first is incomparably the easiest to undertake. It would, doubtless, be possible to achieve it even with the means within our reach, if we bestowed a whole summer upon it.[1] For this purpose, if we encountered the icebergs directly on our entrance into the Kara Sea, we should have to anchor either in Matoschkin Schar or Nikolskij Schar, and then with the first west wind that drove the ice seaward proceed to the eastern shore. In order to carry out this idea a watch might be stationed on some high and suitable point to give notice of the

---

[1] Steam had not then been used as an auxiliary to Arctic navigation.

moving of the ice. The distance from the mouth of
the Matoschkin Schar to the port of Kara is something
more than 190 miles, and from thence the passage can
be made in two days, or even in twenty-four hours, if the
wind be strong enough. In the event of winds from
the east driving the icebergs against the shore, and
the ship being run aground, the escape of the crew
would be easy. They need only go to the shore of
Nikolskij Schar to pick up one of the Samoyede
karbassas, which are always to be met with in that
neighbourhood up to the end of September, and to sail
across to the mainland. This part may be easily accomplished by land in reindeer sledges. The required
number of reindeer must be shipped across from Waygat
to Novaya Zemlya, and kept at Nikolskij Schar, or
some other convenient spot, during the winter. The
southern portion of Novaya Zemlya abounds in wild
reindeer, and there is no fear of scarcity of fodder
there for the winter, to insure success; one might easily
accustom certain of the reindeer to a bread diet,
which, I hear, has been tried with success by some inhabitants of Mesen. In the spring, when the favourable weather had become settled, the coast surveyors
would have only to drive to the shore with the reindeer,
and very soon proceed to Matoschkin Schar.

'Admittance to the eastern part of the northern
island is beset with greater difficulties. The possibility of

accomplishing it with reindeer can neither be affirmed
nor denied with certainty.   But the difficulties of the
enterprise are incalculably increased by the extent of
shore being three times as great, and by the greater severity of the climate.   To survey the coast from the sea
two vessels are required, which in build and equipment
should resemble those vessels which the English
Government fitted out to explore the North-west Passage—ships that can work their way boldly through
the ice without fear of getting crushed, and, above all,
which are prepared to winter wherever their star shall
lead them.   Two such vessels could survey the coast
beginning at Matoschkin Schar, and could complete
the work, if not in one, certainly in two or three years.
Loschkin's voyage, in 1760, proves that the undertaking
is not physically impossible, but the danger and difficulty must be extraordinarily great on account of the
enormous masses of ice which crowd on one side from
the great estuaries of the Obi and Yenisei, and on the
other side from the remaining Siberian rivers, and the
Polar Sea; constant east winds and currents from east
to west are the agents by which it is brought in such
vast accumulations.   When once Barentz's Cape Desire
is reached the greatest difficulty is conquered, for, as a
rule, after this the sailor finds both wind and current in
his favour, which greatly facilitate the voyage along the
north coast, although there may be a good deal of ice.'

Ice this year in the middle of June crept as far south-west as lat. 70° 7′ N., long. 45° 7′ E. On June 17 we ran into a long bay of ice, in company with ten walrus-hunters from Tromsö and Hammerfest. After exchanging news with the skipper of one of these crafts, we steamed away north. The ice, thin and rotting fast, was easily ploughed through, and we soon met with open water, in which a few big seals were disporting themselves.

The next day turning out a dense fog I had to be content with hearing the walruses bellowing from afar. We had to lie to until the evening, when, the fog clearing, we steamed up to the coast of Novaya Zemlya. Here we found three schooners. From one of them five men came off offering a bear's skin for sale. They asked such an exorbitant price that I would not deal, knowing too, very well, I should probably get plenty myself soon. They told me of a sad catastrophe off Kanin Nos. The weather there is proverbially stormy in spring, and, during one of the gales in April, Lammegren, a skipper I formerly knew, with all his crew, lost their lives by the capsizing of their schooner.

There was small temptation to stay about this part of the coast. I had no wish to go ashore in a locality so much harried by Samoyedes and Russians, and so carefully surveyed and examined by others. The sea was just as unattractive to a sportsman; no fair ice, no walruses. It seemed fairly open towards the Kara

K

Gates, in which direction the ' Diana's ' bows were now pointed. The little ice met with was visibly melting, and presented so little obstacle to progress that a few hours' steaming fairly ran us into the Straits, for on the evening of the 19th we could see both shores not far off.

The ice now became heavier, and in pushing through it we broke a blade of the propeller. This compelled us to lie still for the night. Early next morning the screw was hoisted out of its well without much difficulty. On examination the fan (which, according to contract, ought to have been steel) was found to be composed of the worst sort of cast iron, and had broken with the smallest chop against a light piece of ice. Luckily I had brought a spare one, and was able, with some trouble, to replace the broken one.

While the yacht lay idle, to allow the engineer to ship the new screw, I took a long row towards the coast, hoping there might be a chance of getting deer or geese ashore. It was impossible to approach within two miles of the land. We got, however, sixteen brace of guillemots, which make excellent soup, and are always grateful to the crew as a change from salt junk.

On the way back I shot two seals, a very large one and a ridiculously small specimen of the species, commonly known as the ' floe-rat ' (*Pagomys fœtida*).

This is the smallest of Arctic seals. It usually frequents quiet, sheltered waters or basks on the flat ice-floes. Numbers haunt the still waters of the Greenland Fjords, where they are extensively slaughtered for food and clothing, notwithstanding the fœtid odour, especially of the old males. On a calm warm night, when the 'Diana' has been lying amongst floe ice, I have more than once observed this intelligent little animal swim round the ship, and even, prompted by a confiding curiosity, approach and attempt to climb up the sides of the yacht.

The most interesting fact, however, in connection with this seal is its identity with a fossil seal of the Scotch brick clays. Some seal bones had been obtained in sinking a shaft for a pit in the Grangemouth coal-field in 1868, and for some time there was doubt whether the specimen was not possibly a young individual of the *Pagophilus grœnlandicus*, as affinity with any other known species of seal was most conclusively negatived. The cranium of a floe-rat obtained on one of my voyages was submitted to Professor Turner, of Edinburgh. A careful comparison between it and the fossil seal was instituted, and we could have no higher authority than that of so accomplished a palæontologist, who concluded that the seals the remains of which are found in the brick clays of Scotland correspond with the now existing small Arctic seal

(*Pagomys fœtida*). The deduction of more interest to the general reader is that Mr. Turner considers the determination of its bones in the brick clays to be an additional piece of evidence to those advanced from other sources that at ' the time when these clays were deposited an Arctic climate prevailed over Scotland.'[1]

Soon after noon next day the ice seemed to be opening very fast ; we forced our way in ; and, to my great delight, in four hours cleared the loosely-jammed ice, and got to the edge of a vast floe apparently attached tightly to the shore. For miles a fine open water stretched away along the edge of this ice, exactly as I had expected. At last we seemed to be through the much-dreaded Gates, and late at night we anchored to the floe.

Early on the following morning we steamed along the edge of the floe. Eagerly we scanned the ice and the water, all the sloops were behind, and here I felt confident there must be game of some kind which we could approach without annoying interruption. Hardly was the thought framed when, right ahead, standing at the ice-edge, appeared a huge Polar bear. Far from crediting all the ferocious qualities ascribed to this animal, I have always considered him a most inferior sporting beast. True, my experience has been gained mostly in summer, and I can believe

---

[1] Paper in Proceedings of Ryl. Soc. of Edin., Session 1869–70.

that in the winter months, hard-set and hungry, *Ursus maritimus* may be an ugly customer at close quarters. His instinct is to run from man, and on ice and land he is more than his match in speed.

A small boat was lowered, and we rowed gently up to the bear as he moved slowly away, gazing with stupid wonderment at the ship. I was afraid he would suddenly bolt round and make play over the ice, so I fired at about 100 yards, and had the satisfaction of hearing the big round bullet crash into his shoulder. With a savage roar of rage and agony he bounced round and attempted to run on three legs. Jumping on the ice I ran up to him, and on seeing me he attempted to charge gallantly enough, but his leg gave way beneath him, and I then shot him through the heart. All hands on board, including my Newfoundland 'Sailor,' had a full view of the whole hunt. I could not help thinking what a splendid chance this would have been for a lady voyager to have seen a bear killed!

Another boat came off to help us to flense him, and while waiting for them I sat admiring this beautiful animal as he lay bleeding through the two large round bullet-holes placed almost mathematically in the deadliest spots. He was a very large male, in fine condition. His long silky hair, little less white than the snow, hung down over his hard grey claws, while his mouth lay open exhibiting his perfect and terrible array of teeth. His stomach contained a seal entire, except the bones, chopped into chunks of two or three inches square. On such diet the bears put on fat as quickly as the reindeer on the plains. Food is scanty during the winter, but there is no doubt the males roam about in search of it. Some of those wintering in Novaya Zemlya have noticed that the bears left them in November and returned with the daylight. Others have been annoyed with their visits the whole winter through. We learn from M. Payer's account of the Austrian expedition that out of the sixty-seven bears shot in two winters there was not a single female; and, further, they discovered a tunnel-shaped winter-hole, in a snow-cone lying at the foot of a cliff, which was inhabited by a female bear and her cubs. It is probable, then, that the female bear lies dormant all the winter until her accouchement in spring.

Steaming on, we reached the east mouth of the Strait, opposite to Bolvanosky Nos, the north-east point of Waygat Islands. Stephen Burrough was here about the same time of the year in 1556. He has left us an interesting account of the idols seen here, and of the religious rites of the Samoyedes which he witnessed. Hence the name of the headland, which means Idol Cape.

The scheme of religion among the tribes embraces

a belief in a Supreme Being, whose influence, being beneficent, they trouble themselves very little about; and in a malevolent Deity whose wrath they dread; a liberal allowance of priests, who hold the traditions and give counsel; and in idols, which are carried about rather as charms than objects of religious worship. Burrough relates that his Russian cicerone brought him to a heap of the Samoyede idols, which were in number about three hundred, 'the worst and most unartifical worke that ever he saw, the eyes and mouthes of sundrie of them were bloodie, they had the shape of men, women, and children, very grosly wrought, and that which they had for other parts was also sprinkled with blood. Some of their idols were an olde sticke, with two or three notches made with a knife on it.'

The existence of a numerous tribe of idolaters, who still eat their flesh raw, and buy their wives in a reindeer currency, overlapping the very frontier of Russian civilisation, and abutting on Christian Europe within three weeks' sail of our own shore, I respectfully commend to the notice of promoters of missionary enterprise. From time to time other writers have visited this sacred island. Ivanoff, as late as 1824, found the idols just as Burrough described them.

An immense mass of heavy ice jammed the entrance to the Kara Sea, and convinced me of the futility of attempting to push in through the Kara Gates as early as this; and I therefore turned back, determined to see what might be done at Jugorsky Schar. Sailing along the coast of Waygat Island we saw a few walruses, and noticed the Samoyedes gathering eggs along the shore. Towards evening we got into Jugorsky Schar with little difficulty, and anchored in a bay at the eastern end.

The Kara Sea here, too, seemed jammed with ice, but to make sure I set off next morning at four o'clock in a boat, with a four-feet telescope, and pulled to a bluff headland, from which I anticipated we might be able to see farther into the Sea.

We were now on the great Samoyede peninsula, the home, or rather one of the great head-quarters, of the 'swamp ("Sama") dwellers' of Northern Europe and Asia. Formerly, when they were more numerous, that is before they had been pushed out of existence by Yugrian encroachment from the south, the Samoyedes shared with the Eskimos the whole circle of the circumpolar regions. Even now, their colonies at Siererovostochnoi Nos constitute them, with the exception of the Eskimos of Smith Sound, the most northerly inhabitants of the world. Stunted physically, socially, and politically, the Samoyedes have little chance of breasting the wave of invasion which has already, with the help of pestilence, obliterated their allied tribes, the Omoki and the Tukotschi. Probably, in a few years,

Drawn by W. Lucas.

A Samoyede Encampment.

they will be only known by tradition, and we shall
have less substantial traces of them than now exist in
the caves of their predecessors, the metal-finders
and worshippers of *Slata Baba*.

Not far from the shore we saw the conical tents of
a small party of one of these nomadic tribes, and on our
approaching were conducted with barbarous welcome
to their fires. Here were we, representatives of western
civilisation, visitors to a Samoyede camp, commenting
on the tents and dress, and watching the simple forms of
cooking and rude arts which these people had practised
without change or advance any time these thousand
years. The single landmark of civilisation, if such it
could be regarded, in all these centuries, was the levy
of the obrok by the Russians. This tax is still paid,
because they have no instinct to resist an imposition
about which they only know their fathers paid it before
them, probably regarding it as part of the order of
Nature. The men resembled those we had seen before.
The women could only be distinguished from them by
a little faded trimming of coloured material, added to
the reindeer clothing, worn in other respects exactly
like that of the men. The tents were formed of poles,
placed to form a cone, and covered with seal-skins.
Around the encampment their tame reindeer grazed
when not yoked in the rude sledges for a journey.

When we climbed the hill we found our view shut

off by other land.   Miserably disappointed we trudged many weary miles over undulating, swampy ground, in hopes of getting an uninterrupted view, and of seeing open water beyond the ice, but one spiteful hill rose up after another, and the Kara Sea, as far as we could see it, was still crowded with ice.

In the course of the walk we found several Samo-yede fox-traps, in the plank-and-trigger or figure-of-4 form so universal all over the world ; and in one of them was a beautiful white fox, long dead and flattened out like a pancake.   I had carried only cartridges with No. 1 shot, expecting to get some geese.   With a bag of small-shot cartridges I would have made a great bag of small birds very rare in Britain.   There were dottrels (*Charadrius Morinellus*), many of those curious birds called Ruffs and Reeves (*Tringa Pugnax*) and I shot a dozen brace of small pin-tailed ducks, about the size of a hen widgeon.

In the evening we steamed out of the Straits, and were unlucky enough to go aground, near the south-east point of Waygat Island.   The bottom was fortunately soft mud, and we contrived to work out of it without much difficulty.

All next day we sailed north and north-west, with a light breeze, and saw no ice till we were again in sight of the Kara Straits.   Heavy ice then appeared coming out of the Kara Sea.   We could get no farther

on a north-west course; and, my sailing-master saying
he saw a schooner making great play into Kara Gate,
which seemed to him more open than four days previously, I consented with great reluctance to another
attempt in this direction. I foresaw the inevitable loss
of at least a day, perhaps two or three, and I felt quite
sure the navigation was as impracticable as ever. We
steamed on, passing the schooner, and at midnight my
opinion was justified. An absolutely impenetrable barrier of ice shut the way, and stretched in every direction as far as could be seen from the crow's-nest.
After mooring to a floe for a few hours to give the
engineers a rest, we steamed back again through much
heavy ice; and meeting four smacks going in I told
them what we had seen.

One skipper replied, 'he would try Jugorsky
Schar, as he had got in there twice before, and that if
necessary he would wait in the Straits till the ice
melted.' This might suit small sloops who would
take, perhaps, a month to go north about, but I con-
ceived that I should be throwing away one of the chief
advantages of steam power if I adopted such a plan;
so I resolved (in spite of the sailing-master's anxiety
to wait for a break-up here) to try the north passage
into the Kara Sea by Matoschkin Schar. I had had such
a sickener of waiting for ice to break up on the north-
west of Spitzbergen last year that I was determined

to back my own opinion here. If all went right, and the ice did not interfere in impenetrable masses and in unusual places, I ought to be at the mouth of the Matoschkin Schar in four days. The Kara Sea ought to clear there long before it did down here; if I got in there I should be amongst loose ice and walruses in two days more. Were things here still against me, I should have more walrus-ground before me on the north-west coast, and I could try Matoschkin Schar again late in July, and, failing a second time, could return to the Kara Gates or cross over to Spitzbergen. Here was a choice which resolved itself into a question of coals. Then, again, I had heard that in Silver Bay near Matoschkin Schar there is such abundance of coal that when the Russian sloops have no walruses in their holds they load up with cargoes of coal before proceeding home.

I brought on board the 'kreng' of one of four gigantic seals I had shot in the evening, and was delighted to find it burned most successfully in the furnaces, when cut up and mixed with coal.

Steaming northwards to Matoschkin Schar we rapidly left behind the icy waters issuing from the Kara Sea. Again we had evidence of the warm Gulf Stream water. In forty-eight hours we had passed from water at 32° Fahr. in the Kara Straits to a temperature of 46° off Goose Land; and for two successive

evenings the air had a temperature of 54°·5 Fahr. at
eight o'clock. We passed several small vessels, rolling
idly in a dead calm and blazing sun. Observing two
sloops coming in from the offing we spoke one and
learned the rest were still kept off by outlying ice.
On the coast we saw several reindeer, feeding close to
the sea, but as the landing was bad and I had every
hope of getting plenty at my old anchorage in Goose
Haven, I would not delay to go after them.

We were at one time in great uncertainty as to the
precise part of the south-west coast we were off, and
therefore took a midnight altitude. We found, by
the unmistakable evidence of the sun, that we were
fully fifty miles further north than we supposed.
The sun *cannot lie*, and therefore the point abreast
of us was South Goose Cape, and not Myss Tschorni,
(Black Cape) as we imagined. Near here, we saw
three walruses on some small ice. A Russian boat
caught one, while one which I shot dead sank to the
bottom.

When off North Goose Cape two vessels were seen ,
in the bay, and six outside; so I judged it better to
give them a wide berth, as they were sure to have
harried the coast, and steamed on past Myss Britwin
(Razor Cape). Our self-denial was rewarded by seeing
reindeer grazing on some splendid meadows on the
shore. We immediately hove-to, and landed some four

miles off, intending to shoot some. I had a laborious stalk, through heavy mud, under a roasting sun, up to one of three troops, which we had marked; but when within four hundred yards or so I discovered, to my great disgust, that a muddy and turbulent river (which mirage had hid from view) ran between me and the deer. The water looked too formidable to allow me to cross it, especially without a sounding-pole, and so I had to content myself with a good look at the deer through a glass. There were fourteen old stags, all asleep except two, and within easy shot of a bank at the side of a river. Their growing horns seemed to be about as long as carrots, and in the bright sun their coats appeared as white as milk. Further on there were two more droves, but all were on the wrong side of the river.

Walking up the glen in hopes of crossing a snow bridge, only one was found a mile off, and so rotten I did not at all like it. There was nothing for it but to retrace our steps, cross the river-mouth in a boat, and commence a fresh stalk. After doing all this, and on reaching the ground we had marked out, the deer were no longer to be seen. For half-an-hour I looked about, but could see nothing of them. I felt quite certain they were still there, and were either lying down on a patch of snow, the whiteness preventing their being seen, or feeding in some slight depression of the undulating

plain, which we could not detect owing to the mirage.
I never saw mirage worse, even on the hot plains of
Africa, than it was here to-day. The deer had looked
like large white ponies, standing on four telegraph
poles! A hot haze simmered through the atmosphere,
and the walking was very bad, over deep tenacious
mud, covered with broken slate-rock, of which this
part of Novaya Zemlya seems chiefly composed.

On walking back to the boat I found my crew had
gathered half a boat-load of excellent dry drift-wood,
and almost immediately after pushing off we all saw
the deer on the slopes, apparently just where I had
been looking for them !

The mirage has a very singular effect in these
regions, especially on hot sunny days. Vessels or land
which are known to be far out of sight and, properly
speaking, below the horizon are seen hove up in the
air by refraction. The irregular masses of floating ice
become dazzling cities, with domes, minarets, and
steeples, of a more composite style of architecture than is
to be seen in any modern capital ; while the floe-
edge is made to represent many miles of fairy palaces
and enchanted castles.

Too tired to renew the fruitless chase, I got on
board the yacht, and, steaming ahead, met the ice between Gribowaja Guba (Mushroom Bay) and Matoschkin
Schar (Mathew's Straits).

It is quite a lottery where the ice lies about this part of the coast during the summer months. This does not depend so much upon what drives through Matoschkin Schar, though that is a considerable amount, as it does upon the indented nature of the coast between North Goose Cape and the Straits. Cape Britwin[1] roughly bisects this stretch of shore-line. South of the headland is Moller Bay, subdivided into many deep bays and estuaries, and in some of them good anchorage is found. Northward are Besimannaja Guba (Nameless Bay) and Mushroom Bay, separated only by the promontory of Perwousmotrennaja Gora (First-seen Mountain.) In all these bays the drifting ice-masses become fixed by the winter bay ice. This frozen mass depends on the varying condition of wind and current for its escape into the open sea ; and as the current tends rather to drive ice into the bays, although it is a warm stream, the coast is sometimes unapproachable the whole summer. An interesting illustration of this was the position of the ice in 1835. Pakhtusof, who was at the east end of the Matoschkin Schar, noticed east-south-east wind drive the ice through the Straits and clear it ; while from other sources he learned that the western mouth and the coast all along to Goose Land was blocked up with ice-floes and stranded bergs, and not till July

---

[1] Britwin Bay affords a secure anchorage. A circle of mountains protects it from winds off shore, while the promontory shelters it from a westerly gale.

29th was the western entrance free. Rosmysslof, after sailing through Matoschkin Schar from the east in 1769, met with close-packed drift-ice, six miles south-west of Matoschkin Schar, as late as August 27th.

And Lieutenant Lasarew was headed off from the Straits by drift-ice early in July of 1819. The pack stretched hence unbroken to Britwin Island and prevented his passing east of Kolguev, and when he again attempted to force a way to the Straits at the end of the month, in latitude 73° 15′, he was unable to effect anything after waiting about until the middle of the next month.

Again, Lutke, sailing from Goose Land towards Matoschkin Schar, in the middle of August 1821, struggled through immense drifts of ice, till, a storm blowing from the land (easterly), he was able to sail round a wall of ice into open water. The following year all this coast was free from ice on August 8th.

We had been enjoying nine days of the most lovely weather imaginable, not a cloud to veil the blazing sun, nor a breath of air to ruffle the calm, glassy sea; but the morning of June 30th saw a change. A brisk breeze from the south-west brought with it a dense fog. We had hove-to off Pilz Bay during the night, and seized an interval of clearer weather to go ashore. The plains were very wet, the air oppressive, and the deer had retreated to the high mountain-land. I shot a swan with a ball at 150 yards' distance, but her wing only being broken she ran so fast that we had the greatest difficulty in catching her after a run of two miles. During the day we heard loud and prolonged thunder. To the south of us was the heavy rain-cloud from which presently fell drenching showers, but no lightning was seen. Pakhtusof, too, heard thunder on June 10th in Matoschkin Schar, though it is considered a phenomena of rare occurrence in such high latitudes.

On July 1st we steamed into the Straits in a terrible mirage. There are some treacherous reefs at the entrance which require wary navigation to avoid. Passing Pakhtusof's winter hut, we anchored opposite Myss Morshewoi (Walrus Cape.) I then went ahead in a boat to explore, and found the Straits blocked with fast ice—checkmate to my fourth attempt to reach the Kara Sea!

It was, no doubt, early in the season for these Straits; and I was hindered, not by the east wind, which, prevailing during the greater part of the year as a result of the difference in atmospheric pressure east and west of Novaya Zemlya, often blows a sailing vessel out after she has approached the entrance with a fair west wind, nor by the ice drifted from the eastward by the same cause, but by ice, as I have said, adhering to the shores and now extended across in an unbroken sheet. Steaming back some distance we found a good

L. Beckmann.

Reindeer-shooting.

anchorage, safe except from drifting ice, near a wooden cross on the north shore. The strong current drove the ice with considerable force, and made a vigilant watch necessary even while at anchor. From the deck I saw eight deer, and, after a most arduous walk, run, and crawl of four or five miles, I shot one, and wounded another. The shyness of the animals in this secluded locality equals that of Scotch red-deer, and so contrasts with the tameness of the rein-deer in Spitzbergen that I attribute it to the existence of wolves. The scarcity of the deer was disappointing and inexplicable, as it was a beautiful piece of country embracing splendid pastures, with a great variety of vegetation, and, moreover, admirably adapted for stalking.

I determined to give up the Straits for the present ; and, early next day, commenced steaming out; but, wind bringing fog, we were again compelled to anchor, where we found ourselves to the lee of Myss Stolbowoi (Cape Column) in company with three Russian schooners.

Cape Column and Pankow Island, just off it, mark the mouth of the Straits to the south ; and, perhaps, the best way to find the Straits (not always easy) is to bear this in mind, after identifying the other landmarks of the coast, viz. First-seen Mountain, Nameless Bay, and Pilz Bay.

With the Russian captains we made some barters,

accommodating to both parties. We got a large basket of guillemots' eggs and a tubful of pickled salmon (*S. Alpinus*) for forty pounds of sugar and one of tea ; and a couple of bears' skins were bought for about twenty shillings each. I might have bought everything they owned very cheaply for *rum*, but I had some scruples of conscience about cheating and demoralising these poor ignorant fellows.

Perched on a pinnacle of rotten slate near the shore, I whiled away the time to some profit in picking off sixty brace of guillemots as they streamed by on their way to a far-off loomery. Failing deer, they formed a welcome addition to the crew's diet. A salt salmon appeared at the cabin mess, and, although lean and hard, it was not altogether bad. This fish, of which I had a specimen carefully skinned for Mr. Buckland, is more like a large sea or bull-trout than a *S. Salar.* Two kinds of salmon are fished for in Novaya Zemlya— *S. Alpinus*, and *S. Omul.* But the former only is of any commercial importance. Two methods of taking them are adopted ; one depends on the salmon ascending the rivers to spawn in the lakes, and consists in intercepting them during the first fortnight of August. A salmon trap is fixed across the river, from which the fish are taken out singly with a landing-net. The coast fishing is carried on by a system of fixed and drag-nets, which enclose the salmon in the shallow water on their return from the lakes. The salmon is salted for the Archangel market. In 1852 two boat-owners took, in the Nechwatowa, between 400 and 500 pud. Previous to that time the trade had been much depressed, owing to the wanton way in which the fishing had been carried on. For in the years 1830–1833, traditionally known as the salmon years, the fish were so abundant that it was impossible to salt and carry away the whole catch, and many were recklessly destroyed. There was no proper division of the spoil to the various crews, but each took as much as they wanted. If a boat were unable, from stress of weather, to bear up for the drying station, the cargo was thrown overboard, and a fresh one taken next day. Is it any wonder that the yearly supply varies and diminishes in the face of such iniquitous proceedings?

Towards evening the fog cleared off, and we steamed out to the ice and hove-to.

As we were passing through a small stream of ice next day, I noticed a round, yellowish mass lying on a slab of ice. With the glass I made it out to be a bear fast asleep beside the krang of a seal; the engine was stopped, and I went at him in the small boat. He had evidently gorged himself with seal, and was so sound asleep we might have rowed up to his very nose. At fifty yards, however, I fired, and gave him my favourite shot in the shoulder. He sprang to his feet with a terrific roar, but instantly fell over on his back, and lay roaring and kicking all fours in the air. Another bullet in the chest seemed to revive him, for he took to the sea and swam, but was evidently dying. A third shot in the neck now finished him, and we towed him behind the boat to the yacht. The foreyard and the very mast shook and trembled with his weight as we hove him on board. 'Sailor' had seen bears before, and contented himself with merely sniffing the carcase with an air of contempt and indifference. 'Nelly' hid herself in her box, and 'Billy' (a half-bred bull-dog belonging to the sailing-master) nearly went into fits with mingled funk and fury, at sight and smell of the bear.

This bear [1] was so old his canine teeth were broken and carious. Still he was very fat; the blubber weighed two hundred pounds, in addition to which we got a

---

[1] I had learned to take unusual pains with the bear-skins, as much of their beauty and value depend on the way they are treated. The best way of treating them is this:—

1. The skins are flensed by the most careful man on board, who has need of great patience and skill to avoid injuring the skin, which is thin and lissome.

2. They are well scraped.

3. Towed overboard for a day or two.

4. Put into a tub and soaked in a mixture of one pound of salt and one pound of alum to a gallon of water.

5. Turned every day for a fortnight.

6. Stretched on a frame made of four boats' masts, scraped again, and dried.

large bucket of internal fat, the veritable bear's-grease, which ' it was a pity,' as my valet once remarked, 'was not worth 3*s.* 6*d.* a pot, as in the Burlington Arcade.' In the stomach were the remains of the seal banquet, in the shape of three buckets-full of muddy oil. Ye powers! what a digestion! The day's bag was completed by securing a large bull-walrus out of several which were seen in the evening. Another, successfully harpooned was lost by the line being cut against the ice.

The bear shot was an exceptionally large one, but I think the biggest beast of his species I ever saw was in Deeva Bay, Spitzbergen, in 1859. I had shot some seals one morning, and a few hours after, while still not far from the carcases which I had left on the ice, I perceived a large bear about a mile off. The dead seals were about equally distant between me and Bruin, and I was at first somewhat at a loss how to proceed, because, close to the bear, there was a large extent of level 'fast' ice, with several wide valleys beyond. It was clear that if we attacked him openly in front he would take to his heels over the flat, and soon, with his superior speed, run us all to a standstill. I then thought I would lay down beside the carcases to wait for his approach, but it had now got so bitterly cold that I feared I should be half-frozen before he came. So, after a minute's consultation with the harpooner, we decided on a middle course. We rowed as fast as we could towards the carcases and pushed the boat into a little creek which fortunately existed in the edge of the ice, exactly eighty yards on our side of the carcases. The bear was still snuffing about on the land, and had not yet perceived us ; and, the boat being white like the ice, it was not likely he would do so, if we kept quite still. I made all the men crouch down in the boat, while I alone watched the motions of Bruin by peeping over the gunwale through an opera-glass.

The bear walked slowly and deliberately for some 200 or 300 yards on the ice, as if uncertain whether he should go up to the dead seals or not. How earnestly I prayed that he might not have had his dinner. Shortly he appeared to make up his mind that a seal supper would be exactly the thing for him, for, sliding stern foremost into the water, he swam steadily and quietly along, close under the edge of the ice, towards the carcases. This is his common method of attack when live seals are floating about on loose drift ice ; he ' first finds his seal ' by eyes or nose—in the use of both of which organs *Ursus maritimus* is unsurpassed by any wild animal whose acquaintance I have ever made—and then, slipping into the water half a mile or so to the leeward of his prey, he swims gently towards him, keeping very little of his head above water. On approaching the ice on which the seal is lying, the bear slips along unseen under the edge of it, until he is close under the hapless seal, when one jump up, and one blow of his tremendous paw, generally settles the business. But how a bear manages to get within arm's length of a seal on a sheet of *fast ice* is more than I can understand.

I perceived half-a-dozen live seals capering round the bear in the water as if making fun of their great enemy, or chaffing him now that he was in their peculiar element, like small birds following and teasing a hawk when they are sure he can't catch them. When the bear came close to the dead seals he peeped cautiously up over the edge of the ice, and then, seeing they were not live seals, he scrambled out quite coolly and began to shake the wet from his shaggy coat like a Newfoundland dog. The instant he had concluded this operation I fired, and smashed the joint of one of his shoulders. He fell on his face on the ice, growling savagely and biting at the wound. According to a preconcerted arrangement I instantly sprang out on the ice and ran towards the bear, while the boat started to meet him in case he should take to the water. While I was running the bear got to his feet, and at first seemed inclined to fight it out, as he advanced a few steps to meet me, growling most horribly, and showing his teeth ; but on my approaching a little nearer he seemed to think discretion the better part of valour, for he fairly lost heart and scuffled precipitately into the sea. I then shot him through the brain as he swam away; and, the boat coming up immediately, they got a noose round his neck and towed him to the ice. He was so large and heavy that we had to fix the ice-anchor, and drag him up with block and tackle as if he had been a walrus. This was an enormous old male bear and measured upwards of 8 feet in length, almost as much in circumference, and $4\frac{1}{2}$ feet high at the shoulder; his fore-paws were 34 inches in circumference, and had very long, sharp, and powerful nails; his hair was beautifully thick, long, and white, and hung several inches over his feet. He was in very high condition, and produced nearly 400 lbs. of fat; his skin weighed upwards of 100 lbs. and the entire carcase of the animal cannot have been less than 1,600 pounds.

When he was skinned his neck and shoulders were like those of a bull, and his whole appearance indicated prodigious strength. The people tell me that an old bear like this will kill the biggest bull-walrus, although nearly three times his own weight, by suddenly springing on him from behind some projecting ice, seizing him by the back of the neck with his teeth, and battering in his skull with repeated blows of his enormous fore-paw; and after seeing the size and muscular development of this individual I can easily believe it. One can form no idea of the enormous size and strength of the Polar bear by seeing the feeble representatives of his species in the Zoological Gardens, as the specimens there must have been caught at a very early age; and captivity, as well as the unsuitable warmth of our climate, prevent them from attaining to half their proper size.

I believe *Ursus maritimus*, in a state of nature, to be the largest and strongest carnivorous animal in the world; but, like all other wild animals (except on rare occasions), he will never face a man if he can help it; and I believe the stories of his extraordinary courage and ferocity which we read in the accounts of the early navigators of the Polar Sea to be grossly exaggerated. Even at the present day, many ridiculous fables respecting them are current; for instance, before I went to Spitzbergen, I recollect an Englishman, who had passed many summers in Norway and could speak the language thoroughly, telling me gravely the following story: 'He heard from the people who went to Spitzbergen that the white bear was a most dangerous and ferocious animal, and always charged right at a man whenever he saw him. Other wild animals,' said my informant, 'might charge *occasionally*, but the white bear *invariably* did so, and the plan universally adopted for killing him was based upon

this well-known habit of the animal, and consisted in
having a spear made with a cross-piece about two
feet from the point; and when the bear, according to
his usual practice, charged, the operator presented this
ingenious implement towards him; the bear then seized
it by the cross, and, in his efforts to drag it away
from the man, he pulled the blade right into his own
chest and so killed himself'! Upon my venturing
to express some slight doubts as to whether bears
really were so infatuated as to make a regular practice
of so obligingly committing suicide after the manner
of the Ancient Romans, my friend replied, rather in-
dignantly: 'Oh! there is no doubt about it, *for I
have seen lots of the weapons they use myself*'! Of
course, I could not civilly express any further doubt
of the entire veracity of the story; but I must confess
that my subsequent experience in Spitzbergen has in
no way tended to confirm my belief in this very
remarkable statement.

Scoresby relates an amusing case of a bear climbing
into a boat and sitting coolly inside it while the crew
whom he had ejected hung on outside until another
boat's crew came up and despatched him, as he sat in-
offensively in the stern. This story, I have no doubt,
is true enough; but, upon the whole, I think the Polar
bear affords less sport and may be killed with less
danger than almost any large wild animal I am

acquainted with. He is generally found amongst
loose ice; and, as he cannot swim so fast as a boat can
be rowed, he is completely at your mercy, and you
have only to select your own distance and shoot him
through the head. Even if attacked on land, I conceive that a cool fellow with a gun runs very little risk,
because, although the bear's speed far exceeds that of
a man, still he is so heavy in his motions that he ought
to be killed or disabled by the first shot at close quarters.
They are sometimes killed with the lance in the
water, but it is as well to make use of fire-arms, if they
are at hand, as I have heard of accidents happening
while attacking bears with the spear. I have read
many accounts of the same nature as the above
absurdity relating to the awful courage, ferocity, and
invulnerability of the grizzly bear of the Rocky
Mountains; but, without having seen the latter animal,
I feel perfectly certain that he is not a bit more
courageous, ferocious, or invulnerable than the Polar
bear, or than most other large carnivorous wild
animals, and not nearly so much so as either the
black rhinoceros or the African buffalo.

Though the weather set in thick, and rain fell
heavily during the night and nearly all next day, we
pushed on northwards. Sserebränka Guba (Silver
Bay) might have tempted us, had not Ludlow dispelled
the traditions of earlier voyagers by bringing away

specimens of the talc and mica which, glittering on the shore at a distance, it is true, look like silver. It was here that Pakhtusof found the wreck of the 'Yenisei' in 1835. Lieutenant Krokow had sailed with him two years previously in this vessel; but, after two years' search, the only trace of his party was the stranded keel and shattered timbers lying on the beach.

The flat low tongue of land, Ssuchoi Noss (Dry Cape), forming a peninsula stretching far into the sea, has its own peculiar share of interest; for here Barentz first sighted Novaya Zemlya in 1594; on its east side he landed in Ssafronowa Bay, and found traces of human residence. Next in order is Melki Saliw (Shallow Bay), where Moïssejews established himself in winter quarters in 1838–1839. The meteorological journal kept by this explorer is one of the greatest keys we have to the climate of Novaya Zemlya; and by his spring explorations, carried out in spite of weather, snow-blindness and sickness, the neighbouring Krestowaja Guba (Cross Bay), long suspected to be another strait of communication with the Kara Sea, was thoroughly investigated, and proved to be nothing but a deep bay or fjord. Cross Bay, in common with all the deep inlets between Matoschkin Schar and Admiralty Peninsula, affords a good harbour; indeed, two anchorages may be found on its west side. Barentz described one of these, with its terraced background rising to the proportions of a mountain, in which multitudes of sea-birds breed.

The Bays, North and South Sulmenjew, are separated, the north from the south, and the latter from Cross Bay, by rocky promontories of about equal area to the bays themselves. Into the former we now ran, in a deluge of rain and east wind, and hove to under the lee of Cape Sidenser. One of the best anchorages of the west coast of Novaya Zemlya is found in this bay behind an island on its northern shore; but, anxious to lose no time, I did not care to bring-up with no particular object in view.

On the morning of July 16th, we found an immense accumulation of bay and drift ice off Maschigin Bay. The yacht lay-to in a lane of water while I went away in a boat to hunt. The afternoon's sport was very good. With eleven bullets I killed a fine bull walrus, and ten seals of the first magnitude, and only lost two of the latter by sinking. There were a great many of these seals lying in good ice, the day being calm and sunny. At 4 A.M. next day we steamed through very close and heavy ice till, having crossed the bay, we anchored in a lake of open water during a gale of east wind in a little bight four or five miles north-east of Borissow Island. There is no good anchorage in this great bay, but a tolerably snug berth was found here over a bank of slaty mud in fifteen

fathoms of water. I was able to get ashore under lee
of the land; and, walking across the barren, bleak,
stormy, wind-swept hills to the promontory dividing
the two bays north and south of it, I had a good view
of both sheets of water, particularly Maschigin Bay.
I was much surprised to see how little effect the gale
had in driving the ice seawards. There was a great
quantity of ice on both sides, due either to a very
strong countertide driving it in, or to north-east wind
on the other side of Cape Speedwell driving more ice
down as fast as one east wind sets it off.

Cape Speedwell is the south point of what is now
termed Admiralty *Peninsula*—Barentz described it
as Admiralty *Island.* It is possible both accounts
are true, and that the island of the sixteenth century
has become a peninsula in the nineteenth by the
process of upheaval which we have evidence of in
Northern Norway and Spitzbergen. North Cape,
Shoal Point, and Cape Sparre, in Spitzbergen, are distinct examples of former islands now united to the
mainland. In the old Dutch maps sounds separated
these promontories from the mainland. At the present time deep valleys, with glacier-marked rocks,
undoubtedly show where the ice-laden sea has retired.
In further proof of the gradual rise of the Novaya
Zemlya coast I may cite the account given me by
Captain Mack, of some barren sandy islands half-way

between Cape Nassau and Ice Cape (Gulf Stream Islands), on the supposed site of a sand-bank described by Barentz and in his time covered with eighteen fathoms of water. A study of these islands would suggest a rise of the land at even a more rapid rate than that which I have shown elsewhere to be raising the Spitzbergen Archipelago.

At Cape Borissow there are the remains of an old and small Russian hut. On it I noticed names engraved in rude Russian characters, with the dates 1836 and 1837. As no exploring expedition visited the Novaya Zemlya shores in 1836, and Von Baer in 1837 did not get farther north than Silver Bay, these marks, probably, only recorded the visit of some idle skipper. The timbers of the hut were rather decayed, but the structure might be patched up so as to make it habitable winter quarters for three or four persons on an emergency. Such are the practical thoughts which invariably rise to the mind on visiting one of these rude shelters. A hundred reflections peculiar to the Arctic regions are suggested by the crashing sounds of the ice in the neighbouring bay; and as one takes temporary shelter from the sweeping gale outside, and looks round at the rotting timbers of the hut, it is impossible not to realize for a few moments the long and dreary winters which have been passed in these shanties.

M

The fast ice joined the island to the shore, and I walked across, thinking there might be a bear among the rocks, searching for eggs. It was soon evident that the island had not been disturbed very lately, for the eider ducks were quietly sitting or hatching their eggs. I gathered a game-bag of eggs, but broke most of them in jumping over the cracks in the ice.

The gale continued through the night and next morning, but employment was found for the crew in going ashore for water and drift-wood. From one piece of timber alone, a log of yellow pine about sixty feet long and three feet thick, two boat-loads of wood were cut, and half of it still left imbedded in the gravel beach. When it calmed in the afternoon we weighed anchor and made sail for the offing, in company with eleven other vessels, Russian and Norwegian, including a hideous steamer, from Trondhjem. We beat up and down and hove-to for the next few days in the most variable weather. The wind veered through every point of the compass, and brought successively fog, heavy rain, thunder, and lightning. On the 11th the ice appeared quite impassable to the north, and we still waited in hopes of its opening.

There were now fifteen vessels, including the 'Diana,' hove-to within a square league; such close quarters necessitated a sharp look-out. On one occa-

Drawn by W. Liveny.

Norwegian Walrus-sloops.

sion we watched the Norwegian steamer run foul of a
schooner, carrying away two of her own boats, and
destroying one of the schooner's. I was pleased to
have the opportunity of entertaining some of the
skippers of these vessels, and gained from them much
practical information. The captain of the steamer told
me that he had seen masses of walruses on the ice in
spring, but could not get at them : he had tried both
Kara and Jugorsky Schar since we were there, and
had finally entered the Kara Sea by one passage,
and quitted it by the other, but farther he could not
steam, as the sea was full of enormous masses of ice.
Captain Mack, who has since distinguished himself by
exploring the sea north-east of Novaya Zemlya, tried
the Matoschkin Schar since we were there, and was
of opinion the ice would be broken up ' about now.'
He remarked that he thought ' there must be land
between Novaya Zemlya and Spitzbergen, as the
walruses all go that way.' I thought this, coming
from so experienced and intelligent a man, worth
recording at the time ; and the discoveries of the
Austrian expedition have substantiated his speculation.

Tobiesen, a famous-walrus hunter, and the hero of
the 400-mile row round the north-east of Spitzbergen,[1]

[1] See p. 251.

came on board, and we had a long talk and exchanged much information. His having been in America, where he learned some English, assisted our conversation. His was one of the five vessels beset in North Spitzbergen till September 14th in the year 1869. He got very few walruses that year, but wished he was there again. The sequel to the wild life of this obscure but gallant Arctic seaman is a most melancholy one. His sloop got beset in the Kara Sea in the autumn of 1872. He sent most of his crew to the River Petchora in the boats, but he and the others were found dead in the sloop the following summer.

Each day fresh ice, driving down from the north and sweeping round Admiralty Peninsula, forbade more decidedly a passage along the coast beyond this point. Admiralty Peninsula in some degree, and Cape Nassau in a greater, are critical points in an access to the extreme north, as the north-west corner of Spitzbergen and Melville Bay in Davis Straits are, in other directions. At Cape Nassau the coast takes a decided trend, forming a corner on which the Polar current impinges and heaps its ice masses. Off Cape Nassau the Gulf current meets the cold stream and is deflected to the north-west. This warm current, before stated to free the west coast of Novaya Zemlya in ordinary seasons, also tends to thaw out a semicircular area from the Polar pack. Cape Nassau, projecting into this basin,[1] causes the ice to cling to the coast northward of it; and not till late in the season—as the ice-blocks push past it to be melted in the warm water—is the mass of ice north sufficiently loose to be navigated. Early in the season, or occasionally during the whole summer the Arctic current beats the Gulf Stream, and Admiralty Peninsula, with the coast to the north of it, is unapproachable. A good chart of Novaya Zemlya shows at a glance that, while every cape and inlet south of the peninsula have been accurately surveyed and sounded, north of it the salient points have been barely named. In fact some half-dozen names would exhaust all those who have sailed past this critical point. So recently as 1835, Pakhtusof, whom no one will accuse of either want of courage or perseverance—a man of four summer and two winter seasons of Novaya Zemlya ice—was unable to penetrate beyond Birch Island, where, his vessel getting crushed, he with difficulty escaped to the shore. The remarkably successful voyage of Barentz—who in his first expedition got beyond Cape Nassau, and in his last round the northeast end of Novaya Zemlya to Ice Haven, and returned

---

[1] The mean temperature of the great warm basin which laps the west coast of Spitzbergen and Novaya Zemlya is, even in 78° N., between 48° and 44° Fahr.

in boats the following spring—can only be explained
by the known alternation of close and open seasons.
Barentz witnessed the immense pressure of the ice in
the former voyage when he was beset for three weeks,
and, endeavouring to bore through the pack, put
his ship about eighty-one times.   The ice drove
Barentz into his winter quarters.   The ice-laden
current, too, drove the Austrians in 1872 *from* the land
and floated them through the unknown, unvisited sea
to Franz Josef Land.

Wood, we know, was in 1676 driven on a reef
and wrecked, and his vessel, the 'Speedwell,' has given
a name to the scene of the disaster.   Lutke found the
ice in 1824 in just the position Wood had described it.
On August 11th, 1822, the latter explorer had sailed
without difficulty to Cape Nassau; and there, endeavouring to push farther on through floe-ice and bergs,
he was stopped by an ice-wall, which adhered closely
to the shore.   On August 1st, 1823, Lutke had coasted
to lat. 76° 30′ without having met with ice, but here
he was stopped by enormous masses of packed ice,
which lay stretched out in almost the same place and
direction as in the previous year.

The voyage of William de Vlamingh in 1662, when
he sailed without difficulty round the north of Novaya
Zemlya into the Kara Sea; of Johannesen, who, in
the year 1870, and of Carlsen, who, in 1871, circum-

navigated Novaya Zemlya, show that quite late in the season there may be open water around the north-west of Novaya Zemlya; but Johannesen in 1869 found the ice-barrier on June 19th distant a mile from Cape Nassau, and extending in a north-east and north-west direction. We conclude, then, that Cape Nassau cannot be passed as early as June or July.

Johannesen described the northern coasts as extremely dreary, sandy, full of stones, and so bare of even the lowest forms of vegetation that he assumed Admiralty Peninsula to be the limit of the reindeer. On the ice walruses were abundant. And he described a great glacier thirty or forty miles southwest of great Ice Cape, which extends far into the sea. Probably this is the source of the bergs seen off the coast.

On the afternoon of the 12th, a fresh breeze from the north-west springing up, we took advantage of it to run away south. Driving snow prevented us seeing the land, but we made our course south by east, allowing two points for east variation, which we supposed to exist here. We were quite right, for at three A.M. next day we found ourselves close abreast of Ssuchoi Nos, and at midday entered the Matoschkin Schar. In going in it is essential to keep the south side, and hold close to the north of a haystack-looking rock which lies near to the south shore, off the mouth of Gribowaja River. There are dangerous reefs under water to the north of this rock. As we steamed farther in, the passage assumed an appearance of grandeur which I never saw surpassed in Norway or Switzerland. About the middle the Straits narrowed to half-a-mile, or less, with steep precipitous mountains, 2,500 to 3,500 feet high, rising up sheer from the water's edge on each side. Above the masts towered these great masses, as if they would fall on us; and over the face of one fell a considerable cascade, which, like the well-known Staubach, was dispersed before it reached the bottom. A good-sized glacier in one place occupied a corrie, from which it brimmed over, and fell some 2,000 feet perpendicularly into the sea. In some places, where the cliffs retired, fine green valleys opened on both sides, and, without leaving the deck, we saw six separate troops of reindeer, close to the shore. They are in such poor condition at this season as to be hardly worth shooting, and I was so eagerly, nervously, anxious to get into the Kara Sea I would not lose time in stalking them. In the evening our forbearance was rewarded by bagging a big seal and a fine bear, within ten minutes of each other. The seal was lying on one of the only dozen bits of ice we saw in the whole fifty miles of strait, so rapidly had it cleared since we were last here. The bear was feasting on a rotten white-fish, which appeared to have died of old age, and was stranded on a gravelly point. The water in the Straits deepens from nine to fifteen fathoms behind Baranji Myss (Cape Ram), at the western end, to ninety fathoms at the eastern. The strong current running through it from west to east showed by its temperature that it is still a branch of the warm stream.

Dr. Petermann, from a study of the journals kept by winter observers here, concludes that the Straits are navigable fifty days out of 365. But, owing to the narrowness of the passage, an unfavourable wind, lasting for but a short time, may quickly block it at any point, when there is a supply of ice at its eastern end ; and, it would, perhaps, be more correct to state generally, *a passage is possible during two months of the year, but a run through can never be predicted with certainty.* For example, we should naturally assume that during the month of September, when the Kara Sea is generally free from ice, there could be no difficulty in getting through the Straits any day in that month. But let us call to mind the experience of Pakhtusof in 1834. On September 7th, after a violent east-north-east gale, he started from his anchorage at Cape Ram, and at Myss Shurawlew (Cape Crane) found the Straits ahead blocked with ice, which the gale had driven in. Working their way through this to Myss Saworotny (Windy Cape) they came upon a continuous wall of ice, all across the Strait. Waiting till the 10th, they experienced a light wind from the east; and the icebergs drifted hither and thither, now following the tide from the west, and now the wind from the east. Taking advantage of the tidal waves, they continued their course eastward, through the drifting masses, till, after passing the mouth of the Tarassowa River, they found the Strait ahead completely blockaded with a solid wall of densely-packed ice. The explorers had no choice but to return to the place selected for a winter hut. This they did with difficulty, by passing through the drifting ice, and breaking through the newly forming ice by bags of ballast hung to the bowsprit.

The 13th of July, when I made the passage, is perhaps, then, the earliest date at which it is possible to reach the Kara Sea by this route. Johannesen reached it four days later in 1869,[1] and every other passage through the Straits has been made later still.[2]

---

[1] But Johannesen was more fortunate in finding the Kara Sea so clear of ice he was able to sail down the east coasts to Kara Gates and subsequently to traverse the sea in all directions.

[2] Von Baer, waiting and watching in the Straits while he occupied himself with exploring the natural resources of the district, was unable to reach the eastern end until the last day of July. Again, Rosenthal in 1871 found the channel blocked with ice on August 7th, and at the same time the Kara Gates and Jugorsky Straits were impassable.

Although no ice was visible, an ominous yellow haze hung over the Kara Sea, as, for the third time, I entered its gloomy portals at 1.30 A.M. In two hours we had arrived at the edge of a vast semicircular barrier of close, heavy, packed ice! We steamed round the edges of this ice, and, finding no opening, came to an anchor in Klokow Bay, to the north-west of the promontory. In entering Klokow Bay care should be taken to keep in the middle, with the Gulf end on, until the vessel is well inside the promontory. It is necessary to keep the lead going, as there are dangerous reefs, apparently a prolongation under water of the slate rocks at the Point. The water shoals very suddenly, and had I not sent in a boat to sound before us we should inevitably have gone on the rocks.

Leaving the yacht, I rowed along the coast, past Brandt Bay, to the mouth of Schubert Bay. No reindeer could be seen, but we came across the remains of some which had apparently been killed by wolves or bears during the winter. As far as we could see along this east coast the ice lay close to the land, and I could not but be convinced of the impossibility of a ship exploring the east coast while any ice remained in the Kara Sea.

To add one degree of latitude to that already known, Ziwolka occupied twenty-one days battling with hardships and obstacles incredible to anyone

not familiar with Arctic travelling. Pakhtusof, following up this journey in the month of August in a
karbassa, was stopped a few miles farther on by masses
of coast ice, which, putting him in great peril during
the whole voyage, finally stopped his progress at
Pakhtusof Island. From this farthest point land was
still seen beyond the dreary waste of hummocky ice,
and appropriately named Cape Distant. It has since
been touched at by the Norwegian sloops, which
have visited the coast in various places, from here
to the extreme north-east of Novaya Zemlya. Unfortunately their accounts are very meagre. But
we learn from Johannesen's voyage that there is,
along the east coast of Novaya Zemlya, north of the
Matoschkin Schar, a broad margin of deep water.
Sounding between the Pakhtusof Islands gave 100
fathoms. North of this the coast is not rocky; it is low,
and although very bare of vegetation, yet there is sufficient to feed a few reindeer. Drift-wood was seen on
some of the sandy points, and, doubtless, was brought
there by a sort of circular current, which seems to sweep
round the Kara Sea. It is caused probably by the
current from the waters of the Obi and Yenisei meeting
the Polar current and being deflected at the wide end
of the Kara Sea. This composite current, mingled
fresh and salt water, then, as before stated, sweeps
round the concavity of the eastern shore of Novaya

Zemlya, and deposits immense quantities of drift-wood, which is always found in greatest abundance on the north sides of the headlands. In some places it is piled up to a height of ten feet. In Klokow Bay I got eight boat-loads, and we might have had any number of tons. Amongst the pine logs, which are far less worn than we find them after their stormy voyage to Spitzbergen, I found two splendid three-inch planks of yellow pine, in serviceable condition.

The morning of the 15th, succeeding a cold night's rain, was warm and sunny. I was surprised to find but little difference between the temperature of the sea and air at the west coast and here at the confines of the icy sea. The mean of temperatures of the air taken in July, at 8 A.M. and 8 P.M., while we were engaged on the west coast in Matoschkin Schar, and in passing later into the Kara Sea, was found to be 43·11° Fahr. A similar July average of a former voyage in Spitzbergen, along the coast and occasionally at anchor in the bays to the north of King's Bay, and at the Norway Islands, was 41·11°—an interesting general comparison of the climates of these countries in summer. The surface temperature of the Novaya Zemlya seas is also considerably higher than that of the Spitzbergen waters.

In the evening half a gale of north-west wind sprang up. We dropped a second anchor, and lay still for some time in apparently safe quarters. But the wind, increasing during the night, drove the ice down, and threatened to enclose us in the bay, so we were compelled to get up steam and find our way again into the Strait, where we anchored to the east of Myss Poperetschnoi (Cross Cape). It is related of another vessel, caught in similar weather, but farther out to sea, that, running for shelter, she made for Saliw Nesnajemy (Unknown Bay), judging it to be the mouth of the Matoschkin Schar; and, from the similarity of the coast, such an error, easily made, might, late in the season, bring a summer cruise to a disastrous end. There was good holding, half or a third of a mile from the shore, in a suddenly-shelving bank of mud. The best harbour about here seemed to be Gubin Bay, on the south shore of the Straits. It is perfectly landlocked, and has three fathoms of water at the entrance, deepening to seven or eight.

Through the night it continued to blow strongly from the north-west (north-east in the Kara Sea), and I started with three boats at eight A.M. for a general onslaught at the deer. To the west of our anchorage, and between it and Saliw Belushja (Dolphin Bay) is a vast swampy plain, made up of meadow and shattered limestone ground alternately. Here I got three deer with some difficulty, while the sailing-master shot three more at the water's edge in Gubin Bay. Behind a knoll, covered with buttercups and forget-me-nots, we bivouacked, tolerably sheltered from the cold, hard wind, which blew with piercing severity everywhere else; and we dined, and breakfasted next morning on biscuit, deer without salt, and coffee without sugar. Condiments, even with a hunter's appetite, are agreeable when not forgotten, and if omitted are certainly the more hankered after. An occasional night on the shore in fine weather is very pleasant. With a blazing fire of drift-wood, wrapped in furs, agreeable pictures of incidents long gone by wreathe themselves in the smoke of the well-earned pipe, and in the dry climate no ill-effects result, save a certain stiffness of the hip-joints always caused by the first night or two's lying on the hard ground.

The deer were very lean and wild, and no old stags could be seen. We noticed a great many snowy owls, which frequent the rocky places in search of the lemmings, and we secured both eggs and young birds. In addition, we got nine young foxes, and took them on board. The Arctic foxes in Novaya Zemlya are of less value than in Spitzbergen. Of ten killed in the latter place eight will be blue and two white, while in the former country the ratio is reversed. The blue skins are six or seven times as valuable as the white. The hunters erect wooden traps a few miles in different directions from the friendly shelter of some wooden hut. At intervals the traps are visited, and the foxes,

which have been squeezed to death, are collected.
Those who have wintered in Novaya Zemlya judiciously
adopted this method of keeping up their men's interest
in taking exercise; and in their long dark tramps
through the blinding snow, or by the blazing lights of
the aurora, health was maintained, with the single risk
from hungry bears. The Polar bear had also an
interest in the capture of foxes which lay more than
skin deep, and often forestalled the hunters.   .

Dolphin Bay extends some nine or ten miles up
the country, and seems to receive a considerable river,
for it looked muddy high up, but there was apparently
no deer pasture beyond the knoll where we passed
the night. In this bay there is an island marked on
the charts: we found it to be really a peninsula, across
which the boat had to be dragged. On it we found
a wooden hut, which we judged must be the ruin
of the hut Rosmysslof constructed for half of his
wintering party a hundred years ago. No graves
were seen, although half the party never reached
home, and some died of disease in winter quarters.
The cove formed by the peninsula would be a most
excellent winter harbour for a vessel if so unfortunate
as to get beset in the Straits. The shelter is perfect,
and, although Rosmysslof's disaster is partly to be
attributed to his disappointment in not getting fresh
meat, there *appeared* to be good winter feeding-ground

for deer, although there were not many on it at present.

From the top of the highest hill I got a good view over the Kara Sea. There was a great deal of ice in sight, especially south of the Straits towards Klokow Bay. Evidently it was still impossible to pass Admiralty Point, because otherwise we should not have seen a schooner and smack pass our anchorage during the evening. It was very hard to know what to do. The sailing-master believed the whole Kara Sea to be chock full of ice. I felt quite sure it *was not*, but still there might be a belt or barrier of ice sufficiently broad to prevent any access to the open part before the winter. If we remained here, the entire remainder of the summer might be lost doing nothing but hunting deer. The north-west was blocked, and the Kara Gate probably still impassable. Already more than half the short Arctic summer had slipped away, and the rest of the season must be devoted to a determined trial of the Kara Gate, and, failing that, a watch on the outside for the return of the walruses from the Kara Sea in August.

As we again steamed through this beautiful Strait on July 19th, a week of sunshine and showers had visibly increased the vegetation. And yet Novaya Zemlya is less fertile, and therefore less suited for animal life, than many inhabited districts with a lower annual mean

N

temperature. The reason is that the temperature is more equable—warmer in winter, but colder in summer. The summer of Novaya Zemlya is almost the most inclement in the whole world. The summer heat is less than that of Melville Island or Boothia; and a comparative mild winter temperature benefits less than the cold foggy summer injures, for in those countries where the annual temperature is similar we find the winter's cold is deprived of its sting by the protection of the snow, while the greater heat of a short summer perfects vegetation very rapidly.[1]

On getting to the open sea a heavy swell prevented the screw working to any advantage, and we tossed idly about all day, shifting ballast, and whistling for a wind. Fifty tons of coal remained, which, at $2\frac{1}{2}$ tons a day, would give 20 days of steaming—in smooth water—of 24 hours each, at $6\frac{1}{2}$ knots an hour, or 3,000

[1] The mean annual temperatures of stations in Novaya Zemlya are as follows:—

Shallow Bay, 74° N. Lat.	.	.	.	= 18·9° Fahr.
Matoschkin Schar (W. End) 73° 19′	.		= 16·9° „
Kara Gate, 70° 37′	.	.	.	= 14·9° „

From these observations the mean annual temperature of the whole of Novaya Zemlya has been calculated to be about 15° 9′ Fahr.

That of Fort Enterprise in the Hudson's Bay Territory—where there are English Factories and Residents—is 10·16° Fahr., but the mean winter temperature of Novaya Zemlya is 6·6° Fahr., and of summer + 36·5°, while at Fort Enterprise we have a winter intensely colder than at Novaya Zemlya, but a much warmer summer. And the same is, I believe, the case at the centre of extreme winter cold near Nijni Kolynsk in Eastern Siberia.

miles at least. We had already steamed and sailed more than 4,000 miles.

At seven next morning we were able to start the engine, and were soon abreast of Goose Land, now a tract of emerald-green meadows sloping gently to the sea. In the background we could just trace the dark wall of hills, and with a glass from the crow's-nest could see the vast plain dotted with reindeer, and here and there lakes and ponds full of swans and geese. Ah! what a charming country this would be if it were not for the walruses. Here, in snug harbours, far from the ice, one might lie for months, and have such sport with deer, swans, geese, ducks, salmon, and an occasional seal or even bear, as people would pay thousands a year for in Europe: and yet we contemptuously disregard it all, and rage impatiently up and down the coast from place to place, trying, mostly in vain, to reach the inaccessible regions where that prince of sporting beasts, that monarch of the Arctic world, the walrus, takes up his summer quarters.

Again we found a strong current running north along the coast, and I presumed we were just within the combined influence of the Gulf Stream and the current sweeping round from the Kara Sea. The current runs one and a half to two knots an hour; and, the prevailing winds being from south-east to south-west, it seemed all but impossible for a vessel without

N 2

steam to get south at this season of the year. In fact,
I have heard the walrus-hunters say they allow only
seven days for the voyage from the south to the north
point of Novaya Zemlya. But for the return voyage
they can make no calculation.

We steamed right on for the next twenty-four
hours in a dead calm until dense fog compelled us to
heave-to. I was astonished to find the sea becoming
warmer; as it might naturally have been expected the
temperature would decrease as we approached the icy
Kara Sea.

At five A.M. on the 23rd we again went ahead, and
met some small ragged streams of ice which appeared
to be the sole remains of the enormous floes we found
four weeks previously—and no wonder with the sea
at 44° to 45° Fahr. !

After the knowledge I have acquired of Novaya
Zemlya and the surrounding seas, the course I would
recommend anyone on a voyage of sport or geographical research to pursue is as follows :—

1. Leave Hammerfest any day between June 10th
and 20th. Coal-up full.

2. Coal-up as full as you can hold at Vardö, unless
you have burnt none *en route.*

3. Shape a course for North Goose Cape.

4. Go into harbour there if possible and hunt
reindeer for food. If the harbour be blocked go
north.

5. Search all the small bays, north to Britwin Point *in a boat* if there is ice; the navigation is dangerous and intricate for a vessel, but a boat's crew may get a few walruses, bears, and reindeer, eggs, and wildfowl.

6. Look into Matoschkin Schar, if it is clear of ice and fog, but waste no time there if you can't get right through at once to the Kara Sea.

7. Go north to the Pankratjew Islands and Cape Nassau if you can, and stay on that coast as long as you are having tolerable weather and good sport. But *don't go beyond* Cape Nassau unless you have a consort to wait for you in case your vessel is lost.[1]

8. If the animals are scarce, or the weather—as is very *probable*—intolerably bad, go south and try Matoschkin Schar again, say about July 15th.

9. Having traversed the Straits go right across to Yelmert Land if you can, but if you can't do so—

10. Steam as hard as you can round to the south, and go into the Kara Sea by the main gate or Jugorsky Schar, whichever you can, and try to reach Yelmert Land that way.

11. You may find walruses *anywhere* when once

---

[1] The Russian walrus-hunters told me that if their vessels are driven by wind or current beyond Cape Nassau they give them up for lost and escape in the boats at once. Very few vessels which have passed this promontory have ever been heard of again, and I believe *none* have returned the same way.

inside the Straits, or on the west coast, north of Goose Land, according to the ice.

12. You need not be altogether discouraged at finding heavy beds of ice at the east end of either Straits. For the ice of the Kara Sea hangs longest to the Novaya Zemlya side, and there may be open water a few miles east of what looks like an impenetrable barrier.

In the afternoon the light ice gave place to some heavier masses, on which we saw a few walruses. Of these I shot three fine bulls and also picked up three big seals.

Next morning the fog cleared, and discovered two or three hundred walruses on the ice. They were excessively shy, having evidently been hunted for three months by the Norsk sloops, and would not allow a boat to approach within harpooning distance, so that they had to be shot at from thirty to sixty yards. The deadliest plan, if it can be managed, is to get out of the boat, creep up to them behind some high ice, and shoot unseen from a rest. In this way there is plenty of time to select the best tuskers, and to wait until they show *good heads*. I can quite conceive the possibility of killing a dozen on one cake of ice this way, if the day be sunny and the beasts moderately tame, especially if the leader or sentinel of the troop

is killed by the first shot. As it was, I bagged seven
enormous bulls, and the other boat's crew an eighth.
While we were cutting up some of these walruses
on the ice, a great many others alarmed by the shots
came snorting and plunging up to the edge of the ice,
as if in anger or curiosity, exhaling a strong odour of
molluscs. It would have been very easy to shoot
many of them, and, although my boatmen urged me
to shoot at them, I refused to fire, knowing there was
very little chance of a walrus, shot dead, floating till
we could get into the boat and row up to the carcase.
It is a great consolation to me to reflect that in the
course of a long and sanguinary shooting career, I have
seldom if ever murdered inoffensive animals wan-
tonly, when they could have been of no service to me
or to others when dead.

These walruses were enormously fat—one yielded
between 700 and 800 pounds of fat—and the blubber
of the thirteen last killed all but filled a tank out of
which three tons of coal had been started. In flensing them we cut out several bullets, and, curiously
enough, the leaden portion of a 30-gauge steel-pointed
bullet, which must have been shot by myself, or by
one of the only other English party who had ever
visited Novaya Zemlya, last year. My own weapon
now was a Henry Express rifle, and it was beautiful
to see how the diminutive hardened projectiles had

perforated the dense crania of these animals almost without sustaining any injury themselves.

A south-west breeze now helped us to the Kara Gates, as we thought, without steam ; and we began to hope the sixth endeavour to penetrate the Kara Sea might be more successful than the previous ones. Spanking along with this, for once, favouring breeze we passed various islands and points, which we imagined could be none other than the broken coast-line of the south-east corner of Novaya Zemlya ; but, the land trending away to the east seeming to be interminable, we began to have doubts of our real position, and at noon the sun's altitude announced the unwelcome fact that we were in lat. 69° 27', or from forty to fifty miles out of our reckoning, and abreast of Jugorsky Straits instead of working into the Kara Gate, which we must have run past in the fog the day before. Had we not been fortunate enough to have clear weather to see the sun and the land we might have hove-to here for a week. The westerly wind prevented our getting back to the main gate, and we therefore bore up for the small one. Jugorsky Schar, as it is called, seems from old accounts, and from the experience of Norwegian walrus-hunters within the last few years, to be more often free from heavy ice than the Kara Gate.

Arthur Pet—whose name, some think, should distinguish the Strait—endeavouring to discover a north-east passage to China for the Muscovy Company in 1580, found the Kara Straits entirely blocked with ice, but was able a few days later, on July 19th, to enter Jugorsky Straits, and on August 15th the Kara Sea itself. Cornelius Bosman, on a similar voyage of exploration for the Dutch Government in 1625, found impassable ice between Kolguev and Novaya Zemlya, but on August 10th entered Jugorsky Straits, and on the 13th met ice in enormous masses in the Kara Sea. It is worth noting, too, that nine days later he was, by a north-east gale, blown clean out of the Straits, where he lay with two anchors down. On the other hand, we read of voyagers even late in the season being denied access to the Kara Sea by this route. Three Danish vessels in 1653 for sixteen days endeavoured to pass through Jugorsky Straits; and Burrough, the first European who reached Novaya Zemlya, exactly 100 years before this expedition of the Danish Trade Company, waited at the west mouth of Jugorsky Schar from the end of July till August 20th, when it was still blocked with ice. He had already reached Bolvanosky Nos, through the Kara Straits.

On July 26th we sailed through these interesting Straits without any hindrance from ice. On either side verdant meadows, white in places with the flowers of a species of stitchwort (*Stellaria Norvegica*), sloped gently to the water, many tents of the Samo- yedes enlivened the scene, and we watched with some interest the work of transporting their deer in large ferry-boats to pasture on Waygat Island. On we sailed without hindrance for thirty miles, and I began to indulge in the hope that dogged persever- ance would in the end triumph over ill-luck : but no! not a bit of it! We descried two smacks beating up from the east, and naturally concluded they must be going home full. We immediately busied ourselves in getting letters to send home ; when, on nearing one of these craft, which at closer quarters had a most suspicious look of being empty, we learned the un- pleasant truth that Yelmert Land (the great peninsula between us and the Obi) was completely blockaded with heavy, impenetrable ice, and that there were thirty-seven smacks ahead, twenty-five of which were reported to be fast beset in the ice! What was to be done, with everything apparently against us? So far south (in about the latitude of North Cape the sun had already begun to dip at night) the sea temperature, although standing above 40° Fahr. during the day, was lowered so rapidly during the night that in early morning we had already sailed through vast sheets of pancake ice ; the ice rapidly coming down on the land ; and no open water to be seen beyond it. And then those twenty-five vessels beset! This decided the question : reluctantly yielding to circumstances we commenced a retreat ; and, after getting up steam to pass through one pack, we beat up the east side of Waygat Island, between it and the ice, with the intention of availing ourselves of any chance of forcing a passage across the Kara Sea.

During many years it was a pet scheme with the Russian Government to establish regular sea communication between the mouth of the Obi and the northern European ports ; and no wonder, when it is considered what a vast tract of country might be opened up—a country where wheat is only ninepence a bushel! To find a safe route, and to ascertain its annual freedom from ice, has been the object of many expeditions. The most successful may illustrate what could be accomplished in only the most favourable season. In 1734 Murawieff and Pauloff, between August 6th and September 16th, made the voyage from Jugorsky Straits to Mutnaja or Cloudy Bay along the west coast of Yelmert Land, and returned through Jugorsky Straits to the mouth of the Petchora without hindrance. The next year one vessel alone reached Cloudy Bay. In 1737 Malygin and Skuratow, after being headed off from the ice in Kara Straits on July 13th, were able to cross the sea and reach Cloudy Bay on August 2nd. Then coasting on they passed the Sharapow Bank, and

reached the north part of the peninsula on the 4th.
After a delay of three weeks near White Island they
sailed south through the Bay of Obi, to the river of
that name, and wintered at Beresov, some miles distant from its mouth. The return journey, owing to
difficulties from drift ice, occupied two whole years.
Johannesen's voyages in 1869 and 1870 give us
information of shallow water all along the west
shore of Yelmert Land, and of the formation of sand-
banks far out in the Kara Sea—a result, no doubt, of
the river deposit from the Obi. He noticed the current of the west coast of White Island to set to the
north, and at the north-west of this island to run at
from one to two knots in an north-easterly direction.

Laboriously, and in spite of a strong west wind, in
company with two schooners, we beat up to Waygat
Island, where we found another small schooner at
anchor. No opening in the ice to the eastward could
be detected, but we found a lot of ice lying off the Kara
Gate with walruses upon it. The day was extremely
cold; this and the presence of three Russian lodjie
made the animals unapproachably wild.

These lodjie often anchor in the bays, while the
smaller boats pursue the game, and carry on the Russian Novaya Zemlya trade. The objects of capture are
gathered from the sea, the land, and the rivers. The
industry is subject to great fluctuations. In 1834, after

a pause of some time, a few hunters were so successful
that the following year eighty vessels carried a thousand men to hunt the Novaya Zemlya seas and land;
the following year half this number still scoured the
country. The animals were becoming exterminated,
the products naturally failed, added to which unusual
success in the Spitzbergen fisheries, glutted Western
Europe with walrus oil. The Archangel merchants,
with their men and vessels cooped up by the ice in
the White Sea till the season of fishing was half over,
were unable to compete with the traders of other
ports, and discontinued to a great extent their ventures.
Then the old skippers died off; younger ones put to
sea, without experience; and, disasters quickly following, the last sparks of enterprise were well-nigh ex-
tinguished. In 1859 and 1860 barely half-a-dozen
craft were engaged in the trade. Since 1868 larger
vessels from open ports, better educated skippers, and
more deadly weapons, have revived the chase of sea
animals (the walrus, bear, seal, white whale), which
has fallen mostly into the hands of the Norwegians,
while the land and river trade remains where it did,
and is carried on by the Russians and Samoyedes.
Their karbasse—large half-decked boats with one
ample lugsail—come from the White Sea at the end
of July. Each vessel carries from eight to twenty
men, provisions for the time (winter or summer) they

contemplate being out, and materials for constructing a wooden hut. Arrived at Novaya Zemlya the vessel is safely berthed, the moveable house becomes their head-quarters, and each man is set to his particular work, some to set the fox-traps, some to fish the salmon rivers, others to chase the walrus. These latter man the small boats which, five to ten in number, packed one within another, have been shipped from home. In these they seek the open lanes of water between the densely-packed ice-floes, and endeavour to discover a mass of walruses together. If successful in the search, stealthily approaching in their boat from the leeward, or traversing the ice after drawing their boats on to it, they commence the onslaught by lancing the outsiders, and the subsequent despatch of a large number becomes then comparatively easy. Should a walrus succeed in reaching the water the hunter hurls his harpoon, and, having struck the beast, hastily winds the leather line round a spear driven into the ice; if the stake holds, and the thong cannot be broken, the walrus soon exhausts himself in endeavours to tow the ice-island, and is easily drawn up and killed.

We had a race with one of these small boats for a troop of walruses; but as they were far in front at first it seemed but fair to leave the chance to them, and we were careful not to alarm the game. I went aloft to watch the proceeding through the large telescope. Two men only left the large karbassa, in a small punt towed astern. Amidships was a cask or inflated sealskin to be used as a drag or float attached to the line ; for it was quite out of the question holding on to a walrus in such a cockleshell of a boat. They took an immense deal more pains than we do, and were at least an hour in approaching the walruses. Whenever a walrus raised his head they lay quite still ; but notwithstanding all this they failed, for on getting to about forty yards off the walruses began to scuffle into the water ; one man then fired, but did not kill.

The next two days, August 1st and 2nd, it blew very hard from the west and north-west, and ice came down which appeared as if it could never melt that year. But we got a few walruses and a bear, and anchored to the floe at night. From this, however, we broke loose during the night, when the wind rose. The bear was shot from the deck by the surgeon. My old mate was always good for a yarn on the subject of a whale or bear ; and I have always induced my companions at the beginning of a voyage to ask the veteran whaler an innocent question, which elicited the invariable answer, delivered in the broadest Aberdeen, and in a tone that seemed to commiserate the ignorance of the questioner : ' Well, Wully, you've been in Davis Straits a good many years, did you ever see any bears there?' ' Polar bears? white bears? Lor bless ye, sir, A've seen the flaws blark wi' them.' Certainly, they do appear darker than the snow, and what is a yarn but a narrative of facts intensified?

On the 3rd the wind moderated and we kept about the edge of the pack, which was smashed up outside, but was still heavy further in. We were in the middle of the Kara Straits, Olenji Island bearing east and the nearest part of Novaya Zemlya west; and although the wind was cold we managed to have some sport each day. The walruses were mostly half-grown bulls, and on one day six were shot, though one was lost by sinking, and another by the breaking of an old line. One, a large bull, furiously charged the boat and drove his tusks through her bows. I immediately shot him through the head, contrary to my usual custom when a walrus is fairly harpooned, because it spoils the sport. It is, in fact, like shooting a fox before the hounds. The orthodox way to finish a walrus on the line is with the lance. The more I see of walrus-hunting, the more keenly I enjoy it. It is a 'noble game.' It is like elephant-shooting, boar-spearing, and a gigantic exaggeration of salmon-fishing all in one—thus combining three of the grandest sports to which mortal men are addicted.

While the sea continued perfectly smooth walruses were always seen, and fresh ones seemed to be arriving daily; but the calmness of the water made it impossible to approach within harpooning distance, and to shoot a walrus dead at a hundred or even fifty yards, owing to the peculiar conformation and great strength of all the skull but the occiput, is inconceivably difficult. Directly there was a ripple from a gentle north-east breeze we found the difference in being able to get so close as to stab them. I regretted exceedingly not having brought an old duck-punt. I believe with it I might have shot many more walruses, as it would have enabled me to get up to within ten yards or so before alarming the game. A boat to follow the punt pretty closely would, of course, be required; and a harpoon attached to a cask or other float only could be used. The 8-gauge rifle, propelling a shell with $8\frac{1}{2}$ drachms of powder, proved in one instance an awful weapon, but yet not adapted for walrus-shooting. I fired into the back of a large bull after he was harpooned; he jumped into the water quite briskly, but suddenly ceased to struggle, and was pulled up quite dead. On opening him I found the 3-ounce shell had burst and filled the whole cavity of the chest with destruction.

While in full pursuit of a wounded walrus one evening we saw two bears on a large ice-slab. They took the water and I shot them both with the greatest ease. The Russian hunters have an adage, 'God grant we might find the walrus ashore and the bear at sea!'

I had been several times annoyed by the boats of

o

a sloop near us coming noisily up to the walruses after
we had fairly beat them in the race. I therefore got
up steam and *nursed* them for a few hours. The
annoyance soon ceased! On August 11th it commenced
blowing a gale from the north-east, with occasional half-
lulls, sometimes with rain, sometimes with fog; for a
whole week we wore backwards and forwards across the
mouth of the Straits, not knowing whether we were in
the Straits, to the west, or to the east of them. Unable
to see the land or the sun, we sailed the yacht very much
according to the soundings and the colour of the water.
This, in the Kara Sea, just now, except in the immediate
vicinity of the Straits, was of a greenish yellow colour,
and very fresh.

The ice broke up entirely and disappeared early in
the gale, from the combined influence of the rain, swell,
and wind. I shot a white whale from the deck one
day, but he turned over and sank instantly without a
struggle. The white whale (*Beluga* or *Balæna albicans*)
or white fish is abundant in Novaya Zemlya, many
thousands being sometimes seen in one school. They
are hunted in places clear of ice, in summer and autumn,
in the deep bays where they breed, or over the shallows,
where they seek small fish as food. Though the oil is
highly prized, burning in a lamp without smoke, the cost
of the nets used in their capture is so great that the
annual take is quite small compared with their numbers.

When the gale was at its highest we saw a large bear swimming; he was close to the yacht at one time, but kept to windward, so that we could not have got him if killed. We waited a long time in hopes he would swim ahead or go to leeward, but as he would do neither, and then swam farther away, we fired three or four shots at him without effect; the sea was too bad to lower a boat and go in pursuit.

On the 17th there were a few hours of sunshine, and we got a set of chronometer sights at nine A.M., and a meridian altitude which enabled us to fix our position in lat. 71° 5', and long. 58° 19', or about twenty miles north of the Straits. The vessel had, undoubtedly, been making a good deal of lee-way, especially during the worst of the gale, which was always north-east, or north-north-east; and yet we had got into this position against the wind; there must, therefore, be a considerable current running inwards, or to the north-east through these Gates. This is contrary to the opinion of Petermann and other geographers, who assert that there is always a current *out*. I suspect it varies with the season, or the state of the great rivers of Siberia.

On getting these observations we steered in until we saw the land. Sailing along this, and doubling Cape Menschikow, we saw two sloops at anchor to the lee of a small island, and brought up alongside of them in 4½ fathoms. It was a fairly comfortable shelter from any but a south wind. We spoke the smacks and gave one charge of a letter in case she got home first.

These vessels had been at Yelmert Land, on the other side of the Kara Sea. In company with numerous others they reached that place by following the shore all the way into Kara Bay, so close that they were sometimes in 1½ fathoms of water. Frequently beset on the way, they always got free again in a day or two, because the ice was still, and there was little or no current running. Several vessels, however, were lost, and the crews escaped into other vessels. The ugly steamer and Mack's schooner got across from Matoschkin Schar by patient and resolute pushing through the ice, and waiting for it to open. There was no ice at all on the other side of the Kara Sea, nor had they seen any in the voyage from the east.

This was additional proof of what has been stated elsewhere, that the last ice in the Kara Sea adheres to the Novaya Zemlya shores; and, as I had always maintained, there must be a large open water to the east side of the Kara Sea, long before it is possible to get across the icy barrier and into it. This, probably, occurs every summer.

The ships at Yelmert Land encountered stormy weather, mostly from the north-east, but had got from ten to twenty walruses each, and these smacks each about thirty-five. All these were cows or poor young bulls such as I had got the year before on the west coast of Novaya Zemlya. This year, keeping about the mouths of the Straits later in the season, almost all I got were first-class old bulls. One of these skippers told me that all the walruses disturbed or driven away (and, with seventy or a hundred boats at them, they were rather wild) came away to the west. This made me doubly regret the premature breaking-up of the last hunting-ground, for I was sure at the time that the walruses coming from the east were using that ice as a stepping-stone, or resting-place, *en route* for their favourite rendezvous in the rocks at the north end of Waygat Island. The Russians kill many ashore there every year.

The wind, veering round to the south-east, sent a heavy swell right into the Bay, so we were compelled to be off. Outside it was still blowing a gale of wind. This, with dense fog, and a very low barometer (29°) and several hours of darkness during the night, all combined to make it appear a complete break-up of the Novaya Zemlya season. It was far too late to attempt to go north again, yet for an Arctic country it was still mild; on August 18th the sea temperature was 38° and that of the air 39°. Spitzbergen, although colder, has certain advantages. There I have shot deer at midnight on August 22nd; here the early dark nights are a grave objection to a late stay.

With that indescribable feeling of regret, mingled with a certain relief from chronic, restless anxiety, which the Arctic voyager feels when he turns his back on the last gleam of ice, and sees the last inky cliff dip, we dashed through the Straits in full sail, and bid farewell, most of us for ever, to Novaya Zemlya—the stormiest, wildest, bleakest, and least habitable country in the known world.

IN GOOSE HAVEN.

Section II.

BARENTZ SEA AND FRANZ JOSEF LAND

'The fair breeze blew—the white foam flew,
   The furrow followed free;
 We were the first, that ever burst
   Into that silent sea.'

COLERIDGE

BARENTZ SEA AND FRANZ JOSEF LAND.

An account of ice and currents to the north, north-east, and north-west of Novaya Zemlya having already been incorporated with a description of the north part of that country, to complete the knowledge of the seas between Novaya Zemlya and Spitzbergen prior to 1869, it is only necessary to mention the voyages of Hudson, William de Vlamingh, and Wood.[1] To the present narrative of the first voyage of exploration in late years, in the north of this Barentz Sea, and the attempt to penetrate the Polar pack between Novaya Zemlya and Spitzbergen, an allusion to the only voyages undertaken previous to it may form an appropriate preface. All these three men sailed with the same object, to reach the North Pole, and were alike unsuccessful.

Hudson sailed directly from the Thames, and met the ice in lat. 75° 29′, on June 9th, 1608. Failing to make any way through it, he followed the edge of the ice without finding any opening in it till he sighted Novaya Zemlya at 72° 25′ north.

[1] Barentz sailed from Bear Island to Novaya Zemlya, but kept always south of the 75° parallel; even then they were often 'forced with great paine and labour to lauere out of the ice.'

William de Vlamingh in 1664, finding the north coast of Novaya Zemlya and the Kara Sea in its vicinity almost totally free from ice, at last directed his ship to the north-west, and, it is said, reached the latitude of 82° 10′, where he found the water getting gradually smoother, approaching, as we now conjecture, the lee of Franz Josef Land.

Again, Wood, in June 1676, came in sight of the Polar pack in lat. 75° 59′, having sailed through an open sea about midway between Spitzbergen and Novaya Zemlya. Examining the ice like Hudson, it conducted him in a similar manner to Novaya Zemlya without permitting further access either north or east.

In spite of such discouraging experiences I decided on leaving the coast of Novaya Zemlya[1] and sailing if possible, to the south-west point of Gillis Land ; failing that, intending to explore the east coast of Spitzbergen, with which I had already some practical acquaintance. Helstadt, the harpooner, told me it was ' useless to think of getting to Gillis Land before August.' I thought differently, though my hopes of a more open route were based on very unsubstantial data.

Scientific men previously to 1869 were equally convinced that from Bear Island the main pack of Polar ice, extended in an unbroken line to Novaya Zemlya,

[1] See p. 117.

and only slightly receded from this coast as far as Cape Nassau at long intervals of years.

The cause of this misapprehension is easily explained. In the days of the Spitzbergen whaling trade 'Bear Island,' passed early in the season, in cranky vessels only adapted and intended for conveying boats and men to the land basis of operations on the west coast of Spitzbergen, was always noticed to be incumbered with ice. From the main track towards the open west coast there was no temptation to diverge eastward. On the voyage home, when the sea might have been noticed clear of ice, the full ships were hastening to port with their cargoes. The walrus-hunters, too, of a late period found plenty of employment at Bear Island, or Spitzbergen, and did not care to ' prospect' farther.

The interest of Arctic exploration either languished or was directed into other channels; and what little information could have been obtained from walrus-hunters was neither recorded nor systematised. It is only, therefore, within the last few years that these seas have aroused any interest, and from causes perfectly natural. The walrus-hunting having fallen off in the accustomed districts, new ground had to be sought; and, the exploration of the Arctic regions having again resolved itself into a question of reaching the North Pole, every possible route suggested by theoretical geographers as likely to lead to it is being tested.

To the order 'Brace the yards for Spitzbergen!' the crew, especially the Norsemen, responded with alacrity and goodwill. No one on board, I suspect, was loath to leave the shores of Novaya Zemlya, with its gloomy pall of almost everlasting snow, rain, and mist. As the coast dipped we fondly imagined that, with the fine slashing breeze from the south, we should see land again in two or three days; but, after a long reach to the west, at midday we sighted the main ice, stretching far south in a cape. Sailing along close-hauled we could not see a living thing upon it; and not for twelve hours, going about frequently to weather fresh points of ice, were we again able to make a course for Gillis Land. Towards midnight we got finally clear of the ice; but, although for twenty-four hours we were able to keep our course with very little obstruction from broken streams or solitary pieces of ice, a heavy yellow sky showed the main pack could not be far distant.

A change of wind to south-west at two A.M. on the 19th still allowed us to lie north-west, but I feared it would involve us in ice again very shortly. The sea was of a deep blue colour, though we had perceptibly run out of the greatest influence of the east branch of the Gulf Stream. This, had it prevailed equally with the current on the coast of Novaya Zemlya, would have given us some thirty miles of northing. By a midnight altitude we had only made seven more than the dead reckoning.

Guillemots, kittiwakes, and Arctic terns were seen in abundance on this and the preceding day, indicating land not far distant. The latter bird more especially frequents the shore.

Subsequent discoveries in these parts may render interesting a passage written in my journal on June 19th, 1869, and which I may be allowed to place before the reader. It runs as follows: 'I should very much like, with fine weather and plenty of coals, to try to get into a high latitude somewhere about here (75° 10′ north, 48° 32′ east), either directly or by going to Cape Nassau in Novaya Zemlya and thence trying to the north-west. I am very strongly inclined to think there must be large lands—perhaps, a continuation of Gillis Land—in that direction. It is quite a *mare incognita*, and has never, as far as I know, been visited or attempted by anyone except John Wood, in June 1676, who tried and failed to get through the ice somewhere very near our position to-day.'

Observations similar to mine were made by Dr. Bessels, who, in one of Herr Rosenthal's steam-whalers, traversed this sea only a few days later in the same year on a voyage from Spitzbergen to Novaya Zemlya. Some surprise was manifested at home when authentic reports were brought of a navigable sea between

Spitzbergen and Novaya Zemlya having a temperature considerably higher than many well-frequented Arctic waters. The wildest speculations of a great branch of the Gulf Stream running directly to the Pole were promulgated, and were well received, since they agreed with preconceived theories. An unusually open season in the summer of 1871 enabled Lieutenants Weyprecht and Payer *apparently* to confirm all that had been offered as surmise. So favourable was the season that Hope Island, which had been unapproachable for a series of years, was easily reached in coming from the westward. Thence they worked gradually eastward in a perfectly navigable sea, until ice was met in 78° north and 41° 30′ east. This was on August 30th. In successive days between this and September 6th, slightly higher degrees of latitude were reached in a more easterly direction. Towards the north, it was said, the ice was light and might have been pushed through, but to the west it was always dense and impassable. At one time unmistakeable indications of land were observed, in the muddiness of the water, the fresh-water ice, and the flight of eider-ducks.

Unprejudiced English geographers gave to these signs the only interpretation they admitted of, and we were all convinced that new lands must be not far from the points sailed to by the Austrians. Curiously enough, an old account of a voyage made by a Dutchman some 300 years ago tells us that land had been visited exactly north of where Weyprecht and Payer met the ice on September 6th. There must have been very little ice that year, for Cornelis Roule sailed, it is said, to $84\frac{1}{2}°$ or 85°. For forty miles his vessel passed between broken land till he emerged into more open water, and, going ashore, from a high hill he still saw open water to the north. The birds he found there, in great numbers, were very tame.[1]

This voyage of the Austrians in 1871 (though it showed there could be no very warm stream running direct to the Pole), together with the accounts of walrus-hunters in the same year,[2] added, to the known Arctic seas which can be navigated in *open* seasons, an area 'equal to that of the German Empire.' Again 'enthusiasm prevailed.' The Gulf Stream was now sent round the coast of Northern Asia, and the bold project of a north-east passage to Behring Straits was entertained. But, so little was it understood that *only an exceptional year* had permitted the new seas to be traversed by the vessels in 1871, that it was assumed to be the normal state of the ice; and when, the following year, the pack came down to its more usual limits,

[1] The approximate longitude of Roule's northerly voyage is that of a meridian running right through Austria Sound.

[2] Notably that of Mack, who, finding open water to the north of Novaya Zemlya in 60° east longitude, sailed on 20° farther, with the help of a strong current running east having a temperature of 44° Fahr.

jamming Cape Nassau, men who should have known
better spoke of a deflection of the ice toward Novaya
Zemlya! If there were any deflection it was one in
the opposite direction, clearing the sea north of Novaya
Zemlya in 1871. But these explorers, holding a clue,
as it were, to unknown lands, and stating that the ice
would have been no bar to farther progress northwards,
chose next year to attempt an uncertain and distant
goal rather than a certain and comparatively near one!

A more arduous and hazardous undertaking than
the north-east passage could hardly be attempted. I
do not say it will never be accomplished, but it is
fraught with more danger than the north-west passage,
and when made will, I fear, be of even less value to the
world. However, be the motives and the risks what
they may, we cannot but admire the pluck and perseverance of the men who plunged into the uncertain
pack on August 21st, 1872, and were carried by fate
where inclination refused to lead them.

The account of the remarkable drift of the
'Tegethoff' from Cape Nassau to Franz Josef Land is
fresh in our minds—drifting towards the north-east at
the mercy of the wind, not of the current, we are
carefully told (although a glance of the track suggests an
eastern drift up to February 4th, 1873, by the current
known to exist here, and a subsequent westward
direction, by the Polar stream, but always northward)—

the frail vessel began on October 13th to suffer from
the terrible pressure of the grinding pack. Preparations for passing a winter were now imperatively
demanded ; the ship was made snug ; active duties were
assigned to each of the crew ; observations, meteorological and other, were systematically kept, and provision
against illness and protection against the Polar bears
were made. On October 28th the sun disappeared,
these human prisoners lost the cheerful society of birds,
and the long nights set in with unusual thickness and
heavy falls of snow. On one occasion — 51° Fahr. was
the temperature registered. After dragging through
the long winter, often in extreme peril from the movements of the ice, the sun was again seen on February
16th. Fresh hopes were revived of getting free, not to
bear up for home, but to make fresh discoveries. But
all anticipations of liberating themselves during the
summer of 1873 were vain. The floe—forty feet thick,
and still, in August, five to seven miles in diameter—
held them in its icy grip. At last, after drifting over
shallow water, on the last day of August land was
sighted. A discovery had been made ! but not till the
end of October were the travellers able to set foot on an
outlying island of Franz Josef Land. It was too late to
make any lengthy exploration of the new country; and
when the sun again sank for the last time on October
22nd the gloomy prospect of a second winter, with every

chance of being floated away into the unknown seas, again presented itself. Fortunately, although the floe was shivered into fragments, a harbour of grounded icebergs enclosed them in security three miles from the shores of Wilczek Island during the winter of 1873- 1874. Again quantities of snow fell with northerly winds, in the darkest days night and day could hardly be distinguished, the snow became hard like rock, the oil of the lamps froze, the mercury of the thermometer remained solid for a week, and the spirits were congealed. In these trying circumstances the hope of being able to explore this marvellous and unknown district, before deserting their ship and trying to get home in the boats, rendered bearable all the hardships.

In the first sledge journey, commenced on March 10th, Lieutenant Payer, with a party of seven men and three dogs, pushed beyond the 80th degree of latitude, and Capes Tegethoff and McClintock were visited, and the Sonklar Glacier crossed, in spite of the risks of sleeping out when the temperature was on one occasion $-58°$ Fahr. This preliminary sledge journey of six days was followed by a longer one occupying thirty. On March 24th M. Payer, with six others, set forth on this arduous expedition. But the anxiety to reach the farthest possible degree of north latitude, with the difficulties of transport, necessitated a division of the party after Hohenlohe Island, in 81° 38', had been reached;

and M. Payer, with two companions, alone reached the limit of their journey at Cape Fligely in 82° 5'.

The ascent of various capes enabled them to select the most suitable tracks by mapping out the proposed route in a survey of the surrounding country from time to time. The chief difficulties were the hummocky nature of the ice and the treacherous crust of recent ice spread over and obscuring crevasses. On one occasion one of the crew, with two dogs and a sledge, disappeared suddenly in a deep crevasse, and could only be rescued by a journey back of twelve miles for help from the main party. Indeed, the safety of the whole party and the important results obtained seem fairly to be attributable to the experience of ice-work acquired by M. Payer in the Tyrol, Switzerland, and Greenland.

The spectacle from the farthest point attained seemed to the travellers that of a vast archipelago; at their feet open water, fringed with old ice and dotted over with lighter masses, sparkled in the sun. Stretching towards the north-east was a wide sound, bounded on one side by land which ended in Cape Vienna. This point was assumed to be in latitude 83°. Farther west Oscar Island bounded the horizon; while the land on which they stood was traced through the clouds to a rocky promontory in lat. 82° 20' N.

Vegetation was peculiarly sparse, being represented by the flora of the Alps at an elevation of 9,000 to

10,000 feet; but the season was early for Arctic growth, and, indeed, during the first sledge journey snow covered every rock and shore. The cliffs near the open water swarmed with sea-birds, Polar bears approached the traveller without fear, and traces of foxes and hares were found everywhere.

The glaciers were characterised by the fewness of the crevasses, the coarse grain of the ice, the small development of the moraines, their slow motion, and the excessive thickness of the annual layers. Icebergs encumbered all the fjords, and from their absence on the Novaya Zemlya coast it was argued they must have a channel of exit in some other direction than through Austria Sound southwards.

Raised beaches were observed on the shores of Austria Sound, and drift-wood in small quantities was seen slightly above reach of the tide, which rises two feet. Dolomite was most common as forming the rocky cliffs and mountains, but other minerals, similar to those of north-east Greenland, and tertiary coal were also seen.

On the return journey another danger, apart from the possibility of the ship having drifted away in their long absence, was encountered. When hardly two-thirds of the 160 miles of their way to the harbour the ice terminated abruptly in open water running swiftly to the north. Without boats it was impossible to cross it, and for two days the party wandered about in a snow-storm endeavouring to get round this water. Finally the ship was reached on April 24th. After a short rest a third sledge journey of forty miles to the eastward enabled M. Payer to survey McClintock's Land to 46° east. Ascending a high mountain the closely-packed icy sea to the south held out little encouragement of a successful homeward journey, which had to be commenced at once. On May 20th the flags were nailed to the mast of the 'Tegethoff,' and the baggage was stowed in four boats. The difficulties of the journey may be estimated by finding that it took two months of incessant labour to reach a distance of *eight miles* from the ship. When the loose pack was reached a southerly wind often drifted them again to the north, and when the ice closed they had sometimes to lie idle for a week waiting for it to open. The state of the ice fully convinced them that no vessel in the summer of 1874 could have reached the land they were leaving. On August 14th the edge of the pack, unusually high, in 77° 40′, being reached, enabled the exhausted crew to set sail for Novaya Zemlya, which they reached a few days later. A perusal of the narrative shows that unless superhuman efforts had been used, another winter, probably a fatal one, would have been spent in the ice.

To return to the voyage of the 'Diana' in 1869. On the evening of June 19th, in lat. 75° 21′ N., long.

44° 8′ E., it fell to a dead calm, and we, therefore, got up steam and went ahead on a west-north-west course for twenty-four hours on end. At one time there seemed to be indications of land, and we bore up for it, only to find it melt away as a heavy bank of cloud. We were depending on a map of Dr. Petermann's, published in 1867, for the position of Gillis Land. If this were correct this country offered a coast-line stretching north and south from 81° to 77° 30′, and would have been distant some seventy miles from the yacht on this day. Mountainous land might be seen at that distance from the mast-head.

Geographers now recognise two distinct tracts of land, widely separated, lying east of Spitzbergen—Gillis Land and Wiches Land. Gillis Land was first seen by Captain Giles in 1707. Who does not envy his opportunity for exploration offered by the open season of that year? We are told he passed more than a degree to the north of seven islands without any hindrance from ice. Thence he went east for some leagues in an open sea, then south-east, and finally south. It was in latitude 80° he saw land, 25° to the east from North-east Land, which has since borne his name. The skipper of a small smack, in 1859, told me that in the month of July of that year he had touched on land to the north-east of Spitzbergen, marked in the charts as Gillis Land, but he could tell me nothing about it. Gillis Land has since been sighted by Carlsen in 1863 and by Tobiesen in 1864. Its position is again fixed in 80°, where the original discoverer figured it, and it might be as well to allow it to remain there till it is further explored. It will then, probably, be found a continuation of the land west of Austria Sound, or to form, with the Spitzbergen islands and the broken Franz Josef Land, part of a vast Arctic archipelago.

While Gillis Land was being confused with land seen from the Ryke Yse Islands by Mr. Birkbeck in 1867, and also by Heuglin from the east end of Walter Thymens Straits in 1870, the discovery of an island to the east of Spitzbergen, extending to 79°, by Captain Thomas Edge in 1617, was forgotten or ignored. After Heuglin's voyage it was re-named King Charles Land; but when Altman, in July, Johnson, in August, and Nilsen, later in 1872, approached it and landed, King Charles Land from its position was shown to be identical with Thomas Edge's discovery. The latter killed a great many walruses there for the Muscovy Company, and Captain Johnson shot a fine reindeer. High hills and steep cliffs, connected by low ground, characterise the country, which does not differ essentially in general configuration from the adjacent parts of Spitzbergen. To the east and north Captain Nilsen noticed the sea clear of ice. But a stream of icebergs were drifting south in the sea between it and Spitzbergen. We are here, probably, meeting the icebergs seen by Payer in the Straits about Franz Josef Land, and which must take their origin in glaciers to the northeast of Wiches Land—there are no glaciers in the whole forty-four miles' extent of Wiches Land.

A deep-sea temperature reading on June 19th, in 149 fathoms, gave 31° Fahr., while the surface sea was 33° 25′ Fahr. The cold Polar current, no doubt, underlies here (75° 21′ N., 43° E.) what remains of the Gulf current. This, more properly speaking, might be termed Gulf *water*, as we have seen the current to be fairly exhausted in the middle of the Barentz Sea ; it would seem to be a sort of overflow driven back over the cold water by the impinging of the Gulf Stream on the west coast of Novaya Zemlya.

For two days we were continually headed off from a north-west course by tongue after tongue of dense ice, parts of the main pack drifting in a southerly direction. It was like the disappointment experienced in mounting a high hill, each obstacle is hoped to be the last and still from it another comes into view. Numbers of Jan Mayen or 'springer' seals (*Phoca hispida*) were scudding through the water like porpoises.

The evening of the 21st was occupied in shooting guillemots, which flew in vast flocks over the yacht in a north-westerly direction. We found good practice for

Drawn by W. Evans.

Wild-fowl Shooting at Midnight.

grouse-driving in shooting them as they rushed past the yacht; and, lowering a boat, we picked up thirty brace. From my knowledge of the habits of these birds I thought we must be near some land at the time, nearer than Hope Island, which is the nearest marked on the charts; and I made a note in my journal to ask Petermann his authority for placing the south point of Gillis Land so far down. The walrus-hunters, I knew, all said, to the best of their knowledge, that it did not extend nearly so far to the south. Heavy banks of cloud brooded over the sea and ice; and above, far up, at midnight, the sun shot a struggling beam of light. Here and there over the pack the vapour was lighted up like the flickering of a great fire.

At seven A.M. on the 22nd the engineers were again at their post, willing fellows! and ready to steam another forty-eight hours again right off as long as Spitzbergen lay ahead; for, as one of them was heard cheerfully to remark, ' he liked a day's shooting himself.' We passed through several local fogs, and saw the peculiar Arctic phenomenon called by the sailors ' Sundog' (parhelion or mock sun). Everywhere the sea was a dead calm, and from time to time we met the ice and had to alter our course; each time the chance of reaching East Spitzbergen by the south-east diminished. There was more life in the sea as we went westward, a flock of rotges was seen, more

than one finner whale was reported in the morning's
watch and whale's food in the water.   The seals were
still abundant, and in the evening the look-out in the
crow's-nest shouted cheerily : ' Hundreds of seals on the
ice ! '   It is very unusual to find these saddle-back or
harp seals on the ice in the neighbourhood of Spitzbergen.   It is the seal annually slain by the Scotch
whalers in thousands at what is termed the ' West Ice,'
mostly in the neighbourhood of Jan Mayen—the young
ones in March, the old ones in May.   They were very
wild, and we only got a few dozen during the evening
and next morning.   The sailing-master accounted for
their wildness by saying ' that in May they are casting
their hair and are sick and lethargic, whereas now
they have revived and are on their way to the far
north.'   Blackening the ice as they did for nearly
twelve points of the compass, I was certainly chagrined
at not half-filling the ship with them, but their shyness
necessitated as much caution in approaching them as a
walrus.   With a duck-punt many more might have
been got.   Two brought on board stunk like nothing
earthly, and their stomachs were filled with half-
digested shrimps.   The doctor also was elated to think
he had discovered a new entozoon in the intestines.

'Tommy,' the first young walrus picked up at
Novaya Zemlya, a month ago, to the great grief of
everyone except ' Sailor ' and the cook, was found dead,

with his face immersed in a pail of gruel, and one of the others lying on top of him—clearly suffocated. They were confined in a pen forward well out of the way; for they lately had become a great nuisance, crawling about the deck, always in someone's way, and had taken to roaring like bears down the companion at night. A few nights before his death this little beast had fallen down the hatchway; this might have had something to do with his untimely end. Nothing was found on examination but a total absence of fat, the rest of the dissection was reserved for the Anatomical Rooms of the University of Edinburgh, our late companion and playmate being duly salted and packed in an old pork-barrel.

On the 23rd we passed some of the largest icebergs yet seen, in lat. 75° 34′, long. 23° east. One seemed to be about double the ship's length, at a rough guess. It showed twenty-five feet above the water-line, and we were, therefore, not surprised to find that it had grounded in water only thirty-four fathoms deep. Two days previously, in lat. 75° 35′, long. 27° 40′, the deep-sea thermometer sank to ninety fathoms and stood at 33° Fahr., while the surface temperature was only 30°·5 Fahr. But we were now over the great Spitzbergen bank, which from west of South Cape and from East Spitzbergen extends more than half-way to Norway. The origin of these icebergs excited some curiosity ; but we can now assume that, coming from Franz Josef Land, they had drifted between East Spitzbergen and Wiches Land with the Polar current, which we were now well into. Next day we counted the eighth out from Novaya Zemlya. Observation made us about half-way between South Cape, Spitzbergen, and Bear Island ; yet the ice, point after point, and some of the heaviest we had sailed along, still drove us from our course. Evidently, we could not hope to approach the south-east at present. An unfortunate schooner, fourteen days out from Hammerfest, shared our fate and pitched about in the heavy sea caused by the meeting of Atlantic and Polar currents over this great bank. When the swell moderated a little we clapped on steam, and at 8 P.M. sighted the southernmost promontory of Spitzbergen.

LAND OR MIST ?

Section III.

SPITZBERGEN

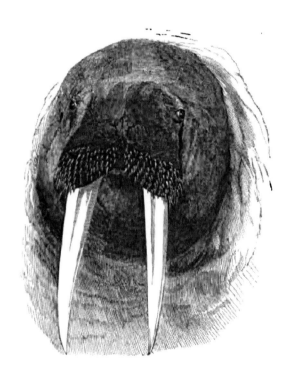

'The sea was rough and stormy,
The tempest howled and wailed,
And the sea-fog, like a ghost,
Haunted that dreary coast,
    But onward still I sailed.'

LONGFELLOW

SPITZBERGEN.

At last, after the sombre skies and fierce storms of Novaya Zemlya, we had reached Spitzbergen—a country which seemed like *terra firma* again—where we need not grope our way with compass and sounding-line—for nearly every convenient anchorage is laid down and the treacherous reefs marked on the charts—Spitzbergen, too, where I had first caught the infection and tasted the wild pleasures of Arctic life. There were clouds of sea-birds, and a pair of immense finner whales, a short distance off. The finner whale, unlike the right whale, does not dive by plunging perpendicularly down; the blowing, too, differs from the graceful curve depicted in all books—it resembles rather the spray dashed up by a heavy shot striking the water. These characteristics, its superior size, and the prominent dorsal fin, render its identification easy even a couple of miles away.

The next morning we bore up for the land. I still hoped to get into my old familiar hunting-grounds of Stor Fjord and the Thousand Isles; but a fresh disappointment awaited us: vast masses of impene-

trable drift ice, fifteen or twenty miles off South Cape,
barred the way eastward and extended for some distance up the west coast. Lord Dufferin, in his graphic
'Letters,' describes the ice in 1856 in a still more unfavourable state; in fact, I think there must have been
more ice clinging to the west coast that year than
has been before or since recorded. Sometimes the
ice is met with in vast isolated floes still farther
south.

Finding early next morning that nothing else could
be done I ordered a course to be made for the west coast,
hoping I might get round to the north-east that way.
The day was clear, and a crisp, bracing air just ruffled
the water. Sharp and defined, the beautiful panorama
of mountain and glacier stood out against the pearl-
grey sky. The view of these splendid and unforgotten
peaks was unspeakably grand and magnificent on such
a day as this. The granite cone of Hornsund's Peak,
the highest mountain in Spitzbergen (4,500 feet), was
well in sight—though between forty and fifty miles off,
the dazzling snow and the rarity of the air reduced the
apparent distance to a fourth. The especial boldness of
this part of Spitzbergen is due to each jagged peak rising
at once to its full height, and thus losing the dwarfing
influence of neighbouring hills, familiar in Alpine landscape. To realise Spitzbergen, let the reader imagine
Switzerland submerged to nearly the line of perpetual

Cloven Cliff.

Prince Charles's Foreland.

snow. The relative position of the glaciers, the process by which the water floats off masses to become icebergs, the flora, the difficulty of habitation, all, with a few modifications, immediately fit into their places. Hence, for the man of science, whatever branch he professes, geology, zoology, botany, it is no exaggeration to say, no country in the world can offer greater attractions. From speculations on the work of past ages in other countries he shifts his ground to the tangible and undeniable phenomena of the great processes of nature going on to-day before his very eyes. Violent convulsions, which older geologists taught were necessary to explain positions of existing strata, give place, in this region of reality and fact, to the beneficent but slow processes of upheaval, denudation, and disintegration. With all respect to records of glacier work in the Alps, I cannot but think that to attempt to explain the phenomena of old glacial periods without a previous study of the mighty existing glaciers of the Arctic regions is comparable to lecturing to a tribe of Red Indians on modern ironclads, in the language of Chaucer, aided by the model of a Roman galley.

We came up to a sloop at anchor in ninety fathoms, just at the edge of the bank, which suddenly shelves to between 1,300 and 1,400 fathoms. This situation is a favourite resort of small smacks hailing from the

Norwegian ports, engaged in shark-fishing. Here, with 155 fathoms of line, we could not reach bottom— the temperature at that depth was 34° Fahrenheit, while at the surface it was 38° Fahrenheit. The sloop had a crew of six, and had been out a month from Bergen, in which time she had half filled up with shark livers. To further enlighten my readers I may state these yield almost their entire weight of a fine fish-oil undistinguishable from cod-liver-oil. That is the secret trade which we now paddled off to investigate. Just before we climbed up the sides, slippery from contact with the slimy skins of numerous and recent victims, two specimens had been dragged on board. A third, having nibbled at the same time, was being rapidly reeled up by a two-handed winch fixed on the gunwale; and we watched with impatience, expecting that a shark of ten or twelve feet would hardly give up his liver for the service of man without having a fight for it. We were amazed at the facility with which the whole business was conducted, and especially at the apathetic way *Squalus Grœnlandicus* treated so serious and personal a proceeding. Without so much as a wag of his tail, following the line (only a cod-line, except a few fathoms of light chain at the end), he reached the surface and was hoisted on board by a gigantic gaff worked by a block-and-tackle, then stunned with a blow on the head from a handspike, his side ripped open with a colossal knife, his liver whipped out, and dropped into a tank, and finally, the stomach being inflated by blowing through a tube, his still quivering body was thrown overboard. Unless this latter precaution were taken the carcase would sink, and all the rest of the sharks would devote their attentions to their defunct friend, to the neglect of the seals' blubber used as a bait.

Near Iceland, where shark-fishing is extensively carried on, strict rules oblige the fishermen to keep the bodies afloat till the end of the fishing. The consequent stench makes it anything but a pleasant business. But it must be a profitable one, if every day prove as lucky as this. Four lines were down; eight sharks had been caught before we arrived; and we learned that the livers of much larger sharks often caught will fill a barrel a-piece—each barrel of oil being worth from 25 to 30 dollars (from 6*l.* to 7*l.*).

These men never eat the flesh, which is white and firm like halibut, but in Iceland the poor buy it in quantities for food. There is a curious parasitic worm (*Lerneopoda elongata*) always found attached to the eyeball of this fish, from whence it takes the name of the ' blind shark.'

We overhauled several sloops working their way north, but could get no information as to the condition of the ice.

The next day we found the ice for ourselves, stretching almost due west from Horn Sound, and were compelled to make a long detour to get as far north as Bel Sound. The entrance to this latter was also blocked with ice, though the warm Gulf water, at a temperature of 37°, was beginning to tell. Another band of Jan Mayen seals was seen, but owing to the unfavourable weather—a cold, cloudy evening with occasional snow-storms—we only got twenty-six. They were far tamer than the last lot, but a heavy swell rendered accurate shooting impossible.

Again we sped away north, in company with six other vessels. Not a living thing was on the ice, but numbers of little auks and sea-parrots rose and fell on the gentle ripple of a south-west breeze. Their cries alone enlivened the scene, blotted out, except in our immediate neighbourhood, by almost constant fog. When we could sight the land near Ice Fjord, towards evening, we found four sloops waiting for the white-whale-fishing. They confirmed our suspicions that Bel Sound was still full of ice; and even in Ice Fjord they could not yet commence operations. Indeed, Bel and Horn Sounds must be always reckoned to be full of ice long after Ice Fjord is clear. The former bays are often inaccessible till late in July. From a number of sea-temperature observations made in several voyages up and down the west coast I have been able, by comparisons of distant points at short intervals of time, to arrive pretty accurately at a satisfactory explanation. I have found the principal influence of the Gulf Stream to be exerted by a broad band of warm water, which, enveloping Prince Charles's Island, laps over each end and flows into Ice Fjord on the south, and King's Bay and Cross Bay on the north. As we recede from either margin of this band the water is found to be cooler; and, of the two extremities, the water in Ice Fjord will be found the warmer. I have seen the surface temperature there 10 degrees higher than to the east of Stor Fjord within the same month, and at a season when any difference in date should tell in favour of the south-east water.

When the fog cleared off, the south end of Prince Charles's Foreland came in sight. Prince Charles's Foreland is a long, narrow island, separated from the mainland by a shallow sound. Although Spitzbergen is eminently a mountainous country it is more properly regarded from a geological point of view as an elevated plateau, whose sides have been broken and cut through by glacier action, to form isolated ridges and pinnacles. It has no great mountain-range, or back-bone. In Prince Charles's Foreland we find the nearest approach to such a regular arrangement of hills. And it constitutes a sufficiently striking mountain-range, occupying nearly the whole sixty miles' length of the island. On the west side the rise from the sea is abrupt and precipitous, but on the east the descent is more gradual to low ground a few feet above the level of the sea. On the latter side the glaciers have considerably encroached. The chain of mountains is broken towards the southern extremity, and gives place to a low, sandy flat, where numbers of sea-birds congregate in summer. With the telescope we could make out the wreck of a timber-vessel, which came from the Petchora river five years ago, had been abandoned at sea by the crew, and was cast up on this shore. About the middle of the island a singular blackrock—or rather mountain, for it is 2,000 feet high—jutting out into the sea, has been termed the 'Devil's Thumb.' Some of these mountains rear their needle-like shafts to an elevation of from 3,000 to 4,000 feet.

We now rounded Fair Foreland, as Poole named it two centuries and a half ago, or Fogel Hook, as it is more appropriately called—a dark perpendicular cliff of great height, swarming with birds, which forms the northern termination of the island. A very extensive prospect suddenly opens out here. On this clear evening we could almost trace the whole eastern side of the island, the winding channel, the mainland with its long perspective of alternate ridge and glacier, and the indentation of English Bay. Directly ahead was

King's Bay, with the Three Crowns and its great
glaciers. On the other side we looked up the gloomy
vistas of Cross Bay, shut in on nearly every side by
grand and frowning mountains. There is some extent
of pasture along the coast between King's Bay and
English Bay, but no reindeer could be seen on it.
We therefore steamed on, and finally dropped anchor
in a small cove known as Coal Haven, where there
was fourteen fathoms of water. A better anchorage
could hardly have been selected; for, looking out from
the deck, the two points at the entrance were seen
absolutely to overlap. Blomstrand's Harbour on the
opposite side of the bay is not so completely sheltered.

It was one of the typical nights one enjoys in the
quiet bays of Spitzbergen. At nine o'clock in the evening the air was positively genial. Wonderfully quiet,
too, was everything beyond the noises of the ship.
Absolute stillness everywhere, save occasionally when
the voice of a wild bird miles away over the glassy sea
was borne to the ear, or the noisy falling of the edge
of a glacier, like the sound of artillery discharges, was
echoed from hill to hill. A clear, unclouded sky permitted the rays of the evening sun to crimson the
snowy peaks, and to throw vast shadows across the
glaciers. Turning in was not to be thought of under
such circumstances; and we divided into parties to ex-

plore, to shoot, to collect, to sketch, and to find water
and coal for future use. We had heard that the
Swedes in 1868 had got plenty of coal 'just below a
cairn, and that there was more and more as they dug
down;' but on this occasion we concluded it must be
buried yet in the snow. Other searches were more
successful. A sketch of those remarkable natural
pyramids, the Three Crowns, is lithographed in our
book. Nearly buried, and overwhelmed by the great
glacier, are some good examples of what are termed
roches moutonnées, isolated masses of rock, which a
more extensive glacier in former times has ground and
rounded to resemble sheep's backs. The summits of
the Three Crowns mark the upper level of a geological formation, which the denuding agency of the
great ice-stream has grooved into valleys. In the
rocky sides of the valleys, where there is other evidence of denuding origin, we often fail to trace the
familiar grooves and polished surfaces of glacier action.
This is due to the disintegration of the rocks by frost.
The tell-tale scratches have been split off, scattered,
and lost; but near the sea level, where the rocks have
been covered by water and snow, and the frost is
possibly less severe, glacier marks are quite common.
On the shore here, some rounded masses of limestone,
which cropped out of the surrounding soil and rocky

débris, plainly showed that a glacier some miles farther up must once have pushed thus far into the bay.

Some seals, a white whale, and a quantity of birds were picked up by some of the boats. The doctor lighted upon some interesting remains of defunct Dutchmen, and gave the following account: 'Descending to a low plain I stumbled on a veritable cemetery, between fifty and sixty graves of the whaling seamen of the last century. Some of them were in regular ranks, with proper mounds of earth over them, and a fragment of stick or fir-wood at the head and foot; others were scattered irregularly around, and a few were so old that the sprinkling of earth had blown away from the coffin, which was exposed in all its nakedness—a few bones, mingled with soil and fragments of rock, and a thick mass of withered herbage, filling up the coffin, the edges protruding above the ground. At the head of one such dismantled grave lay a headboard, upon which was the following inscription, perfectly legible, the black paint still adhering to the surface of the bleaching board of deal: ' Here lieth the body of Edward Sandford, who departed this life August 13th, 1748, aged thirty, late seaman " Elizabeth and Mary," of London. John Adamson, commander.' All that I noticed of poor Sandford, after 120 years,

amongst the stones, earth, and Arctic plants that filled
the coffin, was a single leg-bone. The boards of the
coffin-lid, the head-board, &c., lay scattered around.
But, perhaps, the first grave I came to made the greatest impression upon me. Part of the end of the coffin-
lid had given way, and there, grim and ghastly, a
human skull glared at you from the dark recess. I
could not remove it, as the coffin was full of soil and
ice, which bound its melancholy contents immoveably
in their place. Amongst the rows of graves was one
which, by the inscription upon its broken head-board,
contained the body of a Dutch commander of a
whaler; but the dates had been broken away, or cut
off by some previous visitor. I picked up a fragment
of a head-board, with the date (1740) upon it; another
fragment of board with a Dutch inscription; a lower
jaw-bone, and some of the purple flowers of the
Andromeda from the ridge of a grave. A number of
the coffins were merely buried with the lids upon a
level with the surface, and stones and masses of rock
piled over them to prevent the ravages of bears and
foxes. I counted forty graves, and came upon at least
twenty more at a short distance. It was a weird sight,
reminding me of Tam O'Shanter's discovery in the
old Kirk of Alloway:

'Coffins stood round like open presses
That showed the dead in their last dresses.'

I had always heard of these bays, Cross Bay and King's Bay, as two of the best in Spitzbergen for seals. I therefore set off in a boat, with twenty-four hours' provisions, for a row round them. Large floes of bay-ice, bearing numerous tracks of foxes and bears, were slowly floating out seawards. We rowed up to some islands at the end of King's Bay, said to be much haunted by the eider-duck in the breeding-season. But fast ice still joined them to the mainland; and while this state of things allows the foxes to reach the nests the birds will not lay. Vast numbers of ducks were sitting on the edge of the ice, grumbling and growling at being kept off their hatching-ground. Helstadt told me, what I can readily believe, that a skipper of his acquaintance, happening to hit off the exact time for arriving at one of these islands, got 4 cwt.[1] of eider-down and a great quantity of eggs in a couple of days. Another skipper, a few days later, found almost an equal quantity. The edge of the ice along which we rowed was densely crowded with little auks (*Alca alle*), guillemots (*Colymbus Troile*), and dovekies. The skuas (*Larus parasiticus*), terns (*Sterna Arctica*), and geese are more confined to the bare shores.

---

[1] My informant said twelve vog. A vog is equal to thirty-six pounds Norwegian, or nearly forty pounds English. In Tromsö the down, just as taken from the nests, fetches fifteen dollars a vog, and when cleaned, three dollars a pound; and in England one guinea a pound. Cleaning means taking away all dirt, sticks, &c., and therefore much of the weight.

Hardly any seals, except in inaccessible positions on *bay-ice*, were seen. It is next to impossible to shoot them here. Each seal sits close to his hole; at the slightest alarm he is down and under the ice. I am perfectly sure the vibrations of a boat striking against the ice-edge are conveyed a distance of two or more miles. Directly the bows come in contact with the ice every seal for miles raises his head and is on the alert. I have seen tried a laborious method of approach, which consists in pushing before one a white calico screen— but without success. I remember two seals being killed on bay-ice in 1859 at very long ranges, but my companion was quite an exceptional rifle-shot. Another was also shot on ice attached to the land on this voyage, but it was stalked from the land and shot from behind a rock, so that there was no walking on the ice until the poor beast laid his perforated head down over his hole. This extreme timidity arises from fear of Polar bears. It is most interesting to watch the intelligent manœuvres of a bear when patiently seeking a walrus or seal dinner. The bear, casually lying in wait behind a shelter of hummocky ice, is roused to attention by seeing some poor unconscious beast drag himself up on the ice. Looking round and all seeming secure, the poor seal lies down to sleep. The bear makes his way to the opposite side of the floating ice, climbs up, and begins to roll about as if with the most

harmless and innocent purpose of enjoying the warm
sunshine, but in reality contriving to gradually lessen
the distance between himself and his victim. The seal
becomes suspicious and restless, and instantly the bear
is motionless, commencing after a time, however, to lick
his paws, to clean himself, and to again approach the
beast insensibly. If the seal is now moderately sharp
he will detect the treachery and plunge into the water,
and the bear immediately gives up the game. The
nearer he has been able to get by cunning, the better
chance is there of his superior strength winning the
day. If once a bear is able to grip a seal he is almost
sure of his meal. It is not always so in encounters
between the bear and walrus. My old mate told me
he remembered once seeing a bear swimming towards
a stream of ice in Davis Straits, when a walrus rose
near, and, swimming towards him, rose breast-high
in the water alongside the bear. The walrus, striking
downwards with his tusks, took him, screaming loudly,
under water. After a while the bear came to the
surface again, and did not forget to swim as hard as
he could to the land. The recital of this story ' *drew* '
the old harpooner, who had been twenty years in the
Spitzbergen walrus trade ; and among many other
interesting adventures he informed us that in 1859,
when ashore at North-east Land, he found a large bear
and a walrus, both dead ; the walrus's tusks buried in

the bear's chest, and the bear's paws embracing the head and neck of the walrus. I think it probable that in the water the walrus will get the best of the encounter, but that on land or ice the bear is superior. That such fights often take place, and the walrus escapes, is proved by the frequency with which an old walrus's hide is scarred.

Varying the monotony of the long pull, and interrupting my speculations on the great glacier phenomena spread before my eyes, with these stories, we reached the cape separating King's and Cross Bays, and got a hundred eggs and some eider-down from a neighbouring island. Entering Cross Bay we were unable to penetrate farther than the anchorage on its western shore, on account of a smooth sheet of fast ice which still filled up the farther end. The upper reach of the bay is divided into two inlets, Moller Bay, and Lilliehöök's Bay. In the former is a wooden hut and a stack of driftwood collected by a crew who wintered there some years ago. Two walrus-sloops were lost at Moffen Island, and their crews dragged the boats over the ice to the Norway Islands—an undertaking which occupied three weeks. Finding it impossible to make their escape to the southward in their boats, on account of the ice being jammed on the land, these hardy seamen actually travelled on foot overland from the Norways to Cross Bay. One of their number lost his life by falling down a crevasse, and three others succumbed to fatigue and cold. The remainder contrived to live through the winter, and were released by their countrymen the following spring. During the long winter season they only managed to kill a single reindeer, after many weeks' persistent hunting. They lived almost entirely on seals and bears, devouring the very skins in their extremity. Yet none of them perished in their winter quarters, and it was one of the survivors we met in Novaya Zemlya who told us the story.

After thirteen hours' incessant pulling we got on board, pleased with the change from the confinement of the yacht, but disgusted with the scarcity of game— a small seal, six brace of ducks, and thirteen of guille- mots only lay in the bottom of the boat, and I had fired but seven cartridges the whole time. We picked up the broken blade of a pine-oar, marked ' Vigilant,' on the shore of King's Bay. We concluded it must have belonged to a whaler of that name sailing from Aberdeen, and which was latterly employed as a Government provision-tender to Sir E. Belcher's expe- dition.

An incident which happened to Livesay during our stay in King's Bay is a useful caution to those ignorant of ice. Going out duck-shooting alone, in the slight Siberian coracle, he stood at the edge of some ice, and, about to step in, had cast off the line. Without warn-

ing, the ice gave way, and in falling into the water an
involuntary movement of his outstretched arm pushed
the canoe off a little distance; and it was fortunate that,
loaded with Arctic clothing, sea-boots, and specimens
of rocks, he was able to swim to the boat and return
some two miles to the yacht, with only the incon-
venience of a ducking in Arctic water. Old ice-hands
always break down the overhanging edge of the ice
before venturing upon it.

As the engineers were still busy with some necessary
repairs, and there was no inducement to lengthen our
stay here, where the snow still covered up so much of
the land, we weighed anchor and left the bay in full
sail with a 'soldier's wind,' and, passing Mitre Cape,
where Scoresby made some interesting mountain excursions, we were soon abreast of 'the Seven Icebergs,'
as they are marked on the charts. They are in reality
the extremities of seven glaciers, about equidistant, all
alike in size (about a mile wide and 200 feet high) and
appearance, and all descending to the sea. They are
separated from each other by a series of sharp-pointed
ridges of crystalline schist.

None of the glaciers on this coast are to be compared with the great glaciers on the eastern coast of
Stans Foreland opposite Ryke Yse Islands. As the
east coast is seldom accessible a description of these
glaciers, which I was fortunate to be near only once

out of all my visits to Spitzbergen, may be acceptable. Like all the other coast glaciers, with few exceptions, they are only arms or branches of that vast *mer de glace*, or body of solid ice, which occupies all the interior of the country, and which, like an enormous centipede, extends its hundred legs down nearly every valley to the sea on both sides of the islands. On the coast between Black Point and Ryke Yse Islands there are three glaciers. The two southernmost ones are not of any great size or in any way remarkable; they have each a sea-front of about three miles, and protrude into the water for one-and-a-half or two miles.

The third or northernmost of these three glaciers is one of the largest and most remarkable in Spitzbergen, or, perhaps, in all the world. It has a seaward face of thirty or thirty-two English miles, and protrudes, in three great sweeping arcs, for at least three miles beyond the coast line. It has a precipitous and inaccessible cliff of ice all along its face, varying from twenty to one hundred feet in height; pieces from the size of a church downwards are constantly becoming detached from this icy precipice, and fall into the sea with the noise of thunder, causing a displacement of the water which throws forward a wave for miles. To go near the base in a boat is highly dangerous; the report of a gun will often tumble down a piece sufficient to overwhelm a ship. The surrounding sea is always

R

filled with these fragments, of all sizes and shapes, and many I have observed carrying large quantities of clay and stones imbedded in them. This vast glacier is in three great divisions : the northern and southern divisions are each quite smooth and glassy; but the centre one is broken up, and rough and jagged to a degree that is perfectly indescribable; at a little distance it exactly resembles a great forest of pine trees thickly covered with snow.

This part of the glacier must have undergone some great disturbance, arising either from its sliding over a rocky bed, or from its being forced through a narrow ravine in the underlying hills. Whatever the disturbing cause, it was still actively at work, because I frequently saw enormous *slices* of the smooth division split up and *cave in* towards the disrupted part; and there was a constant succession of tremendous booming reports, resembling loud and prolonged thunder, proceeding from these cracks, and from the whole of the rough parts of the glacier in general. I have questioned men who have frequented the Spitzbergen seas for as many as twenty summers, and they all say that this glacier has always presented the same appearance since they first saw it. Naturally this glacier has no visible terminal moraine, but it may possibly have some connection with an extensive submarine bank, which lies opposite the whole front of the glacier, and extends for fifteen or twenty miles to sea. The soundings on this bank may average fifteen fathoms, with a bottom of bluish clay; it is a favourite resort of the seal and walrus, particularly the latter. From this I am led to suppose that the bank yields in unusual numbers the mollusca on which they feed.

During the evening half a gale of wind blew up, and the sea became so heavy it was necessary to knock off steam. The screw is of no use when the yacht pitches so as to take it out of water half the time. Paddle-wheels are more suitable in a sea, but are inadmissible among heavy ice. For the remainder of the week we endeavoured to beat up to the north, and at times had to lay to, or crawled along the ice edge with the faint hope of picking up a walrus or seal. Thick mist obscured the land and forbade any attempt to run into Magdalena Bay or the South Gat.

We at length rounded Hakluyt's Headland, which we could just identify through the fog. It is a bold granitic cape on Amsterdam Island, and is the most north-westerly point of Spitzbergen. Some loose streams of ice were met with, and with a lessening sea we steamed on past Cloven Cliff and Vogel Sang towards Moffen Island.

In the neighbourhood of this island, and between it and Hinlopen Straits, the harpooner told me he had killed over two hundred walruses in eight days in the

year 1854. The main pack seemed to be coming down
from the north-east on the Norway Islands, but I
determined to lay-to during the night of July 4th, and
see what might happen on the clearing up of the
weather.

At midnight we were among the ice in the calmest
water I have ever seen. It was like a dark and stag-
nant pool for miles—the ice of every fantastic form
imaginable : here a ruined city of Carrara marble ; there
a gigantic swan with outstretched wings. Pinnacled
cathedrals, castles, battlements, colossal mushrooms,
and frosted pine forests in endless variety stretched
away to the golden mist of the horizon, and were
reflected clear and sharp. Every rope and spar reappeared in the dark water. There could have been no
difficulty in making use of this natural looking-glass,
by looking over the ship's side, had shaving been
necessary in the Arctic regions ; but I believe only the
steward and sailing-master ever go through this
laborious process.

Off Red Bay we caught glimpses of the land ;
blinks of sunshine illumined the fog without altogether
dispelling it. On shore was a ruined hut of some size,
and around some lofty poles, terminating in crosses, explained its Russian origin. They are the remains of a
party of Russians who attempted to winter here in 1851.
Twelve graves bear witness to that terrible scourge—

scurvy—for out of eighteen men six only survived the winter, although there was no want of provisions or comfort. The wooden hut was purposely constructed, and brought from the White Sea. It would seem that the forced exercise in the search for food is more salutary than any preparation or forethought in staving off the ravages of disease. We hear of parties making voluntary experiments of wintering perishing miserably, while the hapless crew, escaping to the desolate shore from their foundering vessel, knock together a hut of drift-wood, and, keeping always on the alert to get bare food, have no time for the care and depression of mind which are the malady's best allies.

In the early part of the seventeenth century Spitzbergen became the seat of the most flourishing whale-fishery that ever existed, as many as 400 to 500 sail of vessels, principally Dutch and Hamburgers, resorting here in the season. It then became obvious that it would be very advantageous if something in the shape of a permanent settlement or colony could be founded in· Spitzbergen; and the merchants engaged in the trade offered rewards to their crews, to induce some of them to make the hazardous experiment of trying whether human life could be supported there during the winter. For a long time this was believed to be impossible; and, as no volunteers could be prevailed upon to risk their lives in the solution of this interest-

ing problem, an English company hit upon the ingenious and economical idea of trying it upon some
criminals who were under sentence of death in London.
Accordingly they procured 'a grant' of these culprits,
and offered them their lives on condition that they
would pass, or try to pass, one winter in Spitzbergen.
Of course they were glad to purchase their lives on
any terms, and at once acceded to the conditions. They
were taken out in one of the whalers, and a hut was
erected for their winter quarters; but when the fleet
was about to depart, and they saw the awful, gloomy
hills, already white with the early snows, and felt the
howling gales of north-east wind, their hearts utterly
failed them, and they entreated the captain who had
charge of them to take them back to London and let
them be hanged, in pursuance of their original sentence,
rather than leave them to perish in such a horrible
country. The captain seems to have had more of the
' milk of human kindness ' in him than his philanthropic
employers, for he granted their request and took them
back to London. As hanging them would not have
been of any pecuniary benefit to the company, they
were then good enough to procure a pardon for the men.

This story reminds me of a conversation which I
once heard some of my old yacht's crew holding together. They were discussing the respective merits
of hot and cold countries—the West Indies *versus*

Spitzbergen; and one fellow was urging, that, although 'neither rum nor tobacco grew in Spitzbergen,' still the continual 'blow out' of fat reindeer, which it seemed to afford, might be considered as a point in its favour. To him the other :—' Well, Bob, all I can say is, that I would a blank sight rather go to the West Indies and be hanged there, than die a natural death in this here blank country !'

Soon after the failure of the criminal plan, the experiment of wintering in Spitzbergen was involuntarily tried by a party of nine British sailors, who were accidentally left behind by a whaler. All of these men were found dead the following year, with their bodies cruelly torn by bears and foxes.

In 1630 the same whaler, having sent on shore a boat's crew to hunt reindeer at Black Point, was compelled by ice or bad weather to sail away, and leave these men also to their fate. When all hope of the ship's return had expired, they determined to make for Green Harbour, and reached Ice Fjord after seventeen days of laborious rowing, only to find that all the ships had already left this part of the country. Still believing it possible to fall in with one of the whalers, they spent some time in searches up and down the coast. September 3rd came, and it was now but too plain that they must face the rigour of an Arctic winter. Bel Sound was fixed on for their winter quarters, and they

set resolutely to work to build a hut, and provide a winter stock of food.   Sixteen reindeer and four bears were
fortunately killed.   The skins, sewn together with bone
needles, supplied clothes and bedding.   Two walruses,
which floated into the bay with the ice on September
12th, added further to their stock of provisions, but on
four days of the week their loathsome food was the
refuse of ·whale blubber after the oil had been extracted from it.   Without books, pens, ink, or paper,
nothing could relieve the monotony of the long dark
winter, nor divert their minds from the recital of other
fatal wintering attempts.   From October 14th to February 3rd, the sun was never seen.   But spring came at
last, and with it the bears about the beginning of
March, and the birds a little later.   Thus, when starvation was most threatened, a fresh supply of food came.
On May 24th the ice round the coast at length broke
up, and a few days later all, eight men, were rescued
by their countrymen after a sojourn of ten months in
latitude 77° north.

Shortly after, four Russians were similarly cast
away on a desolate part of the east island of Spitzbergen.
These poor fellows had nothing but what they stood
up in, with one gun and a few charges of ammunition;
but they appear to have been men of a very different
stamp from the London gaol-birds who had first faced
the prospect of a winter's stay.   They at once set to

work to make the best of things, and built a hut, killed some reindeer with their gun, and then, their ammunition being exhausted, they manufactured bows and arrows, spears and harpoons, of drift-wood. They pointed their weapons with bones and pieces of their now useless gun, and twisted their bowstrings out of reindeer's entrails. They made traps and nets for birds and foxes. With these rude and imperfect weapons they not only provided themselves with food and raiment, but kept off the assaults of the Polar bears. It is almost incredible; but these men not only survived, but preserved health for six long years. It seems extraordinary that such energetic fellows as they clearly were should not, in all that time, have contrived to travel across the country or round by the shore to the west coast, where they would have been certain of relief every summer, especially as they were on the most desolate part of the island, one often inaccessible and always little frequented by the whalers. In the sixth year of their captivity one of the four died, and the survivors began to lose all hope of deliverance and to fall into a state of despondency, which would certainly soon have proved fatal to them all, had not a vessel at this time fortunately approached the coast and rescued them. Thus these few men, more than two centuries ago, totally unprepared, survived a banishment and hardships, in comparison with which

a winter or two in a well-found ship seems merely
child's play. During their long banishment these
poor Robinson Crusoes had killed such quantities of
bears, deer, seals, and foxes, that the proceeds of the
skins and blubber made a small fortune for them.

In the loose pack, which now prevented our making
any further progress north we descried a sloop. We
steamed up to her, and learned she had narrowly
escaped being beset with two others at Moffen Island.
Our taking her in tow to the sheltered anchorage
between the Norways, where we brought up in four
fathoms of water, led to a curious misconstruction on
the part of a sloop which was already at anchor when
we came in. No steamer had ever before been seen
in Spitzbergen waters ; and when the rakish-looking
masts and clipper hull of the 'Diana' hove in view, and
she glided round a corner of cliff apparently towing a
prize, those on board the sloop put us down for *pirates*,
and imagined we had come in on a cutting-out expedition, intending to take possession of their vessel also.
This unfortunate sloop had sent out a boat's crew
eleven days previously to hunt seals ; only two days'
provisions were taken, and unless they had fallen in with
game, or other vessels, the men must have died of starvation by this time. It left the vessel, too, so short-handed
that unassisted they could never hope to work her back
to Norway.

The skipper of the sloop we had towed out of the pack came on board in the evening, and, after we had loosened his tongue by appropriate means, he told us an interesting account of a celebrated boat's voyage in which he took a part in 1864. This long row of 400 miles, which occupied fourteen days, was necessitated by the loss of three vessels engaged in walrus-hunting on the east side of North-east Land. Previous to this year, vessels had hardly ever ventured to the eastward by sailing past the Seven Islands or down Hinlopen Straits, approaches to the east coast known as the 'North' and 'South Gates' respectively. But it happened this season that the former 'Gate' was clear of ice in the middle of July, and the latter early in August. The sloop in which our guest was harpooner, and two others, were in the neighbourhood of the Seven Islands on August 3rd. The three skippers, Tobiesen, Aarström, and Mathilas, finding the sea unusually open, agreed to sail together round the north-east point of North-East Land. For a time all went well, and, sailing down the little-visited east coast, great numbers of walruses were killed. But when the excitement of the chase was over, and they attempted to return, the ice had come down on the north-east corner and blocked the way. From day to day it drove still farther south, and at last, finding themselves hemmed in by the ice on all sides, a council was held, and they resolved to

abandon the ships. After encountering great dangers
from a gale springing up, from ice falling and swamp-
ing two of the boats, and from the impossibility of preventing the boats drifting out of sight of each other,
the seven boats arrived at the Southern Gate or south-
east entrance to Hinlopen Straits. They were now
within thirty miles of the Swedish Expedition, which lay
at anchor in Ginevra Bay, at the extremity of Stor Fjord.
But at that time it was not known that Stor Fjord com-
municated with the eastern seas through Hell's Sound.

In 1859, leaving my yacht, the 'Ginevra,' in the
bay which now bears its name, I pulled and walked
a great distance through this sound, and expressed
my conviction, from the depth of the water, the rise
and fall of the tide, and the nature of the ice passing
through, that Stor Fjord must have an outlet here
which would enable a vessel to reach the east coast
somewhere near the south entrance to Hinlopen Straits.
My surmises were not verified until a sloop in 1864
navigated the sound.

The boats' crews, as I have said, not knowing of
this short cut, divided, to attempt the arduous task of
reaching the west coast by Hinlopen Straits and the
north-west. Four boats kept to one and three to the
other side of the strait. It was a row for life; the
season was getting late, and there was every chance
of the ice having already beset Verlegen Hook and the

Norways. All their summer's gains had been left in
the sloops; and of the immense numbers of walruses
they saw in Hinlopen Straits—sufficient, he told us,
to have filled several ships—only a few were killed
for food. At last Verlegen Hook was reached without any vessel having been met with, and it was
thought advisable that Aarström, with four boats,
should search for the walrus sloops in Wide Bay
and Love Bay, while Tobiesen and Mathilas, with
the other boats, should press on to Ice Fjord. At
Amsterdam Island and Seal Bay some tinned provisions from a depot there were taken on board in
prospect of a winter on the coast, and, having reached
King's Bay and rested, a further division of the boats
was made. Tobiesen arrived in Advent Bay on the
31st, where he was fortunate enough to find some of
his countrymen. Mathilas, keeping the shore of the
mainland, fell in with the Swedish Expedition, and
not long after Aarström, with his four boats, also
arrived. The crews of the three sloops were distributed among the vessels in Advent Bay and taken
home, but they had left some 3,000*l*. worth of spoil on
board the three sloops in the pack. The vessels have
never since been heard of.

Fair Haven is in many respects a most convenient
anchorage. Four islands—Vogelsang, Cloven Cliff, and
the Inner and Outer Norways, with their high granite

cliffs—enclose a labyrinth of smooth water with many
outlets, so that with the ice in this year's position,
and it is by far the most usual one, it is an admirable
station to watch for an opening in the pack to the
north. And, should the ice drive down quickly, it is
always possible to escape by one or other of the
channels. I resolved to remain at anchor here a few
days, and twice a day sent a look-out to the top of a
hill, 700 feet high, at the east end of the Outer Norway.
The daily report of the state of the ice was pro-
vokingly monotonous.

One day I clambered over the bare low grounds
and up some stiff bits of cliff to the top of the hill, to
see if there was any change since we sailed along the
ice. Stretching from Welcome Point and enveloping
Moffen Island, the ice appeared to be in one dense unbroken sheet. Streams of ice were carried hither and
thither by varying currents which prevail here.[1]
But the main pack seemed absolutely impenetrable.
Yet I knew that a few hours' favourable wind might
clear the whole seas to the Seven Islands or even much
farther. Parry, in his memorable voyage, was detained
at Amsterdam Island, waiting for the ice to clear, from

[1] Phipps, lying becalmed two and a half leagues N.N.W. of Cloven
Cliff, found the current running to the westward; his consort, not far off,
was drifting in a current running to eastward: and it is quite common to
see two blocks of ice almost touching each other drifting in opposite
directions from their drawing different depths of water, and so being influenced by surface and deeper currents respectively.

Drawn by H. Lucas

The 'Diana' in 80°.

May 14th to June 8th. Then, the sea being cleared by a southerly wind, he was able to sail as far as 81° 5'.

But 1827 was one of the exceptional years. So was 1806, when Scoresby sailed along the edge of the pack trending to east-north-east, and reached the latitude of 81° 30'. This was a degree farther than Phipps, who in 1773 struggled through floating ice to the Seven Islands, and then, getting beset, abandoned the vessels and was about to proceed homewards in the boats, when the ice suddenly opened and allowed the ships once more to set sail. Hudson, it is believed, reached the Seven Islands in 1607. Of modern voyages, we have the Swedish Expedition pushing through lanes of water to 81° 42' in the middle of September 1868. But the risk of such rash navigation is exemplified by the disabling of their vessel by contact with the ice and their subsequent retreat. And again Mr. Leigh Smith reached comparatively open water in 81° north. There was ice then to the north-east though none to the south. This was on September 11th. Mr. Leigh Smith has since revisited the Seven Islands in the 'Diana,' and penetrated to 80° 50 north, in 17° east longitude.

But all these voyages, I repeat, were made in seasons when, from the influence of prevailing winds, the seas were exceptionally open. Barentz, when he first discovered Spitzbergen in 1596, Poole in 1610 and 1611, Baffin and Fotherby in 1614, Tschitschagoff in 1865, Buchan and Franklin in 1818, found the ice much as it was in 1869.

The origin of this ice pack, whose edge, varying each year only within the limits of three degrees of latitude, has persistently kept all vessels on its outskirts, is of considerable interest. Coming from the north-east, we have already seen it blocking the east coast of Spitzbergen; and this it does with rare exceptions every year. But a rarely recurring open season permits of the circumnavigation of North-east Land, as we have seen was the case in 1864, and also in the previous year, when Carlsen first passed the Northern Gate and circumnavigated Spitzbergen. Notably, the boat voyage already recounted shows that the ice first comes down on the north-eastern corner, and thence streams down the east side of North-East Land. At the same time, but more slowly, it flows round the north shore of North-east Land; for we have seen the boats doubling Verlegen Hook when the south entrance of Hinlopen Straits was closed. The Swedes, at the end of August 1868, found the Southern Gate similarly blocked, while the north entrance of the Straits was not only open, but permitted the 'Sofia' to pass nearly due north a fortnight later. Leigh Smith's experience in 1871 was exactly similar; at the end of August the Southern Gate was closed, but it was after this he passed the Northern Gate and attained both his greatest northing and greatest easting.

All voyagers have found the ice to come from the north and east. The warm west water and the favourable conjunction of the wind clear the seas, in degrees which vary each season; and up to August the ice is generally more and more loose; after that, however, the cold Arctic waters get the best of it, and, by the regular steps I have indicated, North-east Land, the north coast of the mainland, and the west coast become successively enveloped. The formation of shore ice assists the general block. In still bays it commences in August; on the wave-beaten coast outside it is later; but eventually the whole archipelago is surrounded by a compact icy girdle.

Till very lately it was assumed that the failure of Parry's attempt to reach the Pole was due to his having started so late that the one-winter's ice, binding the blocks and floes together, had dissolved and loosened the pack. But wherever a winter has been passed in the pack or within sight of it, there almost constant motion has been observed. It constitutes the great danger of a vessel beset, and effectually disposes of any hope of reaching the Pole more successfully by seizing the early spring for travelling over the pack, as an improvement on Parry's attempt. Yet Professor Nordenskiold, whose practical knowledge of ice is certainly considerable, wintered in Mossel Bay, and at the end of April of 1873 set out with sledges, only to repeat

Parry's failure; for, having arrived at Seven Islands, the ice was found of such a nature that no serious effort was made to go north.

But expeditions of this nature have their value, although the pre-arranged programme can seldom be carried out. Professor Nordenskiold, from his bases on the west coast in Stor Fjord and on the north coast, with his Swedish companions, has done in geographical survey, in meteorology, and in natural history what the Russians have effected for Novaya Zemlya; and, together with Mr. Leigh Smith's summer voyages, has greatly enlarged our knowledge of north and north-east Spitzbergen, with the neighbouring islands.

Their narratives teach us how impossible it is to predict the lie of ice during the summer, how difficult to calculate the influence of wind and tide, but how easy, on this hazardous and broken coast, it is to get beset. To avoid such a mishap it might be well never to enter a harbour which had not, so to speak, a back door. For most of the harbours on this north coast, across whose mouths the ice drifts, become traps liable to close suddenly at any moment. Such traps are Mossel Bay, where Nordenskiold, during the winter of 1872–1873, out of the provisions intended for the steamer 'Polhem' alone, had to feed the crews of his tender-ships and also those of some sloops, all of which were surprised by the ice in the autumn of 1872;

Treurenberg Bay, whence Parry and his party started for their five-hundred-mile journey to the north; and the various inlets of North-east Land, not excepting those in Hinlopen Straits, which are exposed to the double risk of ice coming in from either end of the straits.

Far the most terrible of the disasters due to this sudden invasion of ice was that of a crew of thirteen men who were beset at Mitra Hook in September 1872. The crew of the vessel (Mack's) that went in search of their countrymen the following spring found them all dead. Five bodies were laid out on the beach under a cloth. In one chamber of the rough hut were six corpses horribly disfigured by the ravages of scurvy. In another chamber were three corpses in bed, while a fourth, who was dressed and had apparently gone out to the last, was lying across a chest at the entrance. Those in bed presented a terrible appearance, and by their side were the remains of their last food, three biscuits, four or five tablets of sugar, and a parcel of dried vegetables. After a vain search for the remains of the two other sailors, who were probably hidden under the snow, the last of the eighteen who had to be accounted for was found to have died before the arrival of his comrades at the huts. The exceptional fatality was, no doubt, owing to neglect of exercise and cleanliness. There was abundance of

provision.   A diary, kept until the last sufferer was too
ill to write, tells us they killed two bears, two foxes, and
some reindeer in October, but that when darkness came
on they gave up hunting.[1] In the beginning of December
the first man fell ill ; on the 19th a second was attacked,
and by the 21st all were more or less suffering.   The
least ill nursed the dying and kept watch day and night.
But as the cold increased the disease was more severe.
Two men died on the 10th of January ; a third on the
21st of February ; and on the 23rd the writing in the
diary changed, and the new recorder says :—'There
is now only one sound man to keep us all.   May the
Lord have pity on us ! '   On the 28th of February the
cold reached its maximum,—45° Fahr. Up to the 4th of
April ten deaths were successively recorded, and on
the 19th a fresh writer registered another. The last
survivor left the only testimony of his death in throwing his weakened body across the chest in the sudden
agony in which this awful malady often terminates.

[1] The darkness of the Arctic winter is greatly exaggerated. Although
the sun is below the horizon from the end of October to the end of
February in the latitude of Spitzbergen, the sun approaches sufficiently
near the horizon to give about six hours of twilight out of the twenty-
four. Pakhtusof, further south, in Kamenka Bay, speaks of only two
hours and a half of morning twilight, and of its being clear for one and a
half hours in Matoschkin Schar during the winter. But Dr. Bessels, wintering with Hall in 81° 23', noted no less than six hours of twilight on the
twenty-first day of December. There may be clouded skies and storms of
snow sufficient to cause *total darkness* occasionally, but there is no doubt
that, five days out of six during the winter, outdoor exercise can be
enjoyed and should be enforced by commanders of expeditions.

I have been betrayed into digressions which are unavoidable in calling up the dismal prospect of the ice from the elevated point at the Norways.

All these efforts to penetrate to the north of Spitzbergen got no farther than the edge or fringe of the pack, or, so to speak, among the sweepings of the great ice-magazine. Although the 'Trent' and 'Dorothea,' the 'Esk,' and in later times the 'Sofia,' have fully experienced the dangers of the closely-packed drifts Parry alone can be said to have been fairly *within* the pack. And to his accounts must we refer for an accurate description of its character. At the outskirts the ice is loosely packed; there are no floes of any great size, and lanes and pools of water are common. Farther in, at the limit of their journey, the floes were larger, some square miles in extent, from fifteen to twenty feet thick, and evidenced, in their crumpled margins, where pieces had been forced up to form hummocks, the immense pressure to which they had been subjected. Occasionally sheets of lighter ice were met with, and these were thought to be the result of one winter's ice forming over pools in the general mass.

I am not disposed to endorse any *theory* as to the disposition of land, ice, or water around the North Pole, nor to do what might be easier still, viz., to originate a new one. I shall be content to close this subject by recapitulating the conditions which Parry found at 500

miles from the North Pole.   The ice—which, from its
thickness, from the absence of icebergs, fresh-water
ice, and shore *débris*, could not have been formed near
land—was less and less pounded up into drift-ice as he
penetrated farther.   Towards the north, whence the
floes drifted, an ice-sky was seen.   The water, freezing
at the surface in the shade, had deepened to more than
500 fathoms.   Lastly, there were no birds.

Unable to get farther in the yacht, we set out in two
boats to see if it was possible to push on to Liefde Bay
and Wüde Bay by following the land-water.   Wüde
Bay is a deep inlet almost separating the north-west of
Spitzbergen from the mainland by approaching within
fifteen miles or so of one of the arms of Ice Fjord, just
as, running parallel to it, Hinlopen Straits makes North-
east Land an island.   It was first explored by the
Swedes in 1868, but yielded little of interest beyond the
study of its monotonous geological shores—a formation
better exemplified elsewhere.   Red Bay is a picturesque
semicircle of aiguille-like cliffs of crystalline schist.
A small glacier which fell at a sharp angle from its
western side showed a curious and interesting section.
It was regularly stratified, and we could trace the
thickness of each year's deposit.   Its point of exit
was between two steep ridges, but farther inland the
ice-field was wide and unconfined.   The effect of the
viscous mass having to push through a funnel-like

outlet was a contorted and wave-like undulation of the annual layers.

A great sheet of ice filled the extremity of Red Bay. It was dotted all over with seals, and, having driven them down their holes, a few were shot at the edge of the ice. But thick fog, and the ice drifting from the east, obliged us to beat a retreat. Another day I got as far as Red Beach, and hoped to fall in with reindeer, which are said to be abundant there. But a great many vessels have hunted reindeer since Phipps's crew killed fifty deer, and Buchan's expedition forty, on Vogel Sang, and Parry seventy in Treurenberg Bay. We got the boat, with some difficulty, past Biscayers Hook, and then found an excellent wooden house on a flat tongue of land. It was the Russian hut we had seen from the yacht, and we were able to examine more closely the crosses which marked the graves of the unfortunate men who perished here. Each cross was about fifteen feet high, and had a larger and a smaller cross-piece above. Half-way up was a third cross-piece, fixed at an angle, and all were carved and lettered with Russian characters. There is here a considerable lake, which on July 10th was still frozen over; it empties into the sea by a small river.

By the toilsome expedient of dragging the boat over half-a-mile of fast-ice I got within telescopic distance of an immense slope tailing off from a hill.

It was all ground suitable for deer, but none were to
be seen; so, after an attentive survey, I got back to the
boat and laboriously worked back again through the
ice, with even greater difficulty than before. We
must have rowed, hooked, and dragged the boat at
least thirty-five miles by the time we reached the yacht
again at ten P. M., knocked up and thoroughly disgusted,
and, moreover, decidedly convinced that it would be
utterly impossible for any *ship*, even the most powerful
iron-clad in existence, to make the smallest progress
through such ice as we had seen.

The crew had mostly gone ashore in my absence;
but these bare shores, clothed in withering lichens, a
few kinds of grass and moss, and a sprinkling of
scurvy-grass,[1] yielded very little but geese, eider-ducks,
looms, sea-parrots, and the skulls of defunct Dutch-

[1] The broad succulent leaves of the scurvy-grass (*Cochlearia fenestrata*)
are the only Arctic materials for making a salad. It grows abundantly in
some parts of Spitzbergen, and in Matoschkin Schar has been much used
by explorers as a prophyllactic against scurvy. Mustard and cress may
be raised in boxes in the cabin or engine-room, but it takes from twelve
to fourteen days to mature. There being such difficulties in procuring so
agreeable and sanitary a form of diet, I venture to offer the following
compound, as a substitute for salad at dinner. Having been discovered and
invented after numerous experiments on board the yacht, I beg to register
it under the name of 'Salade à la Diane.'

Take of   Cold, boiled potatoes,
               Portugal tomatoes, } from tins,
               Portugal onions,
               Capers and anchovies,
               Hard-boiled eider-ducks' eggs,

a sufficiency; season to taste with pepper, oil, and vinegar; garnish with
scurvy-grass, and serve.

men. I was vexed to find these ghastly relics had been rifled from some graves ashore. Nothing could be more repulsive than the brown bones with dried flesh and hair clinging to them. They were not unlike Egyptian mummies, and were still swathed in rotting fragments of the clothes they were buried in, 200 years ago.

Although we had been at anchor in this unproductive locality for nearly a week, and ice streaming between the islands had sent the frightened sloops away, I still thought July 9th was too early to give up the game. I would endeavour to exist here two days longer. All the books on board, including some heavy standard works had been read twice through. Happily, the granite steps of Cloven Cliff were the breeding-ground of countless sea-birds, and we could amuse ourselves with a sort of sea rook-shooting. At the foot of Cloven Cliff one lands on a natural stone jetty; and, although the breeding-ledges are themselves inaccessible, it is possible to climb to a convenient plateau about half-way up, and opposite, about fifty yards distant from, the looms and sea-parrots. They allow their companions to be picked off with a pea-rifle without manifesting much alarm; but if a bird is only wounded he commences to snap at the one who sits next him, and generally ends by being pushed off the ledge, when he drops 200 feet into 'Sailor's' mouth below. Cloven Cliff is not unlike Ailsa Craig, and its true proportions are only recognised when ashore at its base, or in attempting to climb its ragged sides. A marshy piece of ground near it is much frequented by the Brent goose, and at this time of the year was dotted over with buttercups and poppies. Fox-tracks were abundant on the neighbouring snow and a white fox was chased on the Inner Norway Island.

Before leaving these islands I made another ascent to the rude cairn at the top of the hill; and, having traversed nearly the entire coast of the Outer Norway, got at last to a cliff descending perpendicularly into the water, beyond which walking was impracticable. It was, therefore, necessary to climb up a steep, snow-filled ravine, which was sufficiently hazardous, from the inclination of the slippery surface and the upper part ending in a sharp crest overhanging an unpleasant-looking cliff of smooth rock. After cautious climbing on all fours, varied by many a startling slip as the thin crust of snow gave way beneath my weight, I again arrived at the highest point of the island. The heat was overwhelming. Not a breath of air. The unclouded sun, blazing down, was reflected from the dazzling snow or radiated from the rocks, and made one almost forget latitude till the eye again rested on the great icy expanse to the north. Intense quiet prevailed everywhere; the wailing cries of a couple of burgo-

The Look-out from the Norways.

masters, and the shrill chattering of some rotges in the cliffs below, alone broke the stillness. No crashing of icebergs or grinding together of the floes heralded the approach of the advance-guard of the mighty pack; but none the less steadily had it from day to day stolen down on us. The wind still kept north of west, and it was manifestly but waste of time to lie at anchor, and, in addition, to risk getting beset. I left the summit with a very definite picture of the ice engraved indelibly on my brain—a picture which is called up readily in all its clearness whenever I hear wild talking or read vague theories on the subject of traversing the pack to the North Pole! With some difficulty I descended, the break-neck declivities being in some places covered with a thin layer of frozen snow. Half-way down the snow had completely disappeared, and the surface of the rocks and the crumbling soil were covered with a thick mass of spongy mosses. The beach consisted of masses of rocks detached from the precipice by the action of the frost; and where the snow-drifts still lay in shady hollows the surface was so affected by the sun as to make wading through it extremely tiring. I came across the traces of buildings erected by the Dutch as boiling-houses, and repeatedly drove the eider-ducks and Arctic terns from their nests. The former sometimes sit so close they may be knocked over with a stick; but if sufficient

notice is given of a stranger's approach it is not unusual for them to cover up and conceal the nest before
flying off. During our week's stay here we only saw a
single whale, although there was abundance of ·whale's-
food'[1] in the water.

At two P.M. on July 11th we weighed anchor and
commenced steaming for Ice Fjord. Passing out south
of Cloven Cliff and Vogel Sang, we hastened past Foul
Bay and Foul Point—dangerous from reefs and isolated
rocks—and crossed the northern outlet of the Sound so
well known in the annals of Dutch whaling. Smeerenberg Harbour is a deep fjord, opening towards the north,
and sheltered on the west side by a boundary of high
mountains. But this land on the west, instead of being a
simple tongue thrust out from the mainland, is divided
by the Dane's and South Gats into two islands—Amsterdam and Dane's Islands. The former terminates to the
north in Hakluyt's Headland; and in 1871 I found
inside, and to the east of the headland, a very good
anchorage in ten fathoms of water, nearly off a beacon
on the shore. At that time, July 7th, I climbed a hill
700 feet high, and observed the ice in a most hopeless
condition. A few days later I found the ice jamming
all the islands and sounds of Fair Haven (but all the fast
ice seen in the Smeerenberg bays a few days before had
disappeared). Yet in the year referred to, 1871, Mr.

[1] *Clio Borealis.*

Leigh Smith, in September, made the interesting voyage to the north and east already referred to. A comparison of his and my experience of different months in the same year shows that August, and not July, must be reckoned the more favourable month for exploration, and that in September the sea may be even more clear than during the previous months. It should be remembered, however, that such late voyages entail a serious risk of getting beset for the winter. The southern island, known as 'Danes,' is the larger, and has a convenient harbour at Seal Bay. Here the Swedish Expedition of 1868 ran in to examine their little vessel after she had struck on a sunken rock in South Gat. It is remarkable that, although Buchan's expedition had met with a similar accident, they did not mark the treacherous rock in their chart. Other convenient anchorages within the Sound are still visited, but by a smaller number of vessels than those of the Dutch whaling-fleet during the palmy days of Spitzbergen whale-fishery in the seventeenth century. On Amsterdam Island, near Hakluyt's Headland, was the flourishing summer-settlement of Smeerenberg, or New Amsterdam—the rendezvous and boiling-establishment. Smeerenberg (literally Blubber Town), indeed, arrived at such a degree of civilisation and refinement that 'hot rolls' were to be had every morning for breakfast; and, if report speaks true, even the

charms of female society were not wanting to 'emollify
the manners' and lighten the pockets of the successful
fishers.   The whole district around Smeerenberg has
been exhaustively surveyed and described by Parry, by
Buchan and Franklin, and by the Swedes ; and I must
refer the reader to the works published by these explorers for interesting details.[1]

Steaming all day and night, we were abreast of the
middle of Prince Charles Foreland again by *breakfast
time*.   It is customary to look upon this as a definite
period in the day, in distinction from the hour of dinner
—always a moveable feast.   Seldom thinking it worth
while to carry a watch, most ludicrous mistakes are
sometimes made as to the lapse of time.   In the long
hunting-excursions on shore we usually rowed away
quite early; then, perhaps, thick weather coming on,
the sun would be obscured, and, getting on board, as
we have thought, to dinner at seven or eight, the
patient steward has informed us it was midnight, or,
perhaps, two or three o'clock next morning.

The course from the south end of the foreland to
Ice Fjord is a tedious one, because the main points of
the landscape are so gigantic and so well-defined on
a clear day that one appears to make hardly any

---

[1] Parry's 'Narrative of an Attempt to reach the North Pole.'
Beechy, 'A Voyage of Discovery towards the North Pole.'
'Svenska Expeditionen til Spetzbergen.'

progress as hour after hour slips by. If, under these circumstances, the atmosphere becomes hazy, or the sky gets clouded, the land actually appears to recede from a ship which is advancing towards it. It is related of a Danish captain who made a voyage to Greenland that, frightened by a phenomenon of this kind, altogether beyond the experience and calculations of that age, he put the ship about and returned with great precipitation to Denmark, where he gravely asserted that his progress had been arrested by 'some load-stone rocks hidden in the sea'!

The entrance to Ice Fjord is unspeakably grand. To the north Dödmansören (Deadman's ears)—a prominent headland of stratified rock—stands, like a huge sentinel, in all the majesty of its 2,500 feet of height. Perpendicular buttresses, looking as if regularly built in courses, are varied in one place by an appearance as if a large section of the mountain had slid from above, and turned partly over in its fall. This headland consists of a geological formation, known as the 'Hecla Hook formation,' which is very largely distributed in Spitzbergen. There are many reasons for assigning it to the Devonian or Permian periods; but the absence of fossils is as singular as it is embarrassing to the geologist. In Spitzbergen its correct place in point of time seems to be immediately after the granite and crystalline schist. In many places the mountain lime-

stone rests upon it. As the fjord is entered, an endless succession of terrace-shaped mountains arrest the
attention. Of horizontal tertiary strata, they suggest
an origin from a vast level table-land, out of which great
slices and wedges have been cut here and there. The
subsequent action of frost, and the carrying power of
water in the summer, have covered up the feet of the
cliffs, giving rise to level plains between them and the
sea, and have done much to shallow the water of the
fjord.

On the various shores of Ice Fjord nearly all the
strata of Spitzbergen are represented. The granite and
mica schist are wanting, but, commencing with the
Hecla Hook formation, we have mountain limestone on
the promontory opposite Dödmansören, in much-dis-
turbed strata dipping east at 50° and 60° ; again, on the
east side of Safe Haven, perpendicular strata with charac-
teristic ' *producti* ' ; at Gyps Hook more extensive horizontal strata, with shells and nodules of alabaster resembling from a distance strings of pearls ; and, lastly,
on the opposite side of Klaas Billen Bay, grey limestone
and gypsum. The mountain limestone on each side of
Klaas Billen Bay, in common with the triassic mass of
Samieberg, is fringed with a band of hyperite. The
bones of saurians and nautili have been found in the trias.
The traces of the Jurassic age are found along the
south shore of Ice Fjord as folded and horizontal layers

of limestone, clay, slate, and sandstone. Fossils are scarce, but mark the age. Bivalves and indications of cephalopoda are the more common. Miocene formations, in some parts of Spitzbergen reaching the enormous thickness of 1,000 feet, not only rest on the Jurassic beds of the south side of the fjord, but also reappear on the opposite north shore. The north side of the fjord is in reality almost wholly occupied by the descending limits of the great interior icefield. It is broken here and there by ridges of sharp rocks. In the tertiary strata are the impressions of many plants pointing to a former warm or temperate climate. Lastly, there are in Ice Fjord traces of a post-tertiary formation, containing shells of mollusca now extinct on the shores of Spitzbergen, but occurring in the waters of the north of Norway.

Large quantities of ice floating out of Ice Fjord made navigation difficult and slow. We had ample time for gaining a rough idea of the general lie of the harbours on the southern shore. Advent Bay was our destination, but Green Harbour and Coal Haven were successively passed first. In the former we noticed three small sloops at anchor.

I first visited Green Harbour in 1859, and there was then no difficulty in finding plenty of deer. In one valley we picked out thirteen first-class stags, and left many scores of deer unmolested. In 1871 I

T

walked twelve miles through the same glen, and only saw two very shy animals, and a few foot-prints. The wholesale slaughter of the deer, which is making them scarce on all the old hunting-grounds, is carried on, not by the walrus-hunters, who are perfectly justified in getting fresh meat for their crews when possible, but by badly-organised mobs of shark and white-whale fishers, who represent the rabble of Spitzbergen, and range over the shore, and up the valleys, killing, wounding, and harassing the deer with their clumsy fire-arms; and, if they do not fill their sloops with a cargo of deer meat, effectually prevent needy hunters from finding a single beast which can be stalked. There is a curious flat-topped mountain, well seen from this harbour, which is a very apt representation of Noah's ark—at least, of the toy representative of that ancient craft. The name of the bay takes its origin from the peculiar colour of the rocks on the shore.

Coal Haven is less extensive than Green Harbour. I had heard that coal could be got here, a short distance from the shore, and sent a boat off to seek it. But the search was unsuccessful, and all the spoil collected by the crew was some singularly spherical nodules of ferruginous limestone, exactly resembling rusty cannon-shot of various sizes. Some, left ashore as too large to move, were thirty inches in diameter. These

were found half-imbedded in the mural-looking car-
boniferous limestone cliffs, so as to present irresistibly
the idea of large cannon-shot fired into a half-breached
wall. They reminded me of the enormous marble
balls used by the Turks of old, and which are to be
seen still lying about the old castles of Europe and Asia,
in the Dardanelles. Some were so exactly spherical,
and had so much the look of rusty iron, that a sailor,
who had been in the habit of picking up other specimens
for me, stoutly maintained that, if the others were
fossil clams and cockles, these were undoubtedly
fossil cannon-shot!

In spite of a strong tide against us we dropped
anchor in Advent Bay, late in the evening. We had
steamed more than half-way through this great fjord,
and found here a sheltered nook with splendid holding
mud in four fathoms of water.

I contemplated some days' detention here, and the
meteorological instruments were, therefore, got out and
fixed in a hastily-constructed observatory on shore. A
guy, made to represent a sportsman taking aim, was
added to keep the birds from picking at the shining
bulbs of the thermometers. The ship lay about three-
hundred yards from a level plateau, smooth like a well-
kept glacis, and gently sloping away from a line of
earth-work. It was the form taken by the *débris*
carried by a former torrent. The plain was thick

T 2

with a variety of flowers in bloom. The level ground near the shore was chiefly occupied by the golden tufts of a species of cinquefoil (*Potentilla nivea*), by the brilliant purple petals of one of the saxifrages (*S. oppositifolia*) and its allies (*S. cæspitosa* and *S. hyperborea*), and by representatives of the stitchworts (*Stellaria humifusa*) and fly-catchers (*Silene acaulis*). On the drier ground were found specimens of sand-wort (*Arenaria norvegica*), of chickweed (*Cerastium Alpinum*) and of another stitchwort (*Stellaria Edwardsi*). In some places, where the soil appeared too poor to sustain any growth, the eye was dazzled by fields of yellow poppy (*Papaver nudicaule*). On the slopes formed by the *débris* of the cliffs, which had disintegrated to form a very fair soil, the ground was even more closely clad in a variegated robe. The botanist of our party found saxifrages (*S. cernua*), fly-catchers (*Lychnis apetala*), persicaries (*Polygonum viviparum*), the four-angled cassiope (*Cassiope tetragona*), three species of whitlow-grass, the hairy mouse-worts (*Pedicularis hirsuta*), and the kidney-leaved Oxyria (*Oxyria reniformis*), associated with tufts of the Arctic and annual meadow-grasses (*P. Arctica* and *P. annua*).

At four o'clock next morning, having sent away two boats, and directed the crews where to search for reindeer in the grassy valleys which open into Advent Bay, I started myself with a picked crew and a supply of coffee, biscuit, and brandy for two days. I have alluded to the geological features of Ice Fjord. There is no better district for quiet exploration of the botany and natural history of Spitzbergen. The climate has by all explorers been considered the most mild and temperate in the whole country. It is a large inland sea, and stretches its arms of water tempered by the Gulf Stream far up towards the mountains of the interior. Widely-hollowed valleys, having their mouths turned to the sea, are sheltered from the keen winds from the glaciers, and are fully exposed to the warming rays of a sun which does not set for four months. Copious streams, issuing from the melting snows on the high ground, water these grassy valleys, and form scattered lakes covered with water-fowl.

It was one of the great arms of the fjord, which further subdivides into Sassen and Klaas Billen Bays, that we now crossed, and landed at Cape Thorsden. There was not a single seal on the whole of the ice about here, and only a solitary deer, which I shot. We, however, found a dead walrus floating, and, though horribly *high*, we divested him of his skin and blubber —they being nearly as good as those of a newly-killed animal. Recrossing the fjord to Hyperithatt, we bivouacked at the mouth of a neighbouring valley; and, while the men were engaged in collecting drift-wood for a fire, I took a shot-gun and ascended a

neighbouring eminence to look over the valley.
While going up I suddenly found myself face to face
with a stag, coming out of a ravine. I instantly
dropped and waited, as he had not seen me, till he had
walked into another gully; then ran forward and,
meeting him just as he was coming out, killed him
with a charge of No. 4, at about forty yards' distance. I now saw about a dozen deer feeding at
some distance, and, having returned for a rifle, soon
despatched seven out of the number. This was a
pleasant termination to an otherwise blank day; and we
soon cooked a good supper, and passed a comfortable
night, sleeping round a big fire on the beach. We suffered, however, some discomfort from the sun blazing
down on our unprotected faces, and awoke next morning sun-burnt, blistered, and half-blinded. The heat
was considerable, reaching 59° Fahr. in the shade on
deck, and this followed by no cooling eventime. But
the heat we felt was that of the maximum of solar
radiation, ranging on these days from 91° to 106°
Fahr. Camping out always makes one feel ten years
younger. My bo'sen, who was here with me in 1859,
seemed to experience the same feelings. From the
garrulous senility he generally exhibits, ensconced
behind his pipe, sitting splicing and knotting with the
old mate on deck in the afternoons, doling out yarn
after yarn, he had suddenly sprung into life and

activity, ready to lend a hand in all the hard work going on.

I expected to have got some more deer here the next day, but I hate a crowd when hunting, and the unwelcome appearance of two boats' crews of white-whale fishers drove us up the fjord to another promising valley. Here I found six fine stags, and, with five shots from my little 80-bore rifle, killed all but one. The last was at some distance, and on the far side of a roaring and muddy burn, which I did not care to ford.

We again camped out, this time at the head of Sassen Bay, on an extensive flat, through which a moderately-sized, muddy river runs. I examined a great deal of the drift-wood which lay on this low ground, and found unmistakable evidence of its Siberian origin, viz., numerous fragments of boats sewn with birch twigs and withies, half of a Samoyede paddle, and several net-floats, peculiar to the Siberian fishers. They consist of a sixteen-inch quadrant of a billet, thinned at one end, where a hole is made through.

Assuming the chart to be correct, the head of Sassen Bay is only twenty-three miles from Agardh Bay; and as the valley looked very level for a long way up, and the walking good, I should think it would not be very difficult to reach Stor Fjord by walking over. Some interesting excursions of this kind might be made in Spitzbergen: this one, one from Bel Sound to Whale Bay across the mainland, and again from Northern Fjord to Wiide Bay.

Next morning we saw prodigious numbers of white-whales making their way up the bay, and I thought it would not be at all difficult to kill some in the muddy water. There were some thousands of them, blowing, spouting, whistling, and squealing, in the shallows, but after waiting all day for the tide, while the only amusements were eating, sleeping, and gathering shells and flowers, I found I had wasted several hours, for I could not contrive to fire quick enough to shoot them in the head, and firing into their backs with small bullets did little execution. The *Belugæ* were more shy than I ever saw them before; but I question whether the crew considered we had lost a day, for they managed to consume a whole deer, from stem to stern! To catch these fish several sloops usually band together, by which means they can muster some miles of net. These, made of small stuff no thicker than cod-line, they join and stretch across the smaller bays, at particular periods of the tide.

There is some magnificent scenery in Sassen Bay. I was particularly struck by the appearance of one limestone mountain, several miles long. It is all one gigantic, buttressed, mural precipice, from end to end, and has been appropriately named Temple Mountain.

But all our provisions, except flesh, were exhausted, and the boat had a full cargo of one walrus, two seals, and twelve deer; so I reluctantly had to content myself with the distant view of this picturesque object, and commenced the row back to the yacht. With a strong head-wind, this took eleven hours, though the distance traversed was less than thirty miles. I only pulled and rested, hour about, for exercise; but the crew, with the exception of two short rests for coffee and a bite of cold venison, rowed the whole distance without cessation.

When we got on board I found they had been anxious for our safety, and were about to get up steam to search for the boat. They had also shot plenty of deer and a number of geese; and, what was more essential, the engineer had found coal about a mile from the ship.

At first the crew which I sent ashore were able to gather the coal as it lay scattered over the delta of a winter torrent; but twelve bags collected in this way exhausted the supply that was exposed, and led up to a knoll where it lay *in situ*, covered by about a couple of feet of stony *débris*. There was not much difficulty in picking out the coal, but the carrying down of the sacks to the water's edge was serious work, and by no means so popular an amusement as the transport of stags. The way in which these Norwegians carry a

whole deer of 100 or 120 lbs. weight is very clever—
the deer is trussed up and carried like a knapsack.
The porter sits down to get it on his back, but then on
level ground he cannot rise without assistance, and it is
often amusing to watch them loading each other up.
Often they have to trudge five or six miles to the
shore, staggering under such a burden and over ground
which presents every difficulty in its alternate rough,
stony, wet, and boggy nature.

When I paid a visit to the coal-mine I found it
quite a busy scene for a quiet Arctic shore.   The engineer and fireman directed the blasting, my English
hands quarried, while the Norwegians carried the sacks
down the hill.   The old mate, the ' manysidedness ' of
whose character I have so much valued on my various
voyages, was digging away with the rest, though I am
sorry that in the sketch his weather-beaten face is
turned away. All the rest are portraits, and the
reader will notice that Arctic work is not done in the
attractive yacht uniforms known to Cowes and Ryde.

The coal-bed was about three feet thick, and lay
very horizontally between two layers of soft, mud-
coloured limestone.   It was harder to obtain than I
anticipated, because saturated, through all the cracks
and interstices, with water which had frozen into ice
more difficult to break through than the coal itself,
thereby rendering these fissures worse than useless in

Drawn by W. Livesay.

The 'Diana' Coal Mine, Advent Bay.

quarrying.   This is tertiary coal, and is of fair quality,
but contains a good deal of sulphur.   When we began
to burn it, so much water and ice was unavoidably
mixed with it that the engineers had to let it first drain
on deck in the hot sun and then mix it with an equal
bulk of Scotch coal.   Consumed in this way the ten
tons obtained in three days was a useful addition to
the fast-dwindling stock on board.   I learned by experience on this, my first Arctic voyage in a *steamer*, that
it would be far better to have a collier sloop to meet
the yacht in Spitzbergen than suffer the continual
anxiety and harass which the dread of coal running
short gives rise to.   The fear that, at the end of the
season, in a critical situation, the fuel may come to an
end greatly hampers the movements of the whole
summer.

The ' Diana ' coal-mine [1] lies about one English
mile from the wreck of a sloop partly buried in the
shore near the anchorage, and bears from this unmistakeable mark W.½S.   It is on the *far side of the firs
important cairn* arrived at in walking from the wreck,
and is, or was, marked by a large stone cairn which we
built over it.

While the crew were thus actively engaged I made
several excursions ashore, exploring the interesting
geological sections of the thick tertiary formation which

[1] See Appendix.

stretches in almost horizontal layers from Advent Bay to Bel Sound. Gullies and ravines, choked with sharp splinters of rock in many places, led up to level pastures, on which the tracks of deer seen made it only the more tantalizing that none of the animals themselves could be tracked. But these walks were never without interest. Added to the difficulties of progression—in some places over slushy snow and by the borders of treacherous half-frozen streams, in others creeping along the shattered and yielding slopes of *débris*—there was always something to be picked up—the nest of a Richardson's skua (*Larus parasiticus*); a ptarmigan,[1] with her young brood; a truss of that gayest of Arctic flowers, *Polemonium cœruleum*, half-buried in a luxuriant patch of grass; or less portable specimens of conglomerates, chips of rock, and fossils. I came across the remains of fox-traps, and; far up from the sea, the bones of whales.

There is a pond a little in-shore at the end of Advent Bay and about it were large flocks of Brent and Barnacle geese. The latter were moulting, and therefore not able to fly, but they were able to run like hares. I however got a hundred by concealing myself in one direction while I sent round a man to drive them from another. The flesh of these latter is coarse and ill-flavoured compared with the more delicate

---

[1] A species of ptarmigan is found in Spitzbergen, different from the Scotch or Scandinavian bird. They are everywhere very scarce.

meat of the Brent goose, but no one can afford to be
fastidious about fresh meat in Spitzbergen.

A sloop came in one evening, and the captain told
us he had been trying in vain to get up Stour Fjord,
for the ice still stretched across from side to side. He
further brought us the information that one of Captain
Foin's whaling-ships had been burnt at sea, and that
all the walrus-hunting sloops we had seen at Novaya
Zemlya early in the season had returned full to the
Norwegian ports.

I questioned him about the situation of coal in this
neighbourhood; for, far from mining it with the ease I
was led to expect, it was becoming such a laborious
undertaking that the best-disciplined hands were
almost refusing to carry the loads. He replied that
he was told ' it was between Coal Bay and Green
Harbour, in a rocky bluff, and so close to the sea you
might pitch it into a boat;' but, he added, ' he went
there himself, and could not find it.' I got up steam
next morning, and sent a boat off when abreast of the
most likely-looking place; and, although there are
three or four bluffs, they are so perpendicular no snow
could lie on them to conceal the coal-seams; and I am,
therefore, inclined to think the coal must lie farther
inland. We were no more successful in the search at
the place indicated by M. Blomstrand, which he
describes as half a mile before reaching Advent Bay,

and here, he says, ' several beds of coal are to be found
(one two feet thick) in a perpendicular rock of sandstone, which juts out into the sea, almost bare, and
unincumbered by gravel.'   Having given everyone
plenty of run on shore and laden up with fresh meat
and water, I determined to leave Ice Fjord and go
north again.

North Fjord was thus the only part of Ice Fjord I
had not explored, and I had an opportunity of looking
into it on my voyage of 1871. At that time (July 9th)
we cast anchor to the west of a small island off the
nameless point which divides North Fjord into two
narrow arms, and found there was seven fathoms of
water. I then rowed up the east and longer arm
of the bay for at least sixteen or eighteen miles.
We passed very good deer-ground, with plenty of
geese, but neither deer nor even recent tracks were
seen until we got to an immense valley far up on the
east side. Here we saw a few, but although we
divided into two parties and tramped many miles
no one got a shot at them. It looked such promising
ground from the deck that when we started in the
morning I made no doubt of getting a boat-load of
fresh meat round the first corner, and so did not take
any provisions except a little rum, biscuits, and duck-
eggs for lunch. We were away twenty hours, and
but for a shot-gun being luckily in the boat, with

which I killed four eider-drakes and a goose, we should
have been famished. These birds we divided fairly,
cut them in pieces and burned them on hot stones ; for
the faithful old iron baling-ladle, which had served up
many a Spitzbergen stew, was found to be full of holes
at last. There appeared to be many other fine valleys
up this fjord, but want of food compelled us to return to
the yacht, where we found the surgeon and engineer
had been equally unsuccessful, although each had gone
in different directions both days.

Emerging from Ice Fjord on July 20th we found
the ice to have accumulated in great quantity at the
southern entrance of the Foreland Fjord; but I wished
again to see the condition of the pack at the north-
west; and, as forty miles might be saved by going inside
instead of outside of Prince Charles Foreland, we determined to push through. We had not gone far before
a south-west wind enveloped us in dense fog ; and,
banking up the fires, we allowed the gentle breeze to
help us along north. By next morning, more by luck
than good navigation, we had passed the most critical
part of the fjord, where two narrow sand-pits almost
meet and allow only a few inches of water under the
keel, and were opposite English Bay. The picturesque
character of this inlet has not been over-rated by Lord
Dufferin ; in a small compass are some of the most
striking characteristics of Spitzbergen scenery, and
these may be taken in at a glance.

With a slashing south-west breeze we soon reached
the open sea; and, hurrying past King's Bay, the
Seven Glaciers, and Magdalena Bay, we again rounded
Hakluyt's Headland and anxiously sought the limits
of the ice. To our unspeakable disgust it lay just as we
had left it ten days previously. There was no chance
of making any way through it yet, and again were we
doomed to an indefinite period of inaction and hopeless, weary, waiting. A dozen sloops swung at anchor
within the shelter of the Norways. We had had enough
of this already; and, as there is always less fretting for
everyone in action than in idleness, we worked up to
the edge of the pack, and stood off and on, antici-
pating the south-west wind and warm weather would
open a passage before long.

At four next morning Livesay and I started, with a
boat's crew, to reach a distant hill, whence we expected
to get a better view of the ice. We skirted the pack,
which led us to the east side of Red Bay, and thence
rowed to Biscayen Hook, where we went ashore. There
seemed just a possibility of passing the Hook, and after
an hour's laborious cutting and haak-piking to push
the boat through grounded ice-masses we at last came
to a fine lake of open water, across which we sailed
till we again met the ice. Here we landed on Red
Beach—characteristically named from the fragments of
a deep red, argillaceous limestone belonging to the

Hecla Hook formation, which forms the whole soil for miles. Along this broken shore, and across the marshy plain which lies between it and the Red Cliffs, we walked a great many miles, but could see no traces of wild animals. But, arrived at Welcome Point, we soon read in human foot-prints the cause of our fruitless search for game. The pass through this rocky promontory looked as if every individual from each of the sloops had passed and repassed continually for a week; and we were not surprised, on ascending a hill and sweeping the next plain with the telescope, that not an antler was in view. We could, from this point, almost look down Liefde Bay, and in the far distance we could discern Verlegen Hook. Beyond this lay the goal of all our hopes, Hinlopen Straits. But this headland was hopelessly enveloped in ice; indeed, from the low shore below us, as far as eye could reach, the great pack, without a single pond of open water, stretched away to the north and east.

Wiide Bay—which, we had been told, some Norway sloops visit for cargoes of reindeer—was inaccessible; no neighbouring hill offered a better view of the ice; a few flowering plants only repeated the species of Ice Fjord; there was nothing worth sketching; and so, more desponding than ever, we regained the boat, and, some hours later, the yacht.

Some of the sloops had come out from their

anchorage, and for several days we all lay-to at the ice-edge; for, from time to time, the ice perceptibly loosened, small lanes of water appeared here and there; but, although the ice was melting and rotting fast, more of the favourable wind was necessary to drive it off the shore.

But again the wind veered to the north; and, finding that what little ground had been gained in a few days was lost in as many hours, I ordered a course to be made for King's Bay.

It is not the great pack of Polar ice 'heaped up to eternity,' seen by the explorer which makes him restless, irritable, and desponding. This he knows to be one of the great institutions of nature, inseparable from latitude, climate, and other conditions, and one that can only be slightly affected at its outskirts by wind, heat, and current. But it is when he knows there is open water and easy navigation to which he is denied access by a narrow barrier, just persistent enough in its position from day to day to jam the coast around one particular headland. By ice which had set on Verlegen Hook we were kept out of the interesting reaches of Hinlopen Straits, and, probably, of the east coast of Spitzbergen. Tormenting thoughts of Mathilas slaying his hundreds and Tobiesen his thousands filled our minds with envy and inquietude. And, putting sport out of the question, there was more and newer scientific interest here than in the better-known west coast. We learned later, however, that we had much to be thankful for. These skippers, with three others, were beset in Liefde Bay until September 14th, and then got out with difficulty and made sail for Norway. But we had not the comforting reflections of their misfortunes and empty ships when we took what proved to be a final look at this part of the icy seas on July 25th.

My intention was to occupy a few days in another search for coal in King's Bay. The north-east wind, which was unfavourable in every other respect, allowed us to make this short voyage without further trenching on the coal already on board. The breeze was so light that we made but slow progress and had ample time to note the various features of the coast. Magdalena Bay is the only bay I had not entered; and, although only six miles long and two broad, it affords, in a cove at its further end, one of the best anchorages in Spitzbergen.[1] There are four glaciers in Magdalena, which,

[1] The most convenient anchorage in this bay is situated off the south-east end of the first of the glaciers, the marks for which are the centre of the large glacier at the head of the bay in one with the extremity of the low neck of land called the Burying-ground, and the Hanging Glacier in a line with and over the south-east end of the second glacier. Here there are about eleven fathoms water, and vessels must be cautious not to overshoot this spot, as the bottom is rocky in other places, and the water deepens suddenly, particularly towards the second glacier. In approaching this anchorage care must also be taken to avoid Shannon Rock,

from the steepness of the ground over which they creep
towards the sea, present some unusual and interesting
characteristics. The most striking has received the name
of the 'waggon-way.' From a distance the crevasses
running in parallel directions to its length present an
appearance not unlike gigantic cart-ruts. Another
glacier, about 300 feet thick, breaks over the cliff in
two immense steps, and thus has no direct connection
with the sea like most other of the Spitzbergen glaciers.
It is known as the Hanging Glacier.

During even the most favourable month of the
year little dependence can be placed on the weather
in these latitudes. The short run of sixty miles from
the Norways to King's Bay should not take more than
six hours. Owing to fog, variable wind, and heavy
swell, we occupied half as many days, and did not fetch
our former anchorage in King's Bay until late in the
evening of the 27th. The bay had much changed
since our visit a month previously, most of the bay-ice
had floated out, a great deal of the snow had melted
on the hills, and on landing, instead of finding one
monotonous expanse of snow, one trod on a perfect
carpet of verdure, level as a bowling-green for many
square miles. Here were the most harmonious varieties
of colour and shade—the blue petals and leaves of

which is just under water, and lies south a quarter of a mile from a flat
rock, which will be seen on the north side of the bay.

Mertensia maritima contrasting with the gay saxifrages, potentillas, and the naturally-arranged bouquets of *Stellaria Norvegica.*

We had been given to understand that the coal in King's Bay was indicated by a cairn on shore, which we could see from the deck; and, in consequence, we lost many hours in searching for it in this neighbourhood. The cairn really seems to indicate nothing; and the coal, exposed in the old whaling days for 200 or 300 yards, and since mined by the Swedes, lies much further up the bay. We found this coal lying *in situ*, by following up the scattered bits which had been brought down by a stream of water. Its place is indicated in the sketch (Appendix), and it can only be discovered when the snow is off the ground in late summer. Briefly,—pass the small island with an astronomical point indicated by an iron cross, and go up the bed of the first torrent arrived at on the mainland, until the mounds of stony rubbish below the hills are reached. The coal is exposed just below these mounds and in the bed of the torrent.

In four days, by gathering what lay on the surface, and, when this supply was exhausted, quarrying from the beds, we got in all one hundred and twenty bags of coal, or, in other words, the power of steaming 480 additional miles. Looking around at the bleak hills, and treading under foot the scanty and stunted

herbage, it is difficult for an ordinary observer to
picture the former vegetation of Spitzbergen which
now affords this useful fuel.   Yet the Swedes have
found, in the miocene sandstones of this district, undoubted remains of the foliage of the lime, poplar, and
other trees which no longer live beyond the 60th and
70th parallels of latitude.   I myself, in a voyage in 1858,
brought home fossil trees with coal attached which had
been found in beds at Black Point.   With plenty of
willing hands, proper quarrying implements, and a few
wheel-barrows, a steamer might fill up her bunkers
here.   Twelve men ought to get five tons a day.

The British sailors worked well, but I found the
Norwegian division excessively lazy and mutinous.
They seemed to be under the impression that their
position on the ship should be a sinecure when no
fishing was going on, and that I had hired them merely
to slay walruses and bears.   On Sundays I used to
serve out the week's stores to all the crew.   It is a
most hateful business, but I was too experienced a
traveller to entrust it to anyone else.   I knew no one
else would do it properly, and that both waste and
grumbling would follow; as it was, there was only a little
of the latter, which is always inevitable.   All on board
lived like fighting-cocks or colliers—on venison roasted,
boiled, stewed, and baked; on kidneys, roast geese,
roast ducks, loom-soup, duck-soup; and I believe my

dietary was one of unexampled liberality; but the men, knowing there was a large supply of all sorts of provisions on board, laid in in case of wintering, not unnaturally wished to eat them all at once, and would have laid upon me the onus of starving them afterwards. They got literally more best navy-biscuit and peas than they could manage to swallow; and, in addition, tea, coffee, sugar, flour, raisins, meal, rice, pork, unlimited potatoes, and salt-fish; and, lastly, rum whenever they had cold or hard additional work. *Still* they grumbled because they did not get butter, cheese, barley, and molasses besides, because they knew these were not on board.

I had served out rum liberally to the crew, who, I believed, were all equally hard at work quarrying. To the better hands it acted as a salutary stimulus, but the skulking Norwegians drank their allowance without doing enough honest labour to work it off. The consequence was that after dinner one evening we heard such a jabbering for'ard that I thought the ship had caught fire, or that the foreigners had commenced fighting with knives, according to a barbarous custom which obtains in Norway. Soon, however, the six rascals came aft in a body, and demanded to see me or the sailing-master to ask for additional rations; and it was only after a great deal of mutinous conduct and improper language I at length quieted them by reminding them of the black rye-bread, putrid Siberian butter, and obscene seal-flesh which are the staple food of the walrus-hunters' sloops.

August 1st, which, in these latitudes, is the day which divides summer from the short autumn, had now arrived; and as yet I had done but little of what I hoped to have accomplished in sport and geographical research. A gale of wind from the north-west, with snow and rain, had blown all the previous night, and it was not till late in the afternoon that it lulled sufficiently to allow us to leave the bay. The sailing-master and chief harpooner both asserted that the wind at the north must have blown from the same quarter; if so, it was manifestly useless to sail north again. It was with a heavy heart I heard this sentence, but I felt it was only too true. To attain the north-east of Spitzbergen, to sight Gillis Land, and to fight a way along its unknown shores to the extreme north, were not to be parts of our programme this year. Subsequent experiences have shown that such a voyage may be more easily held out as a spur to inexperienced enthusiasts than accomplished in any season, however favourable. Never, I am convinced, will a ship sail from Spitzbergen to the Pole.

Four or five weeks could still be reckoned on for a cruise in Stor Fjord and about the south-east of Spitzbergen, and we lost no time in steaming in this direction. Rounding Quad Hook, we again entered

Foreland Fjord. I was apprehensive that the heavy swell remaining from the late gale might render the channel impassable, by causing a breaking sea; but we got over the shallow part, just south of English Bay, with no difficulty. The soundings are *extremely level*, and I imagine that in a moderately calm and clear day any vessel, even without a pilot, might readily get through by attending to the chart and freely using the lead. But I would not advise anyone to make the attempt earlier than July 18th, for up to that time I have always found more or less ice in the straits. I did once get through on July 13th, and in a dense fog, but I should not care to do it again. We steamed at half-speed all the time, and got into $3\frac{1}{2}$, 3, $2\frac{1}{2}$, $2\frac{1}{4}$, and even $2\frac{1}{8}$ fathoms; so that for about a mile the 'Diana' had only two feet of water under her keel.

I could not now spare time to run into Bel Sound, although I was anxious to make further observations on some glacier movements which have gone on very actively there within the last few years. I had studied the geology, obtained a series of fossils from the limestone formations, and made some notes on what appeared to be proofs of a gradual upheaval of the Spitzbergen Archipelago, in my voyage of 1859. There was at that time a very good anchorage [1] on the north

---

[1] The Dutch whalers used to anchor here, since it was one of the best harbours in Spitzbergen, and plenty of reindeer were always found in the valley now filled up by the glacier.

shore of Van Mijen's Bay, just beyond the island which closes the mouth of this arm of Bel Sound. On each side of the harbour was low, marshy, muddy ground, and at the end of the cove a low glacier of no great extent. In the summer of 1861 this apparently insignificant glacier had descended into the valley, covered the low land, filled the harbour, and protruded into the sea. Professor Nordenskiold, in his visits to Spitzbergen, has made the subject of these glacier movements a particular study. To this newly-formed or developed glacier —we may almost call it his offspring—he has given the name of the ' Frithiof Glacier.' He points out other examples of similar changes—one noticed by Mr. Robert in Recheche Bay—and reminds us that an arm of Horn Sound, marked in the Dutch charts as affording two anchorages, no longer can be found—a large glacier has entirely filled up the valley and water. I entirely agree with the learned Professor that these changes in the direction of the great ice-outlets depend less on an increase of the mass of inland ice than on causes which determine the changes of course in rivers of unfrozen water. But I am hardly prepared to concur as to a similar deviation of the ice having gradually enveloped Edlunds Mount (Stor Fjord) and now threatening to fill up Ginevra Bay, because in my numerous visits to the far recesses of the Stor Fjord I have observed nothing to support such a theory.

But to return to an enquiry into the causes of the phenomena we have *certain proof* of. Only one agency could have determined the course of the Frithiof Glacier, and that seems to be a change in the face of the country over which the viscous mass is spread. That this change of surface is the result of upheaval does not seem difficult to prove. We have raised beaches— three of which I have observed in Ice Fjord, one above another, at heights of about twenty feet; the conversion of islands into peninsulas; and the occurrence of whale-bones, drift-wood, and recent shells at many feet above the sea-level all as evidence. In 1859 I brought home from Bel Sound part of the vertebra and other fragments of the bones of whales, which had been found half a mile from the sea, and one hundred feet above its present level. Not far from the situation of these remains, at a height of eighty feet above the sea, I got the entire cranium of a small white whale, and at lesser heights other bones of the right whale, more or less buried in the soil. In Walter Thymen's Straits I found part of the lower jaw of a very large whale ; and at the Thousand Isles and elsewhere I have seen great quantities of whale-bones (in one place eleven enormous jaw-bones), associated with drift-wood, and scattered about the slopes from the sea-level to a height of forty feet. Those bones lying high above the sea-level were invariably more decayed and moss-grown

than those lower down. On one of these islands I
observed a further most interesting proof of its elevation. This was a sort of trench or furrow, about one
hundred yards long, three or four feet deep, and four
feet broad, which was ploughed up amongst the
boulders. It was about twenty feet above the sea-level,
and extended from north-east to south-west, being
exactly the line in which the current-borne ice travels
at the present day; so that I presume there is no doubt
it must have been caused by the passage of a heavy
iceberg, with a rock embedded in its bottom, while
the island lay under water.

M. Malgrem has also found whale-bones at Förvex-
lings Point one hundred feet above the sea-level; and
fossil-shells of species still occurring on the shores of
Norway have been gathered by Keilhau one hundred
feet above the sea, at Whale-fish Point; and at an equal
height by Mr. Robert on the shore in Bel Sound; and
by M. Malgrem in Advent Bay, Duym Point, and one
hundred and fifty feet above the sea in Safe Haven.
There is also in the Museum of the Geological Society
a specimen of the shell of *Buccinum glaciale* which I
obtained from an elevation between 400 and 500 feet,
and nearly two miles from the shore in Bel Sound.

Again, Professor Nordenskiold repeatedly found
whale-bones and moss-covered drift-wood at varying
heights above that of high-tide on the islands of north

Spitzbergen and the Seven Islands.   He also discovered at Cape Loven, on the north coast of North-east Land, a sandbank, in which, at the height of ten or fifteen feet above the present level of the sea, were found some hafts of whale-harpoons, oars of a different shape from those at present employed by the Norwegian sea-horse hunters, and other remains from the time the Dutch whalers used to frequent these regions.

Now, could an approximation to the age of these whale-bones be in any way arrived at, they would give some chronological data for determining the time which the land has been emerging from the sea and attaining its present level.   It is, perhaps, impossible to judge of the length of time which such enormous bones may endure in a climate like this, where they are bound up in ice for eight or nine months out of the twelve ; but, allowing—what I am disposed to consider as near an estimate as can be made—four hundred years for bones lying at an elevation of forty feet (the highest at which I have found entire skeletons), and adding twelve feet of water for the whale to have floated in when he died there, we shall arrive at thirteen feet per century as the rate of elevation.

From the position of the eleven jaw-bones which I have mentioned, and from the fact of so many lying together in a slight hollow, I am inclined to believe that these are the remains of whales killed by man, and that they were towed into this hollow—*then a shallow bay*—for the purpose of being flensed. We learn from the accounts of the early whale-fishers that their usual practice was to flense their whales in the bays; and, in fact, that the whales were so abundant close to the shore that the ships did not require to leave their anchorage to hunt them. It was about the year 1650 that the whale-fishery *in the bays* of Spitzbergen was in its prime. Thus, supposing these whales to have been killed in that bay two hundred years ago, allowing three fathoms (the minimum) for the ships to have anchored in, and adding the ten feet which the bones are now above the sea-level, we have twenty-eight feet of elevation in two hundred years, or very nearly the same rate arrived at by the other calculation.

The sealers who frequent the coast of Spitzbergen invariably speak of the ' sea going back from the shore;' and it is a general belief among them that this shallowing of the water, more than the persecution of man, has driven the right whale from the Spitzbergen seas.

If my conclusions are correct these speculations of the gradual upheaval of Spitzbergen are interesting, taken in conjunction with the ascertained phenomena of the west coast of Norway, where Sir Charles Lyell has shown to demonstration that the rise is four feet per century. This is rather less than a third of the

rate of elevation I assume for Spitzbergen, but some
connection between the two is suggested by our knowledge that there is no great depth of sea between Spitzbergen and Norway (nowhere 300 fathoms), although
to the west of the former country the lead sinks suddenly to 1,000 and 1,500 fathoms.

Steaming and sailing as the wind was favourable or
fell, we got round to the mouth of Stor Fjord or
Wybe Jans Water—that great arm of the sea separating
Edge Land and Barentz Land from the mainland of
Spitzbergen. It was known to the Dutch and imperfectly
charted by them, but very little was known of it till
my voyage of 1858. It is not navigable till late in
July and August, for the warm Gulf Stream is hardly
felt save at its entrance. The water here late in
autumn is usually about 34° Fahr. South Cape, therefore, separates two widely-different climates—that of
East and West Spitzbergen. This fact is not better
illustrated by the violent winds of the east compared
with the genial calms of the west than by contrast of
the flora in these divisions of the country. So desolate
is the former district that although often ashore we
were unable to find any new species of plants not obtained in the west, and many found in Ice Fjord were
absent here. Still, that there is abundance of a coarse
vegetation is manifest from the number of reindeer
which feed on the east side of the fjord. All the west

side of the fjord, and, indeed, round South Cape as far as Bel Sound, is worthless for purposes of sport. From Ginevra Bay to South Cape the coast, even late in summer, is blocked with bay-ice, and when this has broken away there is little but glacier and rocks to be seen. There are anchorages at Lamont Island, Mohn Bay, Duner Bay, and Fox Nose, and the coast in the neighbourhood of these points has lately been explored by Count Heuglin (1870).

There was no ice now (August 3rd) at South Cape, nor does it usually adhere to the point later than June, but on stretching across the fjord to Whale-fish Point we found heavy ice filling up Deeva Bay and enveloping the Thousand Isles. Half-moon Island, Hope Island, and Ryke Yse Islands, still farther to the east, were presumably unapproachable—very contrary to my experience of 1859, when I hunted the whole of July and the greater part of August to the eastward of Whale-fish Point.

This being the state of things there was no alternative but to push up Stor Fjord and see whether it were possible to get through Ginevra Bay and Hell Sound, and so to the east coast, where I was convinced that (the conditions being similar) open water like that in the Kara Sea must exist, although the ordinary avenues to it were closed.

In threading our way through mazes of very open

Seals on Ice.

ice, we saw a good many large seals, of which I shot several. One of the beasts measured 9 feet long, and had a girth of 6 feet 10 inches. There were many krangs of seals on the floating ice, and during the day we overtook three sloops, which had evidently been having a fine time of it by themselves, fishing in this fjord ever since the ice had loosened. The calm, bright, sunny day changed towards evening; the sky became overcast, and it began to blow hard from west-north-west.

We ran up the fjord, under reefed foresail, stay-sail, and mizen, until midnight, when we sighted the fast-ice extending right across the fjord from Forvex-ling Head to the west side. In this contracted reach of Stor Fjord—frowned on from the north and west by an uninterrupted series of glaciers over which the pre-vailing winds pass, far from the influence of any warm streams—the ice holds its own nearly the whole year through. At the end of August it sometimes clears, but then new ice also begins to form, and it is quickly blocked again. In 1859 I found it more open at the end of August, but Heuglin, at the same time of the year in 1870, got no farther than Forvexling Head in his ship, and to the mouth of Hell Sound in a boat. I had done the same with less obstruction from ice, and was now determined to leave the attempt to get eastward through the sound for a few days only, while we occupied the time farther down the fjord.

My experience since in 1871, when I was here as early as July 13th, has convinced me that unless Ginevra Bay is wholly free from ice it is of no advantage that Forvexling Head can be passed; for the south and east coasts of the bay are so fringed with rocks and long reefs that even should there be an open land-water available for boat navigation it would be quite impracticable for a ship to reach Hell Sound on her way to the eastward. My experience of 1871 was not confined to the condition of ice hereabouts, as it included a very unpleasant and intimate acquaintance with the rocks about the bare Anderson Island, on July 17th of that year. We had already had some narrow escapes from rocks not marked in the charts— one four or five miles north-west of the harbour at Whale Point, where the Russian hut is, and apparently a prolongation of the reef of small islands lying north of this spot—and again from a horrible group of rocks like a herd of walruses, indicated, but not clearly laid down, on some of the charts. They lie in reality about the middle of the fjord, and bear north-west (Mag.) from Whale Point about ten miles off. We had pushed into the fjord through a barrier of very heavy ice; and, finding Disco Bay and Walter Thymen's Straits completely blocked, were steaming merrily along on the west side of the fjord to the anchorage at Anderson Island. On rounding a black haystack-looking rock three or four miles to the west of the island we went full smash on a sunken rock, not marked on any chart—a sort of crown of hyperite not bigger than a schooner itself, bearing west-north-west (Mag.) from the haystack rock. It was nearly high tide and ebbing—the worst possible time for such a catastrophe—when we struck. The force with which we were going carried the yacht well up on the rocks, and she immediately heeled over to port as if she were stove in and filling. 'Lower away the boats!' was the immediate order of the sagacious and experienced old mate, who was in charge of the deck; for there was every fear of her heeling over and sinking in deep water—a calamity which would only be assisted by the weight of the boats. However, it was very soon evident that she was hard and fast for at least one tide; so we set to work and lightened her as much as possible by sending two boat-loads of coal and other heavy things to Anderson's Island, filling three more boatfuls alongside and lashing the spare spars together in a raft alongside. We next lowered the topsail yards on deck, and, moving the cables right away aft, finally got two kedge anchors and warps laid out astern. One consolation was that the carpenter reported no water to speak of in the well—

showing that even the force with which we had struck
had not burst in her stout planking. All this occupied
ten hours of hard, sleepless, *well rummed* work for all
hands, with the ship lying nearly on her beam ends;
and then we anxiously waited for high tide. When
this arrived we backed the screw astern, and hove
taut on both hawsers, one at the capstan and the
other at the winch; but the vessel would not budge,
and, the capstan hawser breaking, it was all up for
this tide. At midnight I sent three more boatfuls of
coal to the haystack rock and hove ten tons overboard, and, giving the sailing-master full instructions
what to do if the yacht broke up, I went ashore with
the surgeon and one of the engineers to see what
resources the shore would afford if we lost the vessel.
The day was warm and calm, and we walked through
the valley and across the high level ground to where
we could see into Walter Thymen's Straits. It was
full of drift-ice, continuous with that in Disco Bay.
Abundant fresh spoor of deer were seen everywhere,
but the heat had probably driven these animals up
to a high snow-covered plateau, where we could
neither see nor follow them. The precarious condition
in which we had left the yacht haunted us the whole
day, and we resumed the march back, anxious to find
whether we were walking homewards or only to
pick up splinters of the wreck on the strand. But

the ship lay just as we had left her; and, lighting a roaring fire of dry drift-wood we encamped for the night on Anderson's Island, and sat down to a meagre supper of ship-biscuit and ducks' eggs. A strong north-east wind now came on, and we sat awake, anxiously looking at the ship with a telescope. I feared the swell would knock her bottom in, but about 1.30 A.M., to our great relief, we saw her move off under sail, and then, knowing all was right, tired out with two nights and a day's hard labour and anxiety, I went sound asleep on a mossy bank for several hours. On awakening we found the yacht snug at anchor behind the island; and, going down to the boat, rowed off and got on board just in time to avoid a squall, which filled and fairly sank one of the coal-laden boats alongside. The yacht had been got off the rock by lightening the starboard side, and so— with the assistance of the wind acting on the head-sails—rolling her bodily over to port. I immediately ordered a second anchor down, as the gale still increased; and all hands, except an 'anchor-watch,' turned in, thoroughly exhausted. On examination of the tanks afterwards a good deal of oil was found to have escaped, but that and the loss of the coals thrown away was a trivial affair when we had saved the ship.

Such was one of my latest Arctic adventures; but, to return to the general narrative, Walter Thymen's

Straits, besides being said to be too shallow and rocky
to admit a large vessel, was unapproachable on
account of packed ice; so we continued our course
down Stor Fjord to Whale-fish Point. Here the
ice had opened very much, and it now appeared possible to work in towards the Thousand Isles by steaming through the interstices of the floating ice.

But we had hardly gone ten miles next morning,
through close and dangerous windings, when we found
it impossible to proceed farther. We were about two
miles from the north-easternmost of the Thousand
Isles, and saw smoke arising from the island. We
concluded a party from some sloop were encamping
there in order to shoot seals in the neighbourhood,
and were making a rough tent, constructed of harpoons
and a boat-sail, the basis of operations. There were
four sloops in sight; one of these we had previously
met with at the north. We learned from her crew that
she had just arrived from the Norways, where the ice
had come down in greater quantity than ever. All
the other sloops had left that part of the seas, so that
we had evidently lost nothing by coming away.

It was very tantalising we could not push farther
in, for it was east of this I had such unwonted good
sport in 1859. A sketch of our proceedings during
one afternoon will give the reader an idea of what
sport might be met with in Spitzbergen fifteen years ago.

We first found five good bull-walruses on a piece
of ice; four were sound asleep with their sterns
towards us, the remaining villain seemed to be acting
as sentry, but permitted us to approach within about
thirty yards, when he snorted and began to kick his
sleeping companions to arouse them. I had covered
the sentinel's head, determined that he should pay for
his alertness with his life, when suddenly a bull with
much better tusks lifted his head above the sentinel's
back; so, quickly changing my aim, I shot this other
bull through the head, and he tumbled forward on the
ice, so dead that he lay with his head doubled under
him, and the point of his tusks thrust into his stomach.
The rest then escaped. In about an hour we found
a solitary old bull asleep on a very small piece of ice;
he lay on his side with his back to leeward—the best
possible position for either shooting or harpooning a
walrus. I felt so certain of this one that I resolved
not to fire, but to allow the harpoon to do the business.
When we got, however, to ten or twelve yards' distance
the brain of the walrus was so beautifully developed
I could not resist the temptation of firing, and I accordingly shot him through the back of the head; but, to
my unspeakable vexation and disgust, in the act of
dying he gave a convulsive half-turn backwards, and,
the edge of the ice giving way beneath him, he sank
like a shot, less than a second before the harpoon

swished into the water after him. This mishap was
my own fault, and I bitterly anathematized my own
impatient folly in firing when it was not the least
necessary. We next found in succession three large
seals, and I killed them all. We secured two, but lost
the third from the edge of the ice giving way, as it
had done with the walrus. After rowing for an hour
or two more we found two lots of walruses on ice
about an English mile apart; one lot consisted of four
and the other of five—all bulls of the first magnitude.
We took the former first; and, by taking advantage of a
sort of screen of ice, we got within six yards of the *partie
carrée* without their perceiving us. They lay very
favourably, two being close together, and the other two
about five yards to the left. I silently motioned to Christian to take those to the right, and like lightning he
darted one harpoon and thrust the other. At the sound
of the harpoons my two particular friends, to the left,
raised themselves on the ice to see what was going on;
and the instant they did so I took them quickly, right
and left, on the sides of their heads, and they tumbled
lifeless on the ice, one falling across the body of the
other. 'Hurrah,' thought I, ' here is luck at last; four
of the biggest bulls in Spitzbergen all secured at one
stalk.' Nothing could have been more complete and
satisfactory. But my exultation was a little premature,
for one of the harpooned walruses was selfish enough

to spoil this very pretty thing by breaking loose and escaping. As we afterwards found, this had happened through the line having got twisted round the animal's body, and cutting itself against the edge of the harpoon. I then finished off the remaining 'fast' one by shooting him, in doing which I unfortunately smashed the fore part of his head, and spoiled a very fine pair of long white tusks. After flensing these victims it was necessary to throw out all the firewood to make room for them, and yet the boat was up to the thwarts with the spoil. We then turned our attention to the troop of five, which were still in sight about a mile off. They lay upon a rather large sloping iceberg. We had no cover, and we were obliged to approach at the high side of the berg to get the wind; so that when we got to about forty yards the walruses took the alarm and began to move. I again shot a magnificent bull, with fine tusks, through the head, but, unluckily, not quite in the fatal spot. He fell on the ice, but succeeded in regaining his feet, and began to stagger slowly down the slope after the others, who had by this time all gained the sea. The rowers ran the boat against the ice, and Christian and I jumped out and ran down the sloping ice to intercept the walrus. Not being able to see the head, I fired an unavailing shot into his shoulder; and Christian, getting to the brink of the ice just as the walrus was staggering in, thrust the harpoon into his posteriors; the line ran to the end, and then, the boat being fast against the ice, it snapped like a thread and the walrus was lost. This was an old much-used line, and had been clumsily knotted at a weak part; but, probably, under the circumstances any line would have given way in like manner. We then found three large bulls, two of which were asleep, but the third, acting as look-out, kicked his friends awake on our approaching to forty or fifty yards' distance. I shot the best one on the side of the head with two barrels, but all three got into the water, the wounded one bleeding profusely. We followed them for six or seven dives, in hopes of securing this one; but, although he was very sick and faint, the others kept close to him, and always gave him timely notice when to dive. At last I shot the two sound ones through the head, one after the other; but there was now a considerable sea running, and the boat was so heavy with skins and blubber that they both sank before we could harpoon them. After his protectors were gone I made sure of getting the one first wounded; but, after getting close to him once or twice more, we lost sight of him at last amongst the ice.

No doubt, such sport may still be enjoyed if one could reach the retreats of the walrus; but each year the walrus recedes to regions more and more in-accessible to ships. I have no doubt that in a few years walrus-hunting, from being no longer remunerative, will cease as a branch of industry for the Norwegian seamen; and it is unlikely that, even in such a case, they will ever return in numbers to their old haunts.

From the rust of the tanks the drinking-water had become the colour of tonic medicine. I have no doubt its therapeutic effects were similar; but, as none of us lacked appetite or energy, we anchored to a large iceberg in order to get a supply of fresh water. This is usually the source of fresh water in the Arctic regions, but it is necessary to test it with a solution of nitrate of silver to ascertain its purity from sea-salt, for under certain conditions the ponds on the iceberg are brackish and unfit for use.

We remained anchored to the ice for the night. It was one of the calm, still evenings experienced when lying far in among the ice, but a red sky between long lines of stratus clouds gave almost an appearance of sunset, and heralded a time, not far distant, when the setting sun would at last break the long Arctic day. Each evening grew more chilly; and for the first time, on this August 7th, ice formed in thin crystals over a sea whose temperature was 31° Fahr. From the deck of the yacht as we lay at anchor I could see High Rock Island, the scene of one of the most successful walrus *battues* I ever heard of.

This island had long been a celebrated place for walruses going ashore, and great numbers had been killed upon it at different times in bygone years. In August 1852 two small sloops sailing in company approached the island, and discovered a herd of walruses, numbering many thousands, reposing on it. Four boats' crews, sixteen men, proceeded with spears to the attack. One great mass of the walruses lay in a sandy bay, with rocks enclosing it on each side, and on a little mossy flat above the bay, but to which the bay formed the only convenient access for such unwieldy animals. Many hundreds lay on other parts of the island at a little distance. The boat landed a short distance off, so as not to frighten them; and the sixteen men, creeping along shore, got between the sea and the bay full of walruses, and immediately commenced stabbing the animals next them. The walrus, although so active and fierce in the water, is very unwieldy and helpless on shore; and those in front soon succumbed to the lances of their assailants. The passage to the shore soon got so blocked up with the dead and dying that the unfortunate brutes behind could not pass the barricade of carcases. Considering that every thrust of a lance was worth twenty dollars, the scene must have been one of terrific excitement to men who had very few or no dollars at all; and my informant's eyes sparkled as he related the details.

He said the walruses were at their mercy, and they slew, and stabbed, and slaughtered, and butchered, and murdered until most of their lances were rendered useless, and themselves drenched with blood and exhausted with fatigue. They went on board their vessels, ground their lances, had their dinners, and then returned to their sanguinary work; nor did they cry 'Hold! enough!' until they had killed *nine hundred* walruses; and yet so fearless or so lethargic were the animals that many hundreds more remained sluggishly lying on other parts of the island at no great distance. Their two small sloops, already partially loaded, could only carry away a very small portion of the spoil; but they reckoned on being able to return from Hammerfest with other vessels to secure the remainder. But at their return they were most justly punished for their wanton slaughter of these useful animals by finding the island surrounded by many miles of heavy and impenetrable drift-ice, which baffled all attempts to get at their walruses!

In their hurry they had not even extracted all the tusks, which thenceforth became anybody's property; and Daniel Danielson told me he happened to be one of the first to revisit the island next season, and that he cut out about a hundred pair of tusks. The skins and blubber were quite useless by that time and thus several hundred walruses were destroyed without benefit to anybody.

When I visited this island six years afterwards, there still remained abundant testimony to corroborate the truth of the story. The smell was perceptible at several miles' distance, and on landing we found the carcases lying as I have described them, and in one place two or three deep. The skin and flesh of many remained tolerably entire, notwithstanding the ravages of bears, foxes, and gulls. So many walruses had been killed on this island on that and previous occasions that a ship might easily load up with *bones* there, and it grieved me, as an agriculturist, to see the materials of so much bone-dust lying unappropriated. I believe the walruses have never again visited the island—on account of the overpowering smell of the remains of their slaughtered kindred.

Many people have been left to perish miserably on these bleak and desert islands, by accidents arising from fog, ice, currents, and *brandy*. One notable case, of a somewhat ludicrous character, but which might have ended very tragically, took place twenty years ago on an island, which I have visited, some thirty miles from High Rock. A great many walruses had been killed there the previous season, and a small sloop from Hammerfest came to the island for the chance of finding bears feeding on the carcases. They found a perfect flock of these animals—upwards of fifty—congregated on the island, holding a sort of carnival on the remains of the walruses. The crew of the vessel consisted, as usual, of ten men, of whom the skyppar and seven others landed to attack the bears, after having anchored their sloop, securely as they thought, to a grounded iceberg, close to the island.

They had a most successful hunt, and killed more than twenty of the bears, the rest making good their escape to sea. But the chase occupied many hours, and meantime the two ship-keepers, who had received strict injunctions to keep a good look-out, took advantage of the captain's absence to institute a search for a cask of brandy known to be kept in the cabin—merely with the harmless intention of smelling it, of course; but from smelling they not unnaturally got to tasting, and from tasting they soon became hopelessly drunk.

While they were in this happy state of oblivion to bears, icebergs, and things in general, one of the sudden dense fogs of the north came on, the tide rose, the iceberg floated, and in a few minutes it, along with the sloop, were out of sight of the island and drifting away in the fog. The hunting party had thought nothing of the fog, as they believed the iceberg to be fast; so when they had flensed all their bears they rowed round to where they had left the sloop, and were mightily disconcerted at seeing neither sloop nor iceberg. They

shouted and fired signals, and rowed all round and out
to sea until they got so bewildered they lost sight of
the island too.   However, after a great deal of trouble
they found the island again, and waited upon it for
several days, expecting that when the weather cleared
the sloop would return.   The fog cleared off, but, no
sloop appearing, there stared them in the face the alternatives of passing a winter of starvation and almost
certain death on the island, or of attempting to cross in
a small boat the stormy 480 miles of sea which divided
them from Norway.

Like bold fellows, they chose the latter chance for
their lives; and, abandoning one [1] of their boats on the
island, the whole eight got into the other one, with as
much bear-meat as they could stow, and rowed for
dear life to the south.   Four rowed, while the rest lay
down in the bottom of the boat; and, being provi-
dentially blessed with fine weather, they actually succeeded in reaching the coast of Finmarken in about
eight days' time, but, as may be supposed, half dead
with hunger, thirst, and fatigue.   The two jolly
fellows in the sloop kept themselves gloriously
drunk, and floated about at the mercy of the winds
and the ice for many days; but instead of going
to the bottom they had the undeserved good luck to

[1] I saw this boat myself on the island, turned bottom up, with all
her oars, lances, harpoons, &c., just as they had been left five years
before.

fall in with one of the other sealers, which, observing
the helpless condition of the sloop, and imagining her
to be abandoned, sent a boat's crew on board to take
possession; but, finding the two worthies asleep in close
proximity to their beloved cask, they were cruel and
hard-hearted enough to throw the latter overboard, and
then lent them a mate and two men to assist them to
navigate the vessel to Hammerfest, where we may form
some idea of the kind of reception they met with from
their justly-exasperated comrades and the owners of
the vessel.

The drift-ice still streamed in from the eastward;
every effort to push through it was unsuccessful, even
twenty miles south of Whale-fish Point; and, free from
the entanglement of the Thousand Isles, the pack was
perfectly impenetrable, and the question whether we
should return to Novaya Zemlya was seriously debated.

On August 10th we again steamed towards the
land, and dropped anchor in ten fathoms of water off a
conical hill at the north end of a large glacier on the
west side of Deeva bay. The low hills which border
this fjord have a very strong resemblance to the long,
dreary ranges of limestone hills which hem in the
valley of the Nile on both sides from Cairo to the
Cataracts; and this similarity exists both in their size,
shape, slope, and general aspect (ice and snow aside) as
well as in the solitude and almost total absence of life

Y

and vegetation. The glacier lies about half-way up this west side, and, extending almost into the water, pushes before it a huge moraine of mud and *débris*, the base of which is washed by the sea, rendering the latter quite shallow and muddy for several miles round. It is wonderful to observe how insignificant even mountains of solid rock are, compared with the enormous power of glacier action. They appear to melt and crumble into mud and dust like mole-hills, in the gigantic grasp of the 'ice-rivers.' Professor Nordenskiold remarks on this subject that 'wherever a glacier advances it crushes the solid rock, and consequently contributes to the destruction of one of the most important conditions of its own existence, namely, rocks or mountains that rise above the snow-line; so that, should no other influences counteract the levelling action of the glaciers, it might be expected that the whole of Spitzbergen would, within a very short period, geologically speaking, form one vast lowland, free from ice in the summer. The mighty denudation at Spitzbergen is, however, counterbalanced, to a considerable degree, by the rapidity with which the land is rising—a rapidity which seems far to exceed that of the upheaval of land in most other parts.'

All over the Highlands of Scotland I have noticed vast accumulations of earth and gravel, the origin of which completely puzzled me for a long time; but

after having seen the enormous existing glaciers of Spitzbergen I have no longer any hesitation in believing
that these mounds are the lateral and terminal moraines
of ancient glaciers, which filled the glens in times when
the climate and aspect of Scotland must have been very
analogous to that of Spitzbergen at the present day ;
when, perhaps, the seal [1] and the walrus sunned themselves (fearless of harpoons and conical bullets) on
fields of ice, drifting about amongst a ' wintry archipelago ' of barren islands, and sought their food on
submarine banks, now fertile land rented at five pounds
an acre. The shells, those insignificant but yet powerful
exponents of the past, show that this is more than mere
hypothesis, for many of the shells of mollusca now in-
habiting the Arctic seas, although no longer found alive
in British waters, are dug up in large quantities in the
pleistocene beds in some parts of Scotland, and particularly in my own immediate neighbourhood, at Ballina-
kielly Bay in the island of Bute.

Snow had fallen during the night, and it was anything but a pleasant day when I went on deck ; but in
Arctic wanderings, where the weather is the worst in the
world, no one stops for it or cowers over a cabin fire
when there is anything to be done.   I started in a boat
at noon, and, expecting to see many large seals, crossed

---

[1] The interesting conclusions of Professor Turner seem to confirm
these speculations.

over to the other side of the fjord. A few head of
game were seen, but they lay unapproachable on fast-
ice. I landed on the long, low island lying athwart
the bay, and fell into a fit of gloomy reflection. Since
I had hunted this bay—every spot of which I remembered so well—ten years exactly had gone by, ten
years of the cream and flower of my life, and what had
I seen since to equal the sport which had marked every
creek and shallow and rock with the red cross of a kill?
Yachting and shooting in Greece, Turkey, and Africa;
salmon-fishing on the dreary coast of Labrador; the
West Indies, Paris, Rome, Naples; the hot pavement
of Pall Mall, and pigeon-shooting at Wormwood
Scrubs, autumns and winters on the brown moors of
my own country; contested elections; three years in
Parliament, had filled up these ten years. Would I
had come here every year instead! But, alas, there is
no longer occupation for a gentleman sportsman; the
country is quite hunted out; there are no longer
walruses, bears, or even seals.

While indulging in this pleasant train of thought a
faint bellowing roar was heard in the distance. We all
pricked up our ears. ' Bear ! ' said Bill; ' Hvalrus ! ' said
the Norwegians. We rowed in the direction the
sounds came from, and soon discovered a troop of walruses on an ice-cake. Nine enormous bulls lay as close
as they could pack, and, with the exception of the in-

variable sentinel, all were asleep with their tails towards us. The cowardly beast on watch jumped into the water at once, without giving his friends the usual notice; but the splash awoke them, and ere we could get to harpooning distance all began to move; but before they reached the water I killed the best by a shot through the back of the head, and he lay in the same position as he fell when we returned after a half-hour's chase of the troop. Two more troops were seen. The long island, to the north of which we had found these walruses, appeared to afford a good anchorage, but there are some bad reefs, dry at low water, lying about south-west of the west end of the island. A sloop lying here had evidently killed a good many seals, as many of the krangs were floating about.

When I got back late to the yacht I found the doctor, who had been floundering about in a marsh ashore in search of the great auk, and a party who had gone along the west side of the fjord to the end, had returned. The latter brought some geese and goslings killed in the water, and had seen a flock of eider-ducks, some four hundred strong, which dived to avoid them when their line of flight was broken by the boat's approach. Their description of a small bight of shallow water and its muddy extremity reminded me that it was the scene of one of my most exciting hunts of bygone years.

One night in 1859 we had only been in bed two hours when the watch on deck aroused us and said they had seen three bears going along the western shore of the fjord. Tired and sleepy as we were, this report brought us on deck immediately; the bears, by this time, however, had got out of sight to the north. The watch said that through the glass they appeared to be an old bear with two young ones; and from the direction in which they were proceeding I imagined they were scenting their way up to the carcase of an unlucky individual of their race who had fallen a victim to my rifle a few hours before. A bitterly cold north wind was blowing, and a very strong tide was running down the fjord, and this, by carrying the sloop before it, was the reason of our losing sight of the bears so soon. As we felt certain they would follow the shore we had no doubt of falling in with them speedily, and we accordingly manned a boat and pushed off in pursuit. During three or four hours since I had left the edge of the fast-ice, it had all become loose, and was floating, nearly entire, down the fjord with the tide. It was an unbroken sheet, perfectly level and smooth, and could not have had an area of less than sixteen or twenty square miles; but, as the fjord increased in width towards its outer end, there was plenty of room for the boat to pass up between the shore and the sheet of ice. A narrow strip of fast-ice still remained attached to the shore all along, where the shallowness of the water had prevented it from floating. After a row of several miles along the shore, against a very swift ebb tide, we at last discovered the bears seated on this strip of land-ice. We then agreed that my companion, Lord David Kennedy, should get out, and, by running, try to cut them off from the hills; while I should continue in the boat, and row as fast as possible up the edge of this ice in case they should take to the water. We got within five hundred yards of the bears before they noticed us. The old one stood up on her hind legs like a dancing bear, to have a good look at the boat, and a moment's inspection seemed to convince her that it was time to be off. She set off at the top of her speed, with the two cubs at her heels, along the smooth surface of the ice. Kennedy, although an excellent runner, could not keep up with them, so he got into the boat again, and we rowed with might and main to keep in sight of the bears; but they got far ahead of us, and, the weather being rather thick, they were nearly out of sight, and we began to think they had beat us, when luckily they got to the end of the strip of ice. Before them lay a great expanse of soft mud, intersected with numerous little channels of water and with much rough ice left by the tide aground amongst it. This seemed to embarrass them very much, as the cubs could not jump over the channels, and the old bear appeared to be getting very anxious and uneasy, but she showed great patience and forbearance, always waiting after she had jumped over a channel until the cubs swam across, and affectionately assisting them to clamber up the steep sides of the icy places. Nevertheless, the mixture of sticky mud, rough ice, and half-frozen water, soon reduced the unhappy 'jungers' to a pitiable state of distress, and we heard them growling plaintively, as if upbraiding their mother for dragging them through such a disagreeable place.

We had got the boat into a long, narrow channel amongst the mud, which contained water enough to float her, and were gaining rapidly on the bears when suddenly the boat ran hard aground, and not an inch farther would she go. This seemed as if it would turn the fate of the day in favour of the bears, as we did not think it possible to overtake them on foot over the mud; but there still remained the chance of a long shot, as the boat had grounded within about two hundred yards of the bears. Kennedy fired and struck the old bear in the back, completely paralysing her. We then scrambled through the icy mud up to where she lay and despatched her. The cubs, quite black with mud and shivering with cold, lay upon the body of their mother, growling viciously, and would not allow us to touch them, until the men, bringing a couple of walrus-lines from the boat, threw nooses over their heads and secured them by coupling them together like a brace of dogs. They were about the size of large dogs, and no sooner did they feel themselves fast than, quite regardless of our presence, they began a furious combat with one another, and rolled about in the mud, biting, struggling, and roaring, until they were quite exhausted.

This old bear had sacrificed her life to her cubs, as she could have escaped without difficulty if she had not so magnanimously remained with them; but I am sorry to have to record the most horrible case of filial ingratitude that ever came under my observation. When we proceeded to open the old bear for the purpose of skinning her, the two young demons of cubs, having now, by a good mutual worrying, settled their differences with one another, began to devour their unfortunate and too devoted parent, and actually made a hearty meal off her smoking entrails. I little thought, when trying to tame and 'lick into shape' these troublesome orphans, or when consigning them to the Director of the Jardin des Plantes, how tragical and historical was their destiny. I had the satisfaction of seeing them in their French home some months after they left my care. They were considerably grown, but their amiable dispositions had not been improved by confinement in one of the warm, dry dens

constructed for the tropical carnivoræ. But a worse
fate awaited them, for when the Germans narrowed
each day their iron girdle around the city we
learned that the hungry Parisians, in their extremity, had fallen tooth and nail upon the zoological
gardens ; and, no doubt, there was many a less choice
morceau rifled from the collection than the cutlets of
my late captives.

Five days and nights were now occupied in reaching
across from the west side of Deeva Bay round Black
Point. At one time sudden fog or a snow-storm kept us
hove-to, at another current and floating ice baffled our
efforts ; but we at last dropped anchor in the spacious bay
now known as Diana Bay, inside of Half-moon Island.
Care should be taken to identify this, and only my
previous knowledge of it enabled me to refute the
harpooner, who wished to pilot us into a small and
dangerous cove at the south end of the island, where
there was hardly room for the yacht to swing. As it
was, before I had corrected the mistake, in trying to
avoid some grounded icebergs we ran stem-on to a
reef, but the engine being promptly backed astern we
got out and fetched Diana Bay. Steam is a great
comfort and security, and without it it would be
often extremely dangerous to go in amongst drifting
ice. Evidences of such danger were seen in two
vessels which we had noticed abandoned among the

heavy ice of this bay. These wretched smacks enter the closely-packed ice without scruple, because they are so short and round as to be easily handled, and also because they are of very little value compared with their probable or possible cargo. When nipped and no longer seaworthy the crew can nearly always escape in boats to other vessels. And as they have little or no property but what they can carry on their backs it is no hardship for them to have to row about for a few days, or to bivouac for a week on an island.

The strength of the current here renders it by far the most dangerous part of Spitzbergen. At Half-moon Island the flood tide runs north and the ebb south, at six or eight miles an hour. This tide, laden with icebergs from the great glacier before described, and with pack-ice which creeps round the south-east corner of Edge Land, oscillates backwards and forwards between the groups of islands known as the Thousand Isles, and between them and the mainland. Where the channel is narrow the current is so swift that I have been sometimes unable, with a good crew, to row against it. I have seen the sea densely packed with ice in the morning, and by night a vessel could sail unhindered where a few hours ago a boat had been dragged over the ice for miles.

Round Black Point the current sweeps with

tremendous force. The most serious mishap that I have met with in my voyages north occurred here in 1871.

At that time, finding ourselves hemmed in on all sides by the ice, in a lake of open water some six miles long by one wide, from which there seemed to be only one outlet between Half-moon Island and Black Point, I resolved to get out of so unpleasant a position as soon as possible. An enormous quantity of fast-ice, some two or three miles wide, girdled the shore, and, joining the great glacier, extended as far as could be seen east and north-east. So much *fast*-ice quite at the end of July was unusual, even at this forbidding part of the coast. It was evidently caused by many hundreds of bergs having grounded on the bank opposite the great glacier, in twelve to twenty fathoms of water, and so riveting, as it were, the winter-ice to the spot long after the time when it should have totally disappeared. After steaming south a few miles we found the ice jammed across the north end of Half-moon Straits; and, fog coming on, we were compelled to anchor to a berg till it cleared. Next morning, at one o'clock, we steamed rapidly (with the tide) through the Strait, which was nearly choked with floating and grounded ice. At six o'clock A.M. we were off Black Point in a tide so terrific, and with grounded icebergs so numerous and closely-placed, that

we fairly lost all control over the yacht. The tide
first dashed her broadside on a grounded berg—this,
fortunately, gave way beneath her without doing much
damage; but she was then thrown upon a reef of limestone rocks, where we hung, in imminent danger of
being crushed to pieces by the heavy ice which
careered by with the tide. Such would inevitably
have been our fate, but for the providential circumstance of a large iceberg going aground behind us, and
acting as a shield or buffer to fend off the others. All
this occurred in a few minutes; no one stood idly to
watch; and instinctively, while one danger followed
quickly on another, we lowered the boats and filled them
with clothes, food, and ammunition, ready to be off the
moment the ship began to break up. We then lightened her aft, and tried with warp and screw to get the
vessel off, but to no purpose. The tide soon left her on
her beam-ends. She was undamaged, for there seemed
to be no leak, and as there was still $10\frac{1}{2}$ feet of water
alongside she was as yet safe, and I had hopes of
ultimately getting her off if the driving ice did not
break her up before high water again. However, I
prepared for the worst, and took two boat-loads of
necessaries—guns, cartridges, instruments, valuables,
clothes, bedding, biscuit, meat, tea, &c.—to the shore, a
mile and a-half distant. Here we landed and stacked
them on a flat spit of gravel beach, not ten feet broad,

between the sea and the steep limestone cliffs. I intended to have left one man to guard the goods; but, finding no one willing to stop alone, for fear of the bears, I decided on remaining myself with a couple of hands and the small boat. A bitterly cold north-east wind blew with cutting severity from the icy mountains, while a thick, cold, raw fog prevented our seeing what was going on at the ship. We had neither fire-wood nor brandy, and had little appetite for a supper of cheese and biscuit. Added to such discomforts big stones continually threatened us with destruction, by rolling down around us from the awful cliffs above. Millions of guillemots and gulls, breeding in these cliffs, incessantly uttering their harsh, monotonous cries, had a most depressing effect upon us. My anxiety became intolerable, and I passed what I think was one of the most wretched nights of my life, pacing up and down the miserable shore, while I alternately smoked and drank mug-fulls of water from a muddy stream which issued from the cliff. I was glad to see my two men, free from care and responsibility, sleeping like tops amongst the baggage under a boat-sail, for I thought there might be much hard work before them. Endless seemed the hours as I listened, breathlessly at times, to the crash of the ice, and knew by the time that the tide must have turned and exposed the yacht and those on board to fresh risks. At last morning came and the

Drawn by W. Livesay.

The 'Diana' in Difficulties.

fog cleared enough to allow us to trace the outline of
the ship, apparently just as I had left her. I sent off
to hear the report and to bring more goods ashore.
At 8.30 the two men returned, and I learned that the
ship, although in a worse position than before, was
still tight and unbroken. It was to be high water at
10.30, and as this would probably be our last chance
of avoiding starvation ashore all winter, or rowing
to Norway, the restless anxiety with which I watched
the yacht getting more and more upright can be more
easily imagined than described. I had made a series
of marks on the beach, and observed with great satisfaction that this tide rose a good foot higher than the last.
Just about high-water mark we saw the ship decidedly
moving and apparently under control, and immediately
after a flag run up to the mizen gave me the welcome
assurance that they had got her off. In another hour
she steamed up to us, and we at once rowed out to
meet them at a large grounded iceberg in $7\frac{1}{2}$ fathoms,
which I had selected as a suitable anchorage.

We remained at anchor at Half-moon Island for
several days—wind-bound and fog-bound. We could
do nothing but take short boat-trips, when we got a few
seals or explored the island. Half-moon Island, though
much larger, is little less barren than the rest of the
so-called Thousand Islands.[1] Like them it is com-

[1] An old and very incorrect name; it includes groups of a few islands,

posed of hexagonal rocks and boulders of hyperite.
A struggling vegetation, quags of soppy moss, and a
number of small lakes half-frozen over, here and there
patches of snow, and finally fast-ice in the sheltered
inlets, are the features of this island at the time of year
when the breezy moors of Scotland and the islands of
Norway seem almost too hot for walking after grouse.
All parts abound with birds breeding, and the noise
made by them at times is almost deafening. It is
made by separate choruses coming from all sides—the
croak of eider-ducks all round the coast, the combined
screech of a colony of terns, who tyrannise over a
small patch of level ground and drive off all interlopers,
and from the little auks, who at the least disturbance
fly up in a dense cloud of many thousands. At
another time of the day, perhaps, and when the wind is
high, and the drifting snow keeps most of the members
of this animated bee-hive sitting close on their nests, the
only sound one hears is the melancholy wail of the
red-throated diver, who wheels round overhead and
seems to rejoice in the gale. We obtained good
specimens of all these birds, and found nests of the
diver. Most of the other nests had been recently
visited by Bruin, who had left his tracks in broken
shells and foot-prints on the yielding moss. But he

some thirty miles apart. To name the groups separately would be of
more practical use.

had left the island, and our efforts to attract him with the savoury smell of roasted seals failed to bring him in sight.

'Red' and 'green snow' occurred in patches on the snow inshore. It is an appearance familiar to all Arctic voyagers. Kane has given an interesting account of it; Parry observed it in the pack always at the edge of the floes, and it gives character to the Crimsòn Cliffs near Melville Bay. On Half-moon Island the red coloration gave the snow an appearance as if the blood of some recently-killed animal had been sprinkled on the snow. I was once disposed to think it was due merely to the droppings of the little auk, since these birds feed largely on shrimps, and in consequence void a reddish substance, not unlike anchovy sauce. But here the coloured snow was found isolated in large fields of snow, and distant from the rocks where the birds breed. Livesay prepared some specimens for the microscope, which were afterwards exhibited at a meeting of the Edinburgh Botanical Society; and it was interesting to distinguish between the simple spherical cells of the red snow-plant (*Protococcus nivale*) and the jointed segments of the green snow-plant (*P. viride*). This difference in structure, and the fact of the two varieties not being associated in the same place, seem to negative the supposition that they are but stages in the growth of one and the same

z

plant. But I still think it probable that the germ of the snow-plant finds a *nidus* in the bird-droppings, and does not germinate on the snow *per se*.

We spoke one of the sloops we had left at Novaya Zemlya. She had taken ninety-three walruses to Hammerfest, and all the rest of the sloops had also gone there, having got good cargoes; but, as far as I could learn, they had done little or nothing at Novaya Zemlya since I had first seen them in May. I was glad to hear my old skipper, Isaac Dolpy—a good fellow, who took excellent care of us in 1859—had been the most successful of the fishers, having got 170 walruses and 100 small seals. This bag was said to have been made near Kanin Nos, at the east side of the entrance to the White Sea, early in May.

After a morning of fog, so thick we could not see the shore a few yards distant, the wind suddenly veered to north-east on the 15th, the dense mist rolled away in a few minutes, and everything came out clear and sharp from the chilly wrappings of fog. We immediately steamed away to see how far we could get eastward, for from the crow's-nest there seemed to be some open water. But in the evening we had reached the limits of navigable ice, and the main pack appeared only eight or ten miles distant, and joined to Disco Point. This was unusually far south, and it was the more vexatious not being able to break through it that it is the general belief of men who know this locality well that when the ice is far south there is plenty of open water on the other side. The ice was much larger, rougher, and heavier than I had seen it before in these seas. This was very large ice for Spitzbergen, although nothing to compare with the bergs on the other side of the Atlantic. About Davis Straits and the coast of Labrador icebergs are often seen aground in 200 fathoms of water. Many here were aground in deep water. But it is not the size of the icebergs which constitutes the peril of ice-navigation. Dangerous ice is made up of pieces of sufficient size to be neither shivered nor moved by a ship, and influenced by wind and currents and floating sufficiently closely to 'nip' a ship. Except from the risk of it toppling over, a ship might travel closely in the wake of a sailing berg, which ploughs a way for itself through smaller ice.

When at the farthest point east reached this year along the coast (25° 10'), we caught a glimpse of the great glacier already described, but we were unable to approach it or the Ryk Yse Islands, which I visited in 1859. Mr. Birkbeck was here in his yacht in 1864, and from one of the islands saw the forgotten Wiches Land in the distance. The same re-discovery was made from the north-east point of Edge Land by Count Heuglin in 1870. But from Ryk Yse Island to

Cape Heuglin the coast is so constantly blocked with
ice, or rendered inaccessible by ice barriers at each
point, that no one has explored it in late years. What
conditions of ice enabled the Dutch in old times to
visit it sufficiently to mark the anchorages in their
charts I am unable to guess at.

No vessel was able to reach even the Thousand
Isles in 1868, and in the following years of 1869, 1870.
there has seemed to be a sort of general movement
south of the Polar ice, jamming the north and east
coasts. In 1871 we find a change, and Leigh Smith
was able to make his northern voyage, and the
Austrians to land on Hope Island.

The Gulf Stream has little or no influence to the
north and east of Black Point and the Thousand Isles.
The ice is always travelling to the south-west, except
when strong southerly gales prevail. Directly the ice
is driven to the south or west of the promontory it
comes within the influence of the Gulf Stream, and is
rapidly dissolved—that is, during June, July, and
August. After the end of August the Arctic current
entirely overcomes the warm water, which has been
struggling with it, so far successfully as to modify its
blighting influence on the south and west shores of
Spitzbergen during three months, and the Polar ice,
aided by the increasing cold, encroaches in great
quantities. It rapidly sweeps round the coast, over-

lapping first Black Point and the Thousand Isles; then Whale-fish Point; next, filling Stor Fjord, it meets with another stream of ice coming in by Walter Thymen's Straits; lastly, it extends up the west coast until it meets, about Prince Charles' Foreland, another vast body of ice which has travelled round Hakluyt's Headland; and Spitzbergen is enveloped for the winter. I believe that the sea itself to the south and west of Spitzbergen would not freeze over, far to the outside of the shallow bays and gulfs, were it not thus crowded and encumbered with heavy drift-ice, continually swept down from the colder regions of the north and east. When once the Arctic current fairly gains this preponderance over the Gulf Stream it is quite inconceivable how rapidly the ice sweeps round the coast and fill up all the bays. A few days suffice to surround the whole of Spitzbergen with an impenetrable barrier. Woe betide the luckless vessel which at this critical period happens to get becalmed up any of these long bays or fjords; for when they at length make their way to the entrance they may chance to find all hope of egress barred for nine months to come—a period synonymous with eternity to most of those unfortunates who have thus been entrapped. On my first visit to Spitzbergen my yacht had a very narrow escape from being beset in a little bay near Whale-fish Point, into which we had entered for the

purpose of setting up the rigging for the voyage home.
A sudden calm came on, and the ice was advancing
with such fearful rapidity that I began to think we
were in for an Arctic winter. No amount of *whistling*
would induce a breeze to spring up, so, after waiting
to the last moment, I ordered all hands into the boats,
and with some difficulty we succeeded in towing her
out of danger. I had been averse to adopt this
obvious expedient sooner, because we feared that the
strength of the current was such that we should not be
able to keep the yacht from drifting against a long and
formidable reef of rocks, which lay *below* the current;
but we eventually got clear of ice and rocks, and drifted
into open water.

Many dismal tragedies are recorded in the annals
of Spitzbergen. The Russian traders in Archangel,
some twenty-five years ago, had organised a regular
wintering establishment, and for many years the men
were left on the coast in September and October for
the purpose of hunting the seal, walrus, bear, and
reindeer. Small parties of two, three, or four indi-
viduals each were distributed in wooden huts constructed in Archangel, brought thence, and erected on
different parts of the coasts and islands of Spitzbergen.
The men were paid by a share of the proceeds, and
were supplied by their employers with provisions,
consisting principally of rye meal, salt-pork, and tea.

A Spitzbergen Cemetery.

They had a sort of head-quarters establishment at Whale-fish Point, which was under the charge of a superintendent, who distributed the supplies to the hunters, and collected the skins and blubber from the different outposts ; and the Company sent over a vessel in the month of May every year to relieve the men and carry the proceeds of their labours to Archangel.

It was, probably, found to be too severe a strain upon the constitution to pass two successive winters in this way, as I believe it was usual for these men only to remain every alternate winter in Spitzbergen. In 1858, I was informed, there was still living at Kola, in Lapland, an aged Russian, who had actually wintered thirty-five alternate seasons at Spitzbergen. Many of these hardy fellows, however, succumbed to scurvy and the hardships they endured, and many hundreds must have thus miserably perished, as the traveller in these awful solitudes frequently comes across the ruins of a small log-hut, with two or three mounds or cairns of stones in front of it ; and it is also common enough to see the skeletons of the hapless Russians bleaching alongside of those of the bears and reindeer they had killed and eaten. The Company's men seem to have killed immense numbers of animals, and the consequent profits must have been large, as, in spite of the number of lives which were lost, the Company was not broken up till eighteen men perished one winter at Whale-fish Point.

· During the summer of the year in question a prodigious quantity of heavy drift-ice surrounded the Point and all the southern coast of East Spitzbergen. The men belonging to the Russian establishment had all come in from the various outposts, and were assembled at the head-quarters, waiting to be relieved by the annual vessel from Archangel. By a concurrence of bad fortune this vessel was lost on her voyage over, and was never heard of again. The crews of the other vessels in Spitzbergen knew nothing of these men; or, if they did, they naturally supposed that the care of relieving them might safely be left to their own vessel, as nothing was yet known of her loss either there or at Archangel. The ice in the summer months prevented any vessel from accidentally approaching Whale-fish Point; and no one went near it until the end of August, when a party of Norwegians, who had lost their own vessel, travelled along the shore to seek for assistance from the Russian establishment; but on reaching the huts they were horror-struck to find its inmates all dead. Fourteen of the unhappy men had recently been buried in shallow graves in front of the huts, two lay dead just outside the threshold, and the remaining two were lying dead inside, one on the floor and the other in bed. The latter was the superintendent, who had been able to read and write; and a journal lying beside him contained a record of their sad fate.

It appeared that early in the season scurvy of a malignant character had attacked them; some had died at the out-stations, and the survivors had with difficulty assembled at the head-quarter station, and were in hopes of being speedily relieved by the vessel; but, the latter not arriving, their stores got exhausted, and the unusual quantity of ice surrounding the coast prevented them from getting seals or wild-fowl on the sea or the shore. In addition to scurvy they had now the horrors of hunger to contend with; and they gradually died one after another, and were buried by their surviving companions, until at last only four remained. Then two more died, and the other two, not having strength to bury them, dragged their bodies outside the hut to await their own fate; and, when one of them died, the last man—the writer of the journal—had only sufficient strength remaining to push his dead companion out of the bed on to the floor, and he soon after expired himself, only a few days before the Norwegian party arrived. The Russians had a large pinnace in the harbour and several small boats on shore, but the ice at first prevented them reaching the open sea, and latterly, when the ice opened out, those who survived so long were much too weak to make use of the boats. The ship-wrecked Norwegians took advantage of the pinnace to effect their own escape to Hammerfest, carrying with them the poor superintendent's journal, which the Russian consul at that port transmitted to Arch-angel.

When I first visited this spot in 1858 I took a photograph of it. Everything then remained almost exactly as the Norwegians found it; and some of the weapons, cooking utensils, and ragged fragments of clothes and bedding, lay scattered around. A great many skulls and bones of bears, foxes, deer, seals, and walruses, also, testified to their success as hunters. We likewise found a curious implement like a miniature wooden rake, the use of which was a complete enigma to me, until our pilot explained that such contrivances were commonly used by the Russians when they suffered from entomological annoyances.

The huts were all formed of logs, dovetailed into one another at the corners, and were tolerably entire, except the roofs, which, being flat and covered with earth, had now fallen in. The principal one, about twenty-four feet square, had been used both as a sitting-room and dormitory; off this was a small wing with a brick fire-place, evidently used as a kitchen. Another hut was the storehouse, and a third—a common feature of Russian stations in Spitzbergen and

Novaya Zemlya—a bath-house of a rude description, in which I suppose they had enjoyed the national luxury of parboiling themselves and then rolling in the snow at a temperature of −50° Fahr. The roof of the main hut had fallen in, and a little glacier, about as large as a boat turned bottom-up, had formed in the middle of the floor. On a gentle eminence two or three hundred yards from the huts they had built up a sort of look-out house of loose stones; and here, we may conceive, they passed many weary hours watching the ice-laden sea before them. They may even have been tantalised by seeing the topsails of vessels passing outside of the icy barrier, but far beyond their reach. On a piece of level ground not far from the huts they had kept themselves in exercise by playing at a game resembling cricket, as was evident by the bats and rude wooden balls they had used, still lying on the mossy ground.

Altogether there was something inexpressibly sad and desolate about the remains of this unfortunate establishment; and by the rude Norwegian sealers the place is regarded with a degree of superstitious awe, which, perhaps, accounted for the huts being in such good preservation several years after.

Our attempts to get farther east during August 16th 17th and 18th were dangerous and unavailing, from the quantity of ice which continually came down with the current as if from an inexhaustible storehouse. We at one time sighted Hope Island in the corrected position I had assigned to it in 1859, *i.e.* about forty-five miles east of Black Point, or nearly one hundred miles further to the north-east than the charts of that period made it. But we were unable to approach it this season. At one time there would be a tolerably clear lead of water towards it, then fog or snow would come on, and by the time it had cleared off either the ice had collected in impenetrable masses or we had drifted far away with the current. The temperature during these days—and, indeed, for the remainder of the time we remained in Spitzbergen—was almost uninterruptedly below freezing; while the thermometer on the surface-water never rose above 32° Fahr., and was often down to 29° Fahr.

The yacht's head was, therefore, again turned to the east, and we ran towards Deeva Bay, and anchored just in time to lie in the shelter of a group of islands during a gale from the north-east, which now blew up. The largest of the islands has been named Ziegler Island. It was a noted resort of the Russians half a century ago, and their ruined huts still remained. There had been a large oblong building and two smaller ones, placed back to back. The walls, four feet thick, filled in with rubble and made tight inside with plaster and moss, seemed very old; and the plants inside grew as luxuriantly as outside. Around were strewn loose timbers and whales' bones. Not far off was a small fresh-water lake, from which a flock of Brent geese—now in full plumage—were startled. The doctor also shot a snowy owl, in its summer plumage. It is a bird far less common in Spitzbergen than Novaya Zemlya.

The stream runs very strong between the islands of this group, and, as I imagine, keeping the narrow gats open nearly all the winter, renders this a favourite resort of seals, sea-horses, and bears. Two dangerous reefs lie about three miles off the anchorage, and bear respectively west and west-by-south from the middle island. Rocks also run out from the west end of the island, and, in approaching, immediately face you. All these rocks are dry at low water only, and the sea breaks over them when there is any swell. On one of them the ' Ginevra ' struck in 1858.

Black Point and Whale-fish Point are the two promontories terminating the chains of mountains which enclose Deeva Bay and stretch out like a pair of compasses to embrace the archipelago of the Thousand Isles. The seaward sides of both these bluffs are curiously scarped away, so as to form very steep precipitous faces of bare rock ; and, at places where it has room to lie, there is an extensive *talus* of muddy and shaly *detritus* brought down from the sides of the

mountains by the action of frost and avalanches. These
mountains are each about twelve hundred feet in
height, and this may be stated as about the height of
the lower ranges on both sides of East Spitzbergen.
The peaks of the more inland range of mountains are
much higher, but are quite inaccessible, and are only
to be seen here and there peeping out from among the
glaciers. Black Point is composed of a dark-grey or
mud-coloured limestone and sandstone of a soft and
shaly description, which is stratified very minutely
and with almost exact parallelism to the sea—only in
one or two places did I observe slight bends or deflec-
tions from the horizontality of the stratification. The
limestone contains a great number of fossils, of which
I obtained a series.

Black Point and Whale-fish Point are both very
deeply furrowed from top to bottom ; and these furrows,
being generally full of snow, while the dark-grey
ridges between them are bare, give the mountains a
sort of ribbed appearance, which renders them very
curious and conspicuous objects from an immense
distance.

All the lower hills of East Spitzbergen, from
Whalefish Point to Forvexling Head, are much of the
same shape and contour. As far as I have examined
them they appear to be composed of the same shaly
limestone and sandstone. These beds, belonging to

the trias, in this long stretch of seventy miles lie on a thick, conformable stratum of hyperite, and the singularly undisturbed position of the whole formation is still further marked by other thinner bands of hyperite. The circumstance of a crystalline rock being thrust in between the strata of a secondary formation, and maintaining all the characters of a sedimentary rock—not only for these seventy miles, but also for double that length, to which it has been traced overlying the mountain limestone of Lovens' Berg with similar uniformity—has given rise to the surmise by the Swedish geologists that it was not erupted, as we are accustomed to regard the crystalline rocks, but that it had its origin in the 'deposits of volcanic ash or of gravel' from destroyed plutonic rocks, which in course of time have hardened and become metamorphosed into that anhydrous rock now called hyperite.'

On the shores of the great inlets of Stor Fjord and Deeva Bay, where the sea is not exposed to the violence of the currents and gales from the north-east, the *detritus* brought down from the mountains, instead of being perpetually washed away from the base of the cliffs, is allowed to accumulate; and, flowing each year, or each flood, over the top of the layer already deposited, it gradually encroaches on the sea, and forms a muddy flat, which slopes at a gradually-increasing angle from the almost perpendicular limestone cliffs to

a nearly dead level. This plain gets by degrees
covered with mosses, but it is for a long time liable to
be deluged again with mud and shale from the mountains, until the slopes of the latter get so much reduced
by this process that they assume a more permanent
shape. These plains are in some places from three to
four miles broad, and although their surface may not
have undergone any of these natural warpings or top-
dressings for ages, they are generally so very soft and
slushy that in walking one goes up to the knees at
every step. The brief Arctic summer is evidently in-
sufficient to dry the ground from the enormous quantity
of water with which it is saturated by the winter's
snow.

The water is generally very muddy in these bays,
from being so heavily charged with sediment washed
off the hills by the melting snow, and the sea is un-
questionably shallowing very rapidly. This is a process which, no doubt, is taking place more or less all
over the world, and by which all subalpine flats and
valleys have been partly formed and enriched already;
but there is no country which I have ever visited or of
which I have ever read in which it can be *observed* to
be actually happening so conspicuously as in Spitzbergen, and more particularly around the two gulfs of
Stor Fjord and Deeva Bay. The actual formation of
flats and valleys by the denudation of the mountains

and deposition of the sediment is there exhibited so plainly to the beholder that 'he who runs may read.' If there still exists anyone who doubts the power of present causes to remodel the surface of the earth, I should strongly recommend him to take a trip to Deeva Bay, and he may rest assured he will come back a wiser man.

We left this interesting bay on the evening of August 20th. This day is one of the dates of the Spitzbergen year. The sun sets at South Cape; but a hundred miles farther north, at Ginevra Bay, whither we were bound, there should still be long, light nights. I had not yet given up all hope of reaching the east coast, Hinlopen Straits, and even Gillis Land by this route; and I was pleased, on the 21st, as the sun sank behind the big glacier on the north side of Ginevra Bay, and we dropped anchor between it and Lamont Island, to make out from the crow's-nest the entrance to Hell Sound apparently clear of ice. We should not have occupied thirty hours working up the fjord, had I not stopped to kill a couple of immense walruses; but I became so impatient to make use of the open water after this that we steamed right ahead regardless of many seals floating by on the ice.

I sent a boat early next morning to shoot deer on the opposite side of the bay, and they returned in

A A

eighteen hours with ten head.[1]   Another was shot on
a point of land which partly formed the anchorage.

At the same time I set off to explore Hell Sound.
I ascended a rocky hill at the mouth of the sound,
from which I had a magnificent view of this extraordinary gorge and the East Sea beyond it.   The sound
itself appeared like a winding river, being not more
than four or five hundred yards across, and two miles
long.   High precipices—a continuation, no doubt, of the
lowest bed of hyperite, which fringes the east side of
Stor Fjord—bounded the sound on the side where I
stood, and on the other a low rocky island divided it
from the smaller sound, which I partially examined in
1859.   Between these contracted shores a tremendous
tide was running out at some eight knots an hour, and
carrying with it quantities of ice.   On the opposite
side an enormous glacier projected from Barentz Land
far into the East Sea.   Behind me, on the mainland of
Spitzbergen, White Mountain rose to a height of three
thousand feet.[2]

The East Sea itself was very like what I feared we
should find it.   There was a sort of lake of water—

---

[1] These had been killed on a plain and valley to the south of Forvexling
Head—an excellent place, as I gathered, from the extent of the pasture
and the facilities for stalking.

[2] The Swedes ascended this in 1864, and sighted land across the East
Sea.   They believed this to be a continuation of Gillis Land, but more
mature observations have shown it to be identical with Wiches Land,
discovered in 1617.

more or less clear of ice—six or eight miles in diameter—extending from the open sound, and evidently
kept clear by the tide; beyond this all was ice, ice, ice,
to all appearance very thick, heavy, and densely jammed
together.

This state of the ice seemed a complete refutation
of the theories which maintain that the main-ice pack,
always met, sooner or later, by Arctic voyagers, is a
*mere drifting belt of ice with open water again to the
north of it;* for here we were examining the ice seventy
miles north of where we were stopped by the main-
ice off Disco Head, and yet we found it heavier and more
densely packed than it was there! On the other hand,
it may be possible that Hell Sound is as analogous to
Matoschkin Schar as the south-east corner of Edge Land
is to the south-east corner of Novaya Zemlya ; and we
have already seen that when both of these exits of the
Kara Sea are blocked, and the coast between them
encumbered with ice, there is often a great area of
open water beyond. There are, however, in the latter
case conditions for which there is no parallel to the
east and south of Spitzbergen, namely, a land boundary
with great and comparatively warm rivers. The source
of the ice to the north is similar, a north-east current
bringing it between Ice Cape and Cape Taimyr into
the Kara Sea, and between North-east Land and Gillis
and Franz Josef Lands. But these are speculations only.

A A 2

Parry's sledge journey and the Austrian return journey tell us of no loose barrier of ice floating separately at a distance from a main pack (bounded by the sharp perpendicular section which unauthentic voyages have suggested) ; and, no doubt, when such a quantity of ice is met with as to maintain a constant drift the main-pack which feeds it is not far distant, unless some exceptional conditions of current, as *e.g.* that running east at the north of Novaya Zemlya, is strong enough and warm enough to, at times, isolate the drifting barrier from the pack itself.

It could be of no use going down the sound at present, because I saw more from this elevated situation than I could from the far end. I therefore rejoined the boat, with two deer I had shot near the Swedish cross ; and, after waiting for several hours while the ice drifted south out of the way, crossed the mouth of the sound and landed on a rocky, desolate shore, much scratched and polished by the passage of ice, to a curious columnar hill which I had examined on my previous voyage. It was a truncated cone of plutonic rock, of a singularly grand and picturesque appearance. It seemed to be about six hundred feet high and two or three miles in circumference at the base. The lower two-thirds of its height consisted of a steep *talus* covered with beautifully-variegated mosses, while the upper third was composed of a series of bright russet-coloured columns of rock arranged perpendicularly, and looked exactly like a number of half-decayed trunks of enormous trees bound together in a sort of Titanic faggot.

Another hill on the opposite side of the bay has an equally striking appearance. It is some fifteen hundred feet high and is composed of the same triassic shales and limestones which enter into the formation of all the hills on the east side of Stor Fjord; but it had a perfectly flat or tabular top, and the upper stratum, as well as another band about the middle of the hill, were black and apparently harder than the other strata, for they stood up perpendicularly at the ends, instead of participating in the otherwise uniform 45° slope of the hill. At the left hand or south-westerly side of the hill I could perceive that the lower band gradually thinned to nothing. I was not within several miles of the hill, but I estimated the thickness of each of these black bands at about twenty feet. This distinguishing feature of these hills may possibly be coal, but is more probably due to the horizontal bands of hyperite already referred to, and their black appearance is a result partly of the action of the weather on the dark-red rock, and partly of their contrast to neighbouring snow and adjacent lighter strata of sandstone.

I shot here four more deer; two of them were fat old stags, and had their ears marked in the manner already referred to.[1]

[1] P 110.

As it was now after ten, and the shore was strewn
with drift-wood, we hauled up the boat, made a supper
of stewed deer, kabobs, coffee, and biscuit, and encamped
for the night. 'Kabobs,' I may add, are the best form
of cooking fresh-killed meat; and the mode of preparation is as follows :—

First catch a fat deer, then cut a number of wooden
skewers, and thread upon these alternately pieces of
meat, fat, and heart or liver, each cut to about the
size of a walnut; broil upon the glowing embers,
season with pepper, and bite them off while smoking
hot. If hungry, you fancy this the most delicious
thing you ever tasted. For my knowledge of this most
attractive *plat* I was indebted to a one-eyed Arab
cook, yclept Hadgi Mohammed, whom Sir F—— S——
and I had on an expedition in Egypt and Palestine
some years ago. I have also seen kabobs retailed to
the faithful by itinerant cooks in the streets of Con-
stantinople and Cairo.

In spite of a cold wind blowing from the glacier we
had a few hours' refreshing sleep; and, after repeating
the evening meal under the name of breakfast, again
pulled along the coast. After rowing six or seven miles,
I descried ten deer on a smooth hill-side in a very unfavourable situation. I knew that by stalking them I
could only expect to get one deer, and that by a very long
shot. I therefore walked half-a-mile along the shore and

cnsconced myself in a gravelly water-course, while I sent Helstadt round the far side to move the deer and get a shot if he could. This plan answered admirably; for, although Helstadt consumed an hour and a-half in crawling for a shot, missed the deer, and nearly shot me by his bullet ricochetting off a stone and entering the ground with a *thud* a few feet from me, the deer came up at a run close to where I lay flat. I knocked over the two best, right and left; then, while the remaining deer stood about irresolutely, not knowing from whence or how their two leaders had met their death, I managed, lying on my side, to reload my little muzzle-loader, and again shot two—then they went on a bit, and I followed and killed another—having now seen me, three fairly took to their heels and got far away, but two unhappy calves, who would not leave their mothers, fell easy victims; thus making seven killed out of ten, with one muzzle-loading rifle, at a single drive.

On the way back to the ship I observed a great commotion among the birds on a small island near Forvexling Head; and, rightly divining the cause, I directed the men to pull gently round the rocks. We soon discovered a young bear asleep, when a shot in the stomach woke him from one sleep, and a second in his head sent him into another.

A fierce gale from the north-east next day kept all

hands on board. The sea was lashed into fury, the snow only occasionally ceased, to permit a view of the ragged clouds tearing across the sky or enveloping the lofty top of White Mountain. We lay with two anchors down, and sixty fathoms of chain out; and the thick ice driving against the ship, and at times completely surrounding her, might have threatened the horrors of besetting us had we not reflected that the next tide must take all the ice away again. A small fox appeared skipping over the ice, not at all discomposed by the weather, and would, probably, have arrived at the ship had he not been frightened back by one of the men.

Towards night the wind began to fall, and by seven o'clock on the following morning I again set off to make a vigorous effort to pass through Hell Sound. We got in and through on the top of the flood-tide, which runs to the north-east. Half-way down I shot a big seal, which was floating on an ice-cake. And while engaged in flensing it we were insensibly drawn on into a sort of vortex of water, boiling like a huge caldron in a circle of about three hundred yards. In this whirlpool lots of heavy ice were churning and seething in an unpleasantly threatening manner. My Norsk crew now began to get into a precious stew, exclaiming that 'we should be driven out into the East Sea and never be heard of again.' I only laughed at them, and told them to keep cool, as the worst that could happen to us was a detention of five or six hours till the tide changed; but I was far from being in a comfortable frame of mind myself, for a sudden fog or gale might be very disastrous, and we stood a considerable risk of having the boat stove in by the whirling ice. I, therefore, had the boat hauled into the centre of a large flat cake of ice, where we were more safe from the consequences of a collision; upon this we took several turns of the whirlpool until we got near an open and comparatively still place; here we suddenly launched the boat, and, pulling might and main, got out of this infernal caldron into an eddy at the south side. At last, by pulling and holding on by the rocks, we got into quiet water, and went ashore to boil coffee, and wait three hours and a-half for the turn of the tide. While the men rested and slept I walked with rifle and telescope to the top of a rocky hill, and had a grand view of the sea on both sides from the summit. The East Sea was much as I had seen it two days before, *i.e.* covered with ice in every direction, save the small area at the mouth of the straits. I searched the horizon in vain for Gillis Land (at that time said by competent authorities to be distant only sixty miles), but could make out Northeast Land, and some of the large islands at the south end of Hinlopen Straits, at a distance of forty miles.

Bah! what was theory as to where ice might lie and should lie in the face of such a hopeless spectacle!

When the tide began to ebb we got back through the smaller sound without difficulty; but the time occupied in this appropriately-named sound lost all the best of the day. In returning I picked up a couple more seals, and another bear, which I found under precisely the same circumstances as the last; viz. by noticing the disturbance among the birds on an island. We paddled quietly round a corner, when I saw Bruin busy gathering and eating ducklings. I then jumped ashore, crept up to about forty yards, and gave him an explosive shell in the tail region as he turned to fly, and finished him with another. This ended the day, seven hours of which had been wasted in the straits.

The other boats, which had started in search of deer and seals, returned at the same time as myself, tolerably well laden. We had upwards of thirty deer on board; the rigging was festooned with haunches and forequarters; and the poor cook was hard at it, boiling, frying, roasting, day and night, to suit our variable hours and ravenous appetites.

Thus the last attempt to reach the east coast of Spitzbergen had failed like all the rest; in each case I had pushed up, with the advantage which steam gave, to the very edge of the impenetrable pack, which would admit neither ship, boat, nor sledge to advance farther.

It was too late in the season to remain any longer so far from the open sea, so we steamed away, and, shortly after midnight on August 27th, dropped anchor under the lofty shelter of Lees Foreland at the entrance of Walter Thymen's Straits. Soon after a sloop arrived at the same anchorage. The skipper's name was Adrian, or 'young Adrian' as he was known, to distinguish him from his father, the owner of the vessel. Young Adrian had killed seventy-two walruses in Novaya Zemlya, off Gooseland, where he met with them in great numbers. He told me that Neilson's sloop (which I had towed out of the ice at the Norways) had lost a boat and three hands only a few days before at the Thousand Isles. The harpooneer, whom I remembered, having been on my deck several times— a fine, tall, blue-eyed, fair-haired young fellow, a fit model for a Viking or Berserkar—had stuck two big bull-walruses at once, and they fairly dragged the boat under when the water bubbled in over the bows: the other men roared to him to cut the line, one handing him a knife for the purpose, but he rashly held on, and lost his own life and that of two others— the fourth man being saved by scrambling on the ice.

Another smack alongside had been at Novaya Zem-lya, and had also lost two men and a boat in consequence of the line getting foul round the captain's foot, while fast to a walrus. In the hurry and excitement

of extricating his foot the walrus was allowed to pull
the boat under water, and boat and two of the crew
were never recovered. This accident shows the importance of having a sufficiently long line—at least
twenty fathoms—wound round a small bollard while
working the beast; by this means a moderately hard
pressure might be kept on all along, instead of allowing him to run all the line out slack, and then bringing
him up with a sharp jerk. Such casualties illustrate
the risks and dangers of walrus-hunting. Four ships
cast away, as many beset at the north of Spitzbergen,
four boats and nine of their crews lost, made a
disastrous chapter of accidents, a heavy set-off, in
property and men's lives, against the miserable profits
of the trade in one short summer. And there were,
probably, many more such casualties of which we had
not heard. I once came across a stranded boat in
Ice-Fjord with two walrus-lines snapped off short, and
have no doubt that her crew had been dragged under
water, and had all perished in the manner related above.

At midday I started with Livesay and four hands
for a two days' excursion in Walter Thymen's Straits.
After pulling for four miles along the south shore we
noticed two boats hauled upon the shore and some men
descending the cliff loaded with deer. It was a most
unpropitious-looking place for game, but we were told
that a small gorge led up to a magnificent plain, above

Walter Thymen's Straits.

Fair Haven—A Bird's-eye View.

Drawn by W. Livesay.

the cliffs, celebrated for deer. A mile farther on I went ashore and shot a solitary deer. The cliffs now encroached so closely on the water that it seemed unlikely we should get anything on that side of the straits, and we therefore rowed three or four miles across the straits to a huge plain communicating with broad valleys among the hills, where I had killed many deer in previous years. But, to our disgust, we noticed through the telescope a party of marauders feasting round a fire, and others bringing in loads of deer. As it now began to snow heavily we ran ashore under the lee of a low cliff and boiled our midday coffee, and then pressed on to a small valley, where Hans assured us his party had killed twenty deer close to the boat some years ago. But a survey of the ground from the top of a hill disclosed nothing, and only wasted an hour of our time. A mile farther on we landed on a flat shore, like a well-kept parade-ground, at the foot of the cliffs. A valley here extended inland; and, having hauled the boat up and set the men to work cooking the supper, we scaled some steep ground overlooking a broad upland. A deep gorge sloping on the opposite side, but composed of a perpendicular wall of shaly limestone with snow-drifts and frozen streams on ours, prevented our descent to the table-land on which we observed a few deer feeding. But a mile of walking revealed a slip in the cliff, down which we clambered. By crossing the water and snow we reached the shelter of a ridge unseen by the deer, and, posting ourselves, managed to kill all five of the deer, which were feeding together. Although it was now getting dusk we made out more deer feeding half-a-mile off. A wide water-worn gully, up which a column of men might have marched without being seen from the plain, enabled us to stalk these at our leisure. We shot five, and wounded the last one, which was at a longer distance from the gully.

We now returned to the shore, where a blazing fire of drift-wood and a hot supper awaited us; and, sending the men for the deer, rolled into our wraps on the hard shore for the night. It was intensely cold, as the wind came down in icy gusts from a glacier near, and blew through the narrow gorge like a funnel directed on our camp. However, in spite of wind and frequent snow-storms, we managed to get a few hours' sleep undisturbed by bears, whose fresh tracks we lay down on, and which we hoped might have been attracted by the smell of the cooking.

At six o'clock in the morning we got off and steered for the opposite shore of the straits, for below where we had passed the night a glacier some miles long evidently terminated the pasture on the north side. At some distance down the south side we could see a wide valley opening out to an immense extent of plain next the shore. Here, we felt sure, the deer must swarm; but the time was getting so short I determined to chance our luck at the first valley we came to. This valley we found full of reindeer; we stalked them by creeping along the bank which suddenly terminated the level ground at the shore; and, after shooting as many as the boat could possibly hold, walked across the field of slaughter, on which seventeen deer lay dead.

Then we found them so tame we might have shot any number by simply standing still in full view till they came up to be shot. It was like the wildest hunter's dream—the rich pasture with its variegated flowers, dotted all over with these unsophisticated animals, who grazed peacefully close to us, approached within ten yards in a state of puzzled curiosity, followed us as we walked, or gambolled about, heartlessly snuffing up to us as we disembowelled their companions.

We were now about fifteen miles from the yacht, with the wind and tide dead against us; the deer, deprived of heads and feet, formed one great stack amidships in the boat, and the men squeezed in at each end, rowed two abreast, while we either walked along the shore or tried to keep ourselves warm by taking a hand at the oars. When a few miles from the ship we observed the doctor gesticulating on the top of the cliffs, whither he had gone in search of ptarmigan; but the boat was far down in the water, and I did not think we could take another man or deer on board, till I soon after saw a fine stag clambering about the cliffs. Then, remembering that we had now killed ninety-nine deer on the voyage, I determined we should have this one to make up the hundred. I jumped ashore, and killed him, by a bullet through his heart, at 200 yards. The weight of the heaviest stag, without his head, neck, and feet, cleaned and skinned, was 131 lbs.; but I fancied none of these deer were equal to some I had shot in 1858 and 1859.

I had not seen a single seal during these two days, but found the sailing-master had killed three in our absence.

We had now more fresh meat than we could use on the voyage home; and, while we dropped down the fjord under easy sail, I had some barrels of hams salted and packed while we still remained in a cold country.

On the afternoon of August 30th we were again among the Thousand Isles, but the ice was thicker than ever. A few seals were killed, but I did not care for the chance of an occasional seal in company with eight or nine sloops when there appeared nothing else to be done, and therefore took advantage of a favourable wind to beat up to Deeva Bay, and anchored in our old quarters. A small Hammerfest sloop brought up close to us, in order to ride out a north-east gale, which began blowing on September 1st. This vessel had got seventy-one walruses, thirty seals, and a couple of bears at Novaya Zemlya. The skipper, Howin, advised me to wait about the Thousand Islands for a short time, saying 'that if the wind continued it would bring all the ice away from the east, leaving Hope Island free; and that, as the walruses cling to the last remnant of the ice, they would either float about near the islands or go ashore on them. In July 1864 he got more than enough to fill his ship in this manner.'

I acknowledged his advice in the currency of the country—reindeer—and determined to adopt it. We filled up with water from a pond on the island, sufficiently thick with new-formed ice to skate on; and on the 3rd put out into the snow and fog to see what the late gale had done in moving the ice. At Black Point we found the ice worse than ever; not a seal or walrus was seen, although we wore backwards and forwards for a day and a night.

At 4 A.M. on the 5th, finding the weather atrociously bad, and the wind against any prospect of the ice clearing, I called all hands, stowed the boats on deck, and put the helm up for Norway.

So ended, in some respects, an unlucky expedition; but I was convinced no human exertions could have accomplished more in discovery or exploration that season in the Spitzbergen seas, owing to the persistently unfavourable lie of the ice. Had walruses been my only object I might have had splendid sport by

remaining in Novaya Zemlya ; but, making a voyage in
the first steamer that had visited this part of the Arctic
seas, I always considered it my first duty to prove that
steam could carry us where sailing-vessels were unable
to go. This kept me restlessly hammering at the ice at
every possible avenue to the unknown regions, and prevented my making a voyage remunerative in a sporting
point of view.

Still, our rapid movement from place to place
largely added to my knowledge of the lie of ice in
Spitzbergen and Novaya Zemlya, enabled me practically to test many theories broached in ignorance of
existing conditions, and finally enabled me to enjoy
months of exciting hunts, and days and nights, never
to be forgotten, in earnest contemplation of some of the
grandest and most interesting phenomena of nature.
A long farewell, then, to those rugged cliffs and gale-
swept shores, more and more shrouded each day in
the mist and snows of winter and the increasing
darkness of the polar nights.

A stormy voyage of five days brought us to the
North Cape, where we were able to watch the coloured
splendour of the Northern Lights, of which we sometimes see a faint reflection in our more southern islands.
Again, after the endless white of the Arctic hills,
our eyes rested on the verdant pastures around the
Norwegian homesteads, on the blazing sunsets lighting

up the purple stretches of moor, on the shadows playing under the birch-trees, and the busy life of the fishing stations.

At Tromsö we discharged the sinful Norwegians, and quickly found ourselves ankle-deep in letters and newspapers. Each day we moved from island to island for a fresh grouse-preserve. Among the rugged Loffodens we anchored behind the great peaks, and enjoyed the calm moonlight nights and the genial sunny afternoons. And hence, passing the ill-famed Maelstrom we crossed the great Vest Fjord, shot red-deer at Hitteroen, and dropped anchor in the wide harbour of Christiansund, previous to our voyage home-ward to Dundee, where we arrived on October 6th.

LEE'S FORELAND.

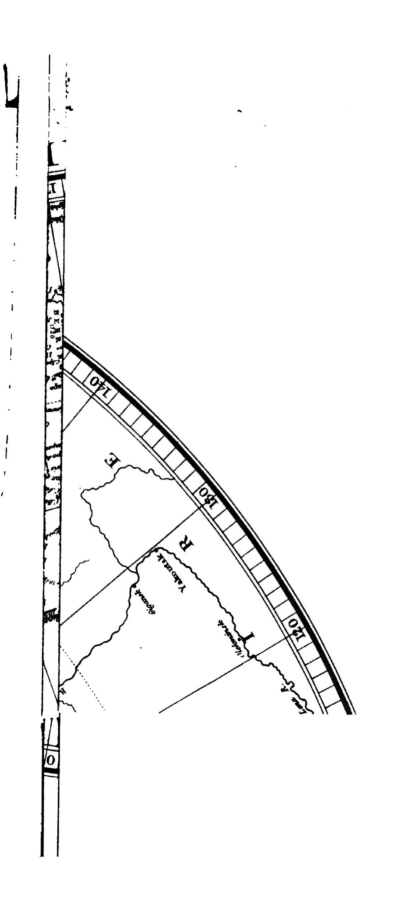

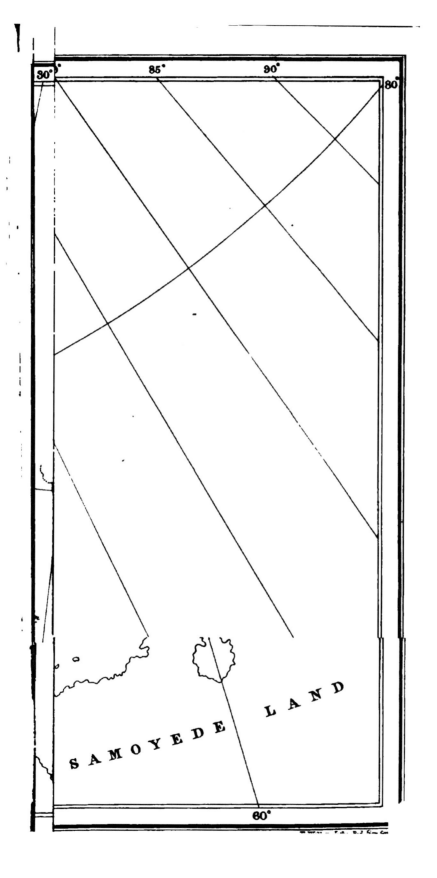

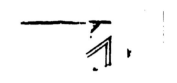

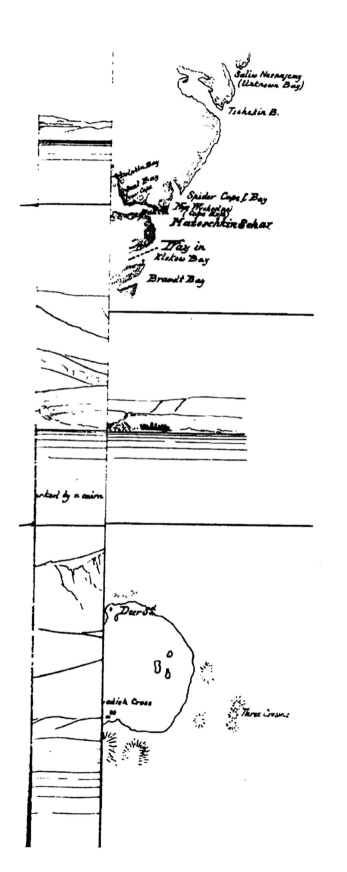

APPENDIX II.

CHRONICLES OF THE SPITZBERGEN

AND KARA SEAS.

CHRONICLES OF THE SPITZBERGEN, BARENTZ, AND KARA SEAS.

From the voyage of Ohthere (890) to Nordenskiold's passage to the Yenisei (1875).

Name	Nationality	Name and description of vessel	Date	Results
Ohthere . . .	Norwegian		890	Sailed round the North Cape.
Willoughby, Sir Hugh	English	'Bona Esperanza,' 120 tons	1553	Discovered Goose Land, Novaya Zemlya, and was afterwards frozen to death in a harbour of Lapland.
Muscovy Company .	English	Was founded in .	1554	For the purpose of trading with the northern ports of Russia.
Burrough, Stephen .	English	'Serchthrift'	1556	Discovered Waygat or Kara Straits.
Pot, Arthur . .	English	'George,' barque	1580	Discovered Jugorsky Schar.
		'William,' commanded by Jackman		
Cornelis Corneliszoon	Dane	'Swane'	1594	Sailed through Jugorsky Schar, and reached, it is said, to the longitude of the Obi.
Nai		'Mercurius,' commanded by Brant Tetgales		
Barentz, William .	Dutch	'Mercurius' .	1594	Coasted Novaya Zemlya to the Orange Islands.
,, ,, .	,,	With two vessels, of which Von Heemskirk and Ian Corneliszoon Riip were captains	1596	The two vessels discovered Bear Island, then Spitzbergen, which, it is supposed, they circumnavigated, by passing to the eastward up Hinlopen Straits, and so to the west coast. Barentz, with Heemskirk and one vessel, then traversed the sea between Spitzbergen and Novaya Zemlya, and finally wintered in Ice Haven, Novaya Zemlya.

Name	Nationality	Vessel	Year	
Hudson	English	'Hopewell,' 80 tons	1607	Sailing from Greenland, arrived at north-west corner of Spitzbergen, and probably sighted the Seven Islands.
"	"	"	1608	Examined the edge of the pack between Spitzbergen and Novaya Zemlya in lat. 75° 29′ N.
Poole, Jonas .	English		1609 1610 1611 1612	Made voyages to Spitzbergen for the Muscovy Company, but, unable to get beyond the north-west corner of Spitzbergen, he entered and named many of the sounds on the west coast, and established the Spitzbergen whale-fishery.
Thomas, Marmaduke .	English	'Resolution' .	1612	Alleged to have sailed two degrees north of Hakluyt's Headland.
Fotherby and Baffin .	English	With ten vessels .	1614	Sailed to Spitzbergen for the Muscovy Company, and entered Hinlopen Straits in a boat-expedition.
Edge, Thomas, and others	English and Dutch	In a pinnace and other vessels	1613–1622	Explored North-east Land, Spitzbergen, and the land east of Stor Fjord ; and discovered Wiche's Land (1617), Hope Island, and others.
Williamszoon . .	Dutch	80 tons .	1624	Stated to have examined the pack 3° N. of Spitzbergen.
Bosman, Cornelius .	Dutch		1625	Sailed through Jugorsky Schar into the Kara Sea, in seeking a north-east passage for the Dutch Trading Company.
Whalers	Dutch		1630–31	First wintered in Spitzbergen.
Vlamingh, William de	Dutch		1664	Established the open nature of the Kara Sea, by sailing into it round the north of Novaya Zemlya.

Name	Nationality	Name and description of vessel	Date	Results
Wood, John	English	'Speedwell,' frigate 'Prosperous,' tender	1676	Examined ice-pack between Spitzbergen and Novaya Zemlya in latitude 75° 59' N.
Giles, Cornelius	Dutch		1707	Explored north and east of Spitzbergen, and discovered Gillis Land.
Murawieff and Pawloff	Russian	Large open boats	1734	Sailed through Jugorsky Schar across to Yelmert Land.
Malygyn and Schurakoff	Russian	"	1737	
Loschkin	Russian		1760 1761 1762	Circumnavigated Novaya Zemlya.
Rosmysslow	Russian	Small 10-ton vessel	1768–69	Wintered in Matoschkin Schar.
Tschitschagoff	Russian		1765	Visited north-west corner of Spitzbergen in an attempted voyage across the Pole.
Phipps	English	'Racehorse' 'Carcass'	1773	Attained to latitude of Seven Islands in a voyage toward the North Pole.
Scoresby	English	'Resolution'	1806	Reached 81° 30' N. 19° E., and explored much of the natural history of Spitzbergen.
Rumangoff	Russian	Tender 'Bee,' 35 tons	1807	Made a voyage in search of minerals on west coast of Novaya Zemlya.
Buchan	English	'Dorothea' 'Trent,' commanded by John Franklin	1818	Made a voyage towards the North Pole, but only reached north-west corner of Spitzbergen.
Lasarew	Russian	Brig 'Novaya Zemlya'	1819	Surveyed part of south-west coast of Novaya Zemlya.

Name	Nationality	Vessel	Year	Remarks
Lutke	Russian	Brig 'Novaya Zemlya,' 200 tons	1821	Surveyed the coast about Matoschkin Schar.
"			1822	Surveyed the coast to Cape Nassau.
"			1823	,,
"			1824	Examined edge of pack between Spitzbergen and Cape Nassau.
Keilhau	Norwegian		1827	Explored the geology of Spitzbergen.
Parry	English	'Hecla'	,,	Anchored in Treurenberg Bay, and reached 82° 40' 30" in boats and sledges.
Pakhtusof	Russian	Karbasse	1832–33	Wintered at Kamenka Bay, Novaya Zemlya, and in the spring surveyed east coast as far as Matoschkin Schar.
Pakhtusof und Ziwolka	Russian	Schooner 'Krokow' and Karbasse	1834–35	Wintered in Matoschkin Schar, and explored east coast as far as Cape Distant.
Von Baer	Russian		1837	Scientific examination of Matoschkin Schar and adjacent coasts.
Sven Loven	Norwegian		,,	Explored the geology, &c., of West Spitzbergen.
Ziwolka and Moïssijew	Russian		1838–39	Wintered in Shallow Bay, and explored neighbouring part of west coast of Novaya Zemlya in the spring.
Robert and French Scientific Commission	French		1838	Visited Bel Sound, Spitzbergen.
Nordenskiold	Swede	Yacht 'Frithiof'	1839	Visited north-west part of Spitzbergen.
"			1858	Visited west coast of Spitzbergen, and explored its natural history.
Lamont	English	Yacht 'Ginevra'	,,	Visited west coast of Spitzbergen.
"	"		1859	Visited west coast, and explored Stor Fjord, Ginevra Bay, and Ryk Yse Islands.

378

Name	Nationality	Name and description of vessel	Date	Results
Nordenskiold and other scientific men	Swede	.	1861	Further explored the west and north coast of Spitzbergen.
Carlsen	Norwegian	Walrus-brig 'Jan Mayen'	1863	Was the first to circumnavigate the Spitzbergen group.
Nordenskiold and others	Swede	.	1864	Visited South Spitzbergen and Stor Fjord.
Tobiesen, Mathilas, Aarström	Norwegian	Walrus-sloops	1864	Having sailed round North-east Land were compelled to abandon their sloop, and rowed up Hinlopen Straits, and round north-west of Spitzbergen to Ice Fjord.
Birkbeck and Newton	English	Yacht	1867	Sighted Wiche's Land from Ryk Yse Islands.
Nordenskiold & others	Swede	Iron steamer 'Sofia'	1868	Reached 81° 42' N. 18° E.
Koldewey	German	'Germania'	1868	Reached 81° 5' N. at N. of Spitzbergen.
Lamont	English	Steam-yacht 'Diana'	1869	Visited Novaya Zemlya, explored sea between Spitzbergen and Novaya Zemlya, and visited north-west corner of Spitzbergen and Stor Fjord.
Bessels	German	Whaler	1869	Explored sea between Spitzbergen and Novaya Zemlya.
Lamont	English	'Diana'	1870	Explored Novaya Zemlya and Kara Sea.
Johannesen	Norwegian	Walrus-sloop	,,	Circumnavigated Novaya Zemlya.
Other captains in	Norwegian	Sloops	,,	Reached Yolmert Land.
Heuglin	German	'Nils Isaken'	,,	Sighted Wiche's Land from Mt. Muldendorf, Spitzbergen.
Lamont	English	'Diana'	1871	Visited North-west Spitzbergen, and passed through Hell Sound in a boat.

Explorers and Ships	Nationality	Vessel	Date	Remarks
				... beyond ... relief.
Mack	Norwegian	Walrus-sloop	„	Visited Kara Sea and north-east of Novaya Zemlya.
Carlsen	Norwegian	„	„	Visited Ice Haven at north-east of Novaya Zemlya, and brought home the Barentz relics.
Leigh Smith	English	Yacht 'Sampson'	„	Explored North-east Land, Spitzbergen, and attained to 81° 24′, 18° E.
Altman	Norwegian	Walrus-sloop	1872	Visited North-west of Spitzbergen.
Johnsen	„	„	„	Landed on Wiche's Land.
Nilsen	„	„	„	„
Nordenskiold	Swede	'Polhem'	1872–73	Wintered in Mossel Bay, North Spitzbergen.
Weyprecht and Payer	Austrian	'Tegethoff'	„	Wintered in pack north of Novaya Zemlya.
Leigh Smith	English	'Diana'	1873	Relieved Nordenskiold, and reached the Seven Islands.
Weyprecht and Payer	Austrian	'Tegethoff'	1873–74	Wintered in pack near Franz-Josef Land, which they explored in the spring.
Wiggins	English	'Diana'	1874	Explored Kara Sea to 76° N. 82½° E.
Nordenskiold	Swede	'Pröven'	1875	Reached mouth of Yenisei.

INDEX.

CPSIA information can be obtained at www.ICGtesting.com
Printed in the USA
LVOW132025091011

249740LV00010B/174/P